ORGANS & ORGANISTS:
THEIR INSIDE STORIES

All you (n)ever wanted to know

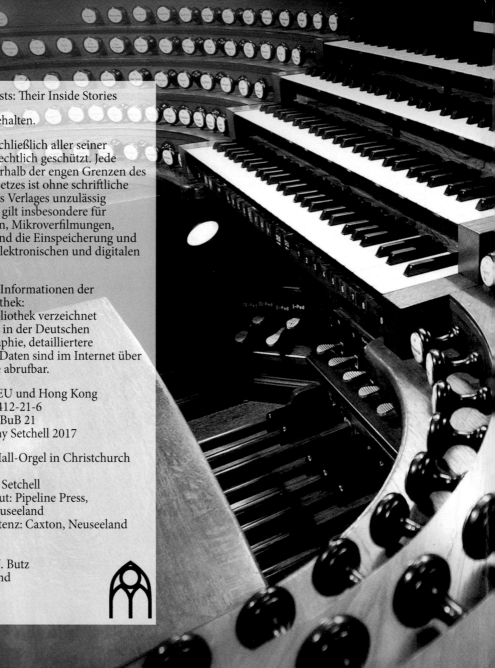

Organs & Organists: Their Inside Stories

Bibliographische Informationen der
Deutschen Bibliothek:
Die Deutsche Bibliothek verzeichnet
diese Publikation in der Deutschen
Nationalbibliographie, detailliertere
bibliographische Daten sind im Internet über
http:\\dnb.ddb.de abrufbar.

Gedruckt in der EU und Hong Kong
ISBN: 978-3-928412-21-6
Verlagsnummer: BuB 21
© Copyright Jenny Setchell 2017

Titelbild: Town Hall-Orgel in Christchurch
(Neuseeland)
Bildrechte: Jenny Setchell
Design und Layout: Pipeline Press,
Christchurch, Neuseeland
Produktionsassistenz: Caxton, Neuseeland

Erschienen im
Musikverlag Dr. J. Butz
Bonn, Deutschland
2017

Marktkirche, Wiesbaden, Germany

Organs & Organists: Their Inside Stories

All rights reserved.

The right of Jenny Setchell to be identified as the author of this work has been asserted by her in accordance with the Copyright, Designs and Patents Act 1988.

No part of this publication may be reproduced in any form or by any means — graphic, electronic or mechanical including photocopying, recording, taping or information storage and retrieval systems without the prior permission, in writing, of the publisher.

Printed in the EU and Hong Kong
ISBN: 978-0-473-41160-2
(Softcover, available Pipeline Press only)
Catalogue no. BuB 21

© Copyright Jenny Setchell 2017

Cover: Christchurch Town Hall organ and design: Jenny Setchell.

Book design and layout:
Pipeline Press,
Christchurch,
New Zealand

New Zealand Production Assistance: Caxton
Printed in China by Everbest Printing
Investment Limited

Published by
Musikverlag Dr. J. Butz
Bonn, Germany
2017

Organs & Organists: Their Inside Stories

All you (n)ever wanted to know

A composting of
organic material

Jenny Setchell

Dr. J. Butz ~ Musikverlag
Bonn
2017

WHAT THEY MIGHT HAVE SAID ABOUT THIS BOOK

"Not nearly long enough." — Richard Wagner

"Pathetic attempt to explain human anatomy, with only one out-dated sketch of a single relevant organ. Who is this female?" — Royal College of Human Anatomists

"To B, or to B♭, that was my real question; forsooth, this uncomely wench hath penned much of the loathsome huffity-puffity wheezebox and more of the silver tongu-ed musick than I ever dared. How base, how vile is this. I will have no more of it." — W. Shakespeare (Mr)

"Ban it." — Donald Trump

"Too many words, my dear Jenny, too many words." — Emperor Joseph II

"Superficial, banal, et surtout a waste de mon temps." — Aristide Cavaillé-Coll

"Simply a must-have for all organists; it's the perfect height for adjusting organ benches." — International Association of Village Organists

"Thank you. Now we know what he got up to." — Maria Barbara Bach, Anna Magdalena Bach

"No technical details about the workings of the 64ft Diaphone Dulzian. Shame on you." — Knobby Ratchety-Scale-Blowerington-Smythe (Mrs)

"No other book, in the history of the organ, has ever explained as effectively the difference between the sound of a 32ft Sordun and an attack of Death Watch Beetle." — Dr C. Thunderpfeifen

"We could have written many more vivid accounts. Very disappointed." — Matthew, Mark, Luke and John (Saints Inc.)

"I'm not in it! I'm not in it! Why is this?" — L. v. Beethoven

"Very nice, dear. Now tidy your room." — Jenny's mum

*This book is dedicated to musicians
and non-musicians who haven't got
a clue about organs or organists.
Long may they continue to discover
the magical world inside the outsides.*

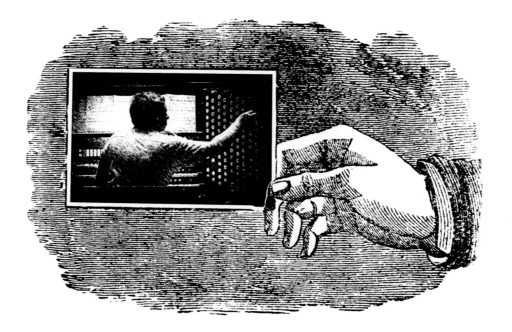

Grote Kerk, Gouda, Netherlands

CONTENTS

PART TWO

~ Martin Setchell ~ On the road with a free-range concert organist

ORGANIST ON THE LOOSE

PART THREE

~ Adrian Marple ~ Organist at your service

THE DAILY ORGAN GRINDER

PART FOUR

Life aloft as seen through the eyes
of other organists ~ and their helpers

LIFE ALOFT AROUND THE WORLD

On the plus side

Appendix

FOREWORD

BY CHRISTOPHER HERRICK

Jenny Setchell has created a delightful book which must surely have instant appeal to a wide spectrum of readers, from those who have but a passing interest in organs all the way through to those passionate people who eat, sleep and dream organs. It is human nature to poke fun at the things we love, and lovers of the organ certainly have plenty of material to chortle over or even to become hysterical about! Jenny, with her world-wide experience of organs and organists, and with her talent to dip and delve in order to tease out the riches and the ridiculous in her chosen theme, is the perfect person, probably the only person, who could do justice to this immense subject and still keep her readers fascinated at whatever level their knowledge.

So who is this book aimed at? I think I may have the answer. Put simply, it is aimed both at me and at my late father.

Steeped in organs since the age of seven or eight, when I was 12, I fell in love with the concept of playing the instrument professionally when turning pages for a BBC recording by Sir John Dykes Bower at the gigantic organ in St Paul's Cathedral, London. Since then, during my career as a concert organist, I have been lucky to travel about quite a bit and have experienced plenty of organic beasts both great and small. Jenny still manages to whet my appetite in her book with awesome images of many organs I haven't yet had the fortune to play!

If this book appeals to me, how much more it would have appealed to my father. Let me explain.

My father started his professional life in the Depression when getting a job at all was quite an achievement. Though he confessed to me that he might have preferred to have been a lawyer or a musician, he settled for a career in local government and rose to the top of that particular tree. His musical outlet was the violin. He told me that he went for only one violin lesson with a certain lady to whom he took an instant dislike. So he never learnt to read music but as a self-taught violinist he played rather competently by ear. I used to accompany him in Gilbert and Sullivan medleys and Kreisler pieces, and in his retirement he would play along to CDs of Mahler Symphonies.

He was a loyal church man all his life and therefore should have been fully aware of organs, not least because I became an organist. In addition, as Church Warden of St Martin's Ludgate Hill, a small Wren church in the shadow of St Paul's Cathedral, he became friendly with the organ builder Noel Mander, with whom he negotiated the restoration of the historic instrument in that church.

However, this sketch of my father is merely

background to the point I want to make and the reason why I believe he would have treasured this book.

When we found ourselves together in Schleswig Holstein, in the north of Germany, an opportunity arose to visit the Marcussen Organ Factory just over the border in the south of Denmark. Imagine my astonishment at my father's reaction upon seeing a large organ in the process of being built, laid out in the factory with all its glorious mechanical intricacies on full display. Somehow my father in his 80s and with a background in churches and a son in the business had no idea that all that stuff behind the organ façade existed; the whole thing was a total revelation to him — pipes galore, wooden and metal parts crisscrossing in great abundance, and a whole wonderful world of mechanical activity at the service of a musician with 10 fingers and two feet seated at an impressive bank of keyboards!

Indeed, how privileged I have been to be that person (some would say, that octopus) making wonderful music on so many superb organs for 60 years and counting. Johann Sebastian Bach, the organist's patron saint, has been the solid foundation of my repertoire and I have been fortunate to air his complete works in recording on beautiful Metzler instruments

Photo: Igor Pushin

Christopher Herrick

in Switzerland as well as twice in concert, once at New York's Lincoln Center Festival and more recently at the Mariinsky Concert Hall, St Petersburg. I have also been blessed with 10 happy years' playing the Westminster Abbey organ, culminating in a recording for Hyperion Records called *Organ Fireworks*, which in turn led to a globe-trotting series of discs on stunning organs in such far-flung places as Dallas Concert Hall, Melbourne Town Hall, Hong Kong Cultural Centre and Reykjavik's Hallgrímskirkja.

Of course, there have been some interesting hiccoughs on the way. For instance, on three bizarre occasions I have been inadvertently locked in, once into a Danish church with an ear-splitting alarm sounding off, once in a Polish cathedral toilet during a rehearsal break, and perhaps most ridiculously of all I was locked into Westminster Cathedral's organ loft by the POLICE who then forgot to let me out after a big service, attended by loads of VIPs, to pray for peace in Northern Ireland . . .

But that's enough about me. Dear reader, whether you possess greater or smaller organ experience and know-how, I encourage you instantly to turn the page and enter into the magical and at times preposterous world of the organ with Jenny as your expert guide.

Ochsenhausen Abbey, Germany

PREFACE

When I finished writing *Organ-isms: Anecdotes from the World of the King of Instruments* in 2008, I knew one thing for certain: Never, ever again. Never. Not ever. Not for anyone.

Unfortunately, readers apparently enjoyed that book in both the English and German versions, and clamoured for a sequel. I ignored them and instead did a picture book called *Looking Up* which showed organs and ceilings. But they liked it too and asked when that sequel was coming. Sighing, I admitted defeat, and combined the concept to make a marriage of the two styles of book. The result is what you have in your hands now.

However, *Inside Stories* has a more serious (but not solemn) hidden layer. For years I promised myself I would write a book about the organ, which, when distilled into its essence, is aimed at those who don't know, and particularly those who *don't know* they don't know (which includes pretty much 99% of the world population). So I decided to weave the humiliating, excruciating, life-as-she-is-lived yarns from organists into illustrations and information about different organs, how they work, and, of course, with colourful pictures. An educational project, if you like, thinly disguised as a coffee-table book.

Rather than being just another book of funny stories or a further glossy tome of gasp-inducing organ façades for people who know all about the organ world, this is a volume for the families and friends of organists who really have no idea what it is that they do for a living — except that their jobs are slightly peculiar, and a good target for off-jokes. Organists, (others think) are occupational misfits whom normal people avoid at social events because they don't know what to talk to them about. Apart from those inevitable jokes.

The pipe organ is not a joke, and it is not just any old instrument, although old it certainly is. We are dealing with a noisy, mechanical monster that dominates its surroundings as the largest and most complex of all instruments (until the Industrial Revolution and the invention of the steam engine, the organ was arguably the most complicated machine that mankind was able to build). This behemoth is an extraordinary work of art and engineering which has changed little in the centuries since it first became a hit. Yet it is probably the least understood by performers and listeners alike.

The organ makes phenomenal physical and technical demands on its players. Of course, organists are not alone in the struggle to perform under often awkward circumstances.

All musicians can face difficulties with venues, employers, committees, organisers, and the instruments they play, but organists are alone in several unique regards:

- Every pipe organ is different
- Organists can't carry the same instrument around with them
- They have to use most parts of their body when playing
- Organists commonly have to learn new repertoire and practise in public places
- In many instances, players can see only about 5% of the instrument they are playing
- Organists commonly play without seeing (or being seen by) their audience

My first aim is to introduce the awe-inspiring box of whistles known as the 'King of Instruments' to non-musicians who have only a vague idea what it is, and probably know nothing about what is behind the façade. Everyone admires a large organ in a cathedral or concert hall, but few have any idea how it makes such a sound.

It is also the only musical instrument which is frequently played in public by people who range from top-of-the-line, world-class musicians to downright incompetents who should never be allowed near it. Pianists are dragooned into reluctant but noble service by necessity; beginner organists, undaunted by their lack of musicianship or training, flounder noisily around, convinced that cavernous acoustics and playing as loudly

as possible will disguise any massacre of the music. Such people do more damage to the reputation of organ music than anyone realises. Consider this: with no flying training and experience, you would not jump into an A380 jet and expect to pilot it safely, hoping the noise of the engines would carry the day. Or would you?

Hence the second target for this book: those who ought to know better. Organists themselves can be shackled by an insular appreciation of 'their' own instrument and never realise how another's experience may be entirely different. If we organists don't understand one another, imagine how the rest of the world sees us. Organists are a weird mob, but all bring their own richness and individuality. Sometimes their gifts are undervalued or scorned by those with whom they work, and these colleagues and employers too, need to know as much as they can about the beast, its driver and how they collaborate to make music.

The third impetus for this undertaking is personal.

I sit for hours (days even) admiring impressive pipe organs while listening to the sublime music they make (most often performed by my husband Martin, who features throughout this book as an unwitting model), and my heart almost bursts with the desire to share this with others. Through my photos I want to entice 'unbelievers' into this sumptuous 'other' world. Access to organ music of the great composers is easier than ever through CDs, DVDs, downloads from the internet, etc., so my dream is that this chunky tome will act as a catalyst for a blossoming love of a unique, hundreds-of-years-old craft.

Note that although I have most often used the pronoun 'he', 'his', or 'him' in relation to organists, this is a way of keeping things simple. The balance between genders of organists is probably about 50/50, but who knows? Who cares? To me, an organist is an organist, and that is that.

Some of the organs illustrated here have altered since their photos were taken; or they have been upgraded, moved into different venues, sold to other owners or even demolished. This is the fate of anything that lives for a very, very long time, and certainly beyond the life-span of most human beings. I have tried to note where any such changes have happened since their 'photoshoot'.

I offer no apology for the fact that *Inside Stories* is intensely personal. It may be one of the more superficial, nonacademic, least technical tomes ever to (dis)grace the shelves of any literature lover, but hopefully it amuses while it informs.

For organ buffs expecting pages of figures, dates and complex data and details: I have deliberately avoided myriad technical details and data. Recommended reading for those wishing to investigate further is found under 'Thirsting for more?' in the appendix. A few details can be found in endnotes listed on page 407. And before you can ask 'But

what about. . ?.' sorry, I couldn't include every conceivable organ design or quirk — after all, it is not intended to be a comprehensive, scholarly organ textbook.

In addition to providing some answers, *Organs & Organists: Their Inside Stories* should stimulate your curiosity and raise many questions. If, after turning these pages, you want to see more organs, listen to the music produced by them, and encourage more organists to master their craft, the book has done its job.

If, however, it inspires you to become an organist, see a psychiatrist.

Jenny Setchell
Christchurch,
New Zealand, 2017

De Montfort Hall, Leicester, England

ACKNOWLEDGEMENTS

Organists and other musicians unafraid to expose their personal organ-related foibles (and bare legs, even) have volunteered their observations, embarrassing experiences, and even confessions for this book.

To all those who risked their reputations and livelihoods by taking me into their confidence, my heartfelt thanks. I hope I have not done too much damage with my editing, and that you will remain on good terms with your employers and families once the book becomes public. To all of you, but especially people who have given advice, photos, ideas, and saved me from myself, I owe you shoals of chocolate fish.

Organ builders Claudius Winterhalter, Rieger, Klais, Kuhn, C.B. Fisk, Inc. have kindly given their time, information, and material. John Pike Mander of Mander Organs hosts an online organ forum where one can find much inspiration, yarns and advice from fellow organ buffs; many of whom have valiantly offered to help with research and submitted anecdotes and pictures over the last eight years.

Frank Mento helped with a tricky shift into conversational French when I was searching for stories, and German translator Hans-Uwe Hielscher did likewise. Many friends, family, and colleagues, especially Mark Quarmby, Christopher and Richard Feltham, Achille Speranza, Kenneth Aplin, Kevin Bishop, Lynley Young, Lorna Buchanan, Hamish Halls, Paolo Zacchetti, and Philip Ianna waded through my labyrinth of texts and photos to help find the best way to describe a highly complex instrument. Thank you for saving me from the tyranny of autocorrect.

These pages have been animated by the insane scrawlings of cartoonist Al Nisbet. Despite trying to publish his book of earthquake cartoons while being tossed around by 7.8 magnitude earthquakes, he continued bravely filing his drawings to me using whatever means he could. I value his crazy friendship which rather strangely inspires. At the very least Al makes us laugh when we need it most.

I can hardly believe my good fortune to have landed in the gentle and extremely efficient hands of the Butz publishing team under Hans-Peter Bähr. One day I will wake up and find it was just a dream. It must be rare for authors to be guided and encouraged to the degree that I have with this book. Thanks to Hans-Peter's attention to detail in his kind, wise way, my task of writing, compiling and organising *Organs & Organists: Their Inside Stories* has been a labour of pure (if protracted) joy.

Families are the first to suffer when a spouse undertakes a massive project like this. Martin has blossomed into a multifaceted house husband, proving that rehearsal techniques and concert programming principles can be equally applied to cooking, hanging out washing, and ironing. Without his patience and generous love, I would have nothing to write about. Nor would I feel like doing it.

The cats, meanwhile, did little but drool over squirrel videos while spending hours of lap time at the computer (see end page). Much fur has been donated to the cause and the keyboard.

Most of the photos in this book stem from private experiences garnered during several decades of clambering up loft stairs and exploring consoles as I accompanied Martin on his recital tours around the globe. None of my photos is posed, and many candid ones were taken at times of great pressure. After using my powers of persuasion, I am glad to say he has considered his options and has agreed to let me use these pictures. His bruises should heal soon.

Formerly St Andrews URC Church (now restaurant/café) Chester, UK

Montpellier Cathedral, France

 PRELUDE

In the beginning

VICAR: *The organ will now play.*

ORGANIST: *Oh no it won't. I will.*

FIRST, FIND YOUR
ORGANIST

Organists are Great, Swell, and Positif
~ but apparently very bashful

Spotting organists is tricky. Many of these creatures are nocturnal, emerging from their hiding places only after dark when a building is closed to the public. Some organists and their habitats are so well hidden that people doubt they exist. Organs, they assume, play themselves. (Hence the saying "The organ was playing. . .")

Many church authorities help the bashful organist remain anonymous by keeping any forthcoming concert or recital a top-level secret. In parish newsletters, organ recitals are cunningly disguised by publicising book fairs, Bring & Buy Sales, or the latest in underwear for the fashion-conscious vicar. Bible Class sausage sizzles will always rank above anything emanating from the King of Instruments, and this guarantees that potential listeners will remain unaware of any concerts scheduled for the next millennium.

Large posters or hoardings advertising details of dates, times, player and programmes are discouraged or avoided altogether, so that the organist can be confident of exposure to as few people as possible, especially on concert night.

Shy players can sometimes take refuge inside the case. The pipe organ is the only musical contraption that can be operated by the musician sitting inside it, but that depends on the size of the beast (both organ and organist).

Some organs have a separate case of pipes behind the player's back, as well as the pipes in front and above. Although it conceals this shy animal and makes a private canoodle possible, it severely restricts the chance to hold parties or swing cats. And it means organists can play an entire programme safely unaware of the three men and a dog in the audience.

Béziers Cathedral, France

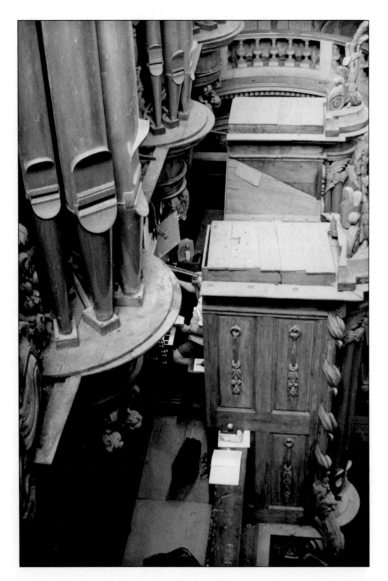

*An organist at
rehearsal ~ as seen
by the pigeons*

An organist at rehearsal ~ as seen by the page turner

To begin with

ORGANIST: Small mousy nocturnal creature, mention of which at social events leads to long silences as people wonder what to say next.

CONSOLE: The dashboard from which the organist drives his spacecraft. It is usually equipped with keyboards, stops, pistons, couplers, music desk, rear vision mirror, and a variety of sweet papers, pens, glasses, false teeth, bits of scruffy paper, mobile phones, pencils with no lead, and sticky notes that have lost their stick.

BAD ORGAN MUSIC PLAYED BY A BAD ORGANIST: Sound that you haven't heard before and think you don't like; and when you do hear it, know you were absolutely right, and sprint for the nearest exit.

GOOD ORGAN MUSIC PLAYED BY A GOOD ORGANIST: Sound that you haven't heard before and think you won't like; and when you do hear it, love it, and rush to buy the organist's CDs. Or the organ.

ORGAN RECITAL: Monologue delivered by a hypochondriac at a party when he realises he is talking to a doctor.

REGISTRANT: Hard-working sucker, sorry, assistant who helps to operate the many confusing and peculiar buttons of the organist's cockpit, turn pages, and mop the organist's brow. Up to three assistants may be used for large, old organs, and a dozen for very large, old organists.

ORGANIST
HABITATS

Where they work and play,
and on special occasions, live.

THE 'ATM' HOLE-IN-
THE-WALL HABITAT

A quietly remote position for a coy instrument, such as one of
the organs in the Constantine Basilica in Trier, Germany.

THE
'WHO'S A NAUGHTY
BOY? GO-STAND-IN-
THE-CORNER'
HABITAT

A rare and punitive corner-dwelling in the Cathedral of Notre Dame, St Bernard-de-Cominges, France. The organists are swallowed alive by the instrument and they must use headphones to hear clearly what they are playing.

THE 'I'M-NOT-TALKING-TO-YOU' HABITAT

Christchurch Town Hall, New Zealand

Organists are musicians who turn their backs on everyone. Look for the only person at a concert with their back to the conductor, orchestra, or choir, and that's your organist. It's nothing personal, it's just how they have to work sometimes. Well, often.

Westminster United Church, Winnipeg, Canada

Church authorities are fond of using playpens to keep their organists under control. It discourages sleep during sermons and prevents premature escape.

York Methodist Central Hall, England

The organist sits so close to the action he can hear the vicar's nostrils flaring.

Performing Arts Hall, Shanghai, China

THE DUAL-PURPOSE, 'YOU'RE-ON-YOUR-OWN' HABITAT VIEW #1

The detached console is connected by an umbilical cord to the main organ,
which can be seen along the back wall of the concert hall.

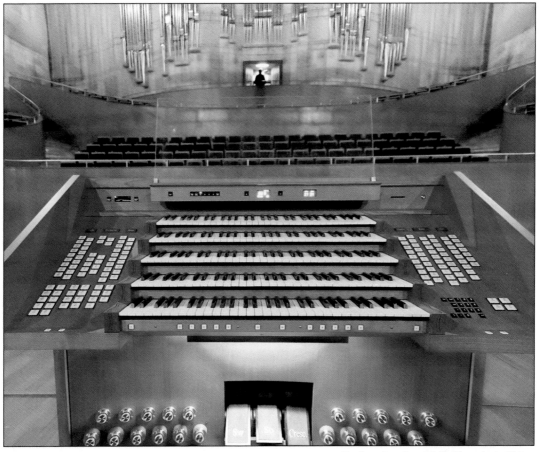

Performing Arts Hall, Shanghai, China

The dual-purpose, 'You're-on-your-own' habitat view #2

The organist can escape back to the main organ if the stage should be
invaded by choirs, orchestras, or worse.

How to recognise an organist

There are two breeds of organist. They are distinguished mainly by their behaviour, but attire, plumage and nesting habits give some clue as to their leanings. Both species are on the World Artist Life Endangered list.

The Domesticated Church Species

The easy-care breed is the domesticated organist, or in the vernacular Latin, *Dogsbodyicus Atyourserviensis Organgrindicum*. Happiest in a familiar landscape of home or parish church, the domesticated types typically do not venture far from their breeding grounds. The skills they exhibit with all four feet and seven arms when performing on their favourite toys amaze other musicians, who regard them as certifiable lunatics or transmutant aliens with genius chromosomes.

Usually endowed with a sanguine, pleasant temperament (provided they are inoculated against distemper and composers post-1898) they respond well to training. The *Dogsbodyicus Atyourserviensis Organgrindicum* organists are strong working animals who give their

owners hours of pleasure if regularly given a pint, shown affection, and taken for walks to music shops, organist conventions, and concerts. They can be trusted to perform unsupervised, although the clergy (bless 'em) and well-meaning members of congregations still like to offer helpful advice and comments on musical matters. This can trigger a snappy instinctive response from the breed, so caution is needed in these circumstances.

See '*The definitely odd life of one of the English Church musician species*' page 245

WILD FREELANCE SPECIES

(A.K.A concert organists)

Just like organs, no two organists are alike. They infiltrate almost every sector of society by posing as normal human beings.

Distributed worldwide (except polar ice-caps), the feral branch of the organist family, *Peregrinatio Digitor Plodicus* faced extinction early in the 20th century but made a comeback thanks to the invention of electricity and affordable, transportable organs. Their native habitats are large secular concert venues and stadia, or large ancient religious buildings like basilicas, cathedrals and abbeys. Here they prefer to shelter in the exotic higher reaches of organ lofts out of the way of predators; they are recognisable by their bright sequined jackets or sparkly shoes.

These feral animals need constant attention as they can become disorientated after a long absence from their breeding and feeding grounds, and the observer must be alert for the many dangers lurking in unfamiliar territory. If disturbed, they can react violently, and it is best not to approach them or attempt to touch them unless they have been recently watered, fed, or have finished their performance.

See *'Organist on the loose' page 193*

A PIANIST IS AN ORGANIST?
NAH. NOPE. NEIN. NADA.

What pianists play

What organists play

No two pipe organs in the world look alike or sound the same.
A bit like snowflakes. But more expensive.

Wesley Uniting, Kent Town, Adelaide, South Australia

❧ PART ONE ❧

A rough pictorial guide to pipe organs

VISITING ROCK BAND LEADER: *Where's the organ?*

VERGER: *At the back, the West End.*

VRBL: *Oh. I need it at the front. Only for tomorrow though.*

IOHN LOOSEMORE MADE THIS ORGAN 1665

Exeter Cathedral, England

FAÇADES & CASES

On the face of it, organs are just boxes full of pipes.
But oh! What beautiful boxes they can be.

— Anon

TOURIST: *Looks nice. What songs does it play?*

On the outside

FAÇADE: The front, the bits you can see.

CASE: (1) The often highly carved or painted exterior framework of the organ. (2) Organist's survival kit containing music, shoes, batteries, emergency tuning gear, fruit, clothes pegs, screwdrivers, heartburn pills, and dozens of broken pencils.

PIPE: (1) A tube, open or stopped, made of metal or wood, which makes all the din. (2) An object for trapping pigeons, mice, cats, and occasional small choristers. (3) Large pipe: a water main.

TRUMPETS EN CHAMADE:

An impressive and fearsome rank of horizontal pipes jutting out from the case at right angles, usually very raucous. They should not be played unannounced within earshot of people with weak hearts.

DIVISIONS: Groups of pipes/stops that belong together and form a unity. They can sometimes be seen clustered together in different parts of the façade. Divisions are given names such as Great, Grande Orgue, Orchestral, Antiphonal, Hauptwerk, Swell, Brustwerk, Solo, Echo, Choir, Rückpositiv, Oberwerk, Bombarde, Récit, Positif, Pedal, Hoofdwerk, Rugwerk, Bovenwerk.

Ask many people what they think an organ looks like,
and they will probably describe something like this

or this:

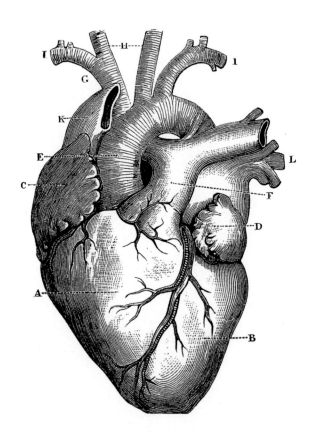

or worse:

and, of course, comedians will
automatically think of this:

Although all organs work along
the same principles, every pipe
organ is unique. Spot the differences
between the following instruments:

Old Radnor, Wales

ANCIENT

St Stephanus, Filderstadt, Germany

MODERN

Temple Church, London, England

THE PRINCE

St Mary's, Crich, England

THE PAUPER

Weingarten Basilica, Germany

EXUBERANT

Dunedin Cathedral, New Zealand

RESTRAINED

Kaiser Wilhelm Memorial Church, Berlin, Germany

ILLUMINATED

St Laurenzen, St Gallen, Switzerland

LUMINOUS

St Eustache, Paris, France

Solid

St Lebuïnuskerk, Deventer, Netherlands

PLAYFUL

Adelaide Town Hall, Australia

ORANGE

Rikkyo University, Niiza, Japan

Blue

Marienorgel, Unserer Lieben Frau, Lindau, Germany

WHITE, WITH A SMIDGEON OF BLING

Mariä Himmelfahrt, Schongau, Germany

BLINGIER

St Anna's, Warsaw, Poland

BLING SUPREME

Koseinenkin Kaikan Hall, Kyushu, Japan

GUARANTEED (ALMOST) BLING-FREE

Mormon Conference Centre, Salt Lake City, Utah, USA

BIG. REALLY BIG

Lutheran Church, Bethany, South Australia

SMALL

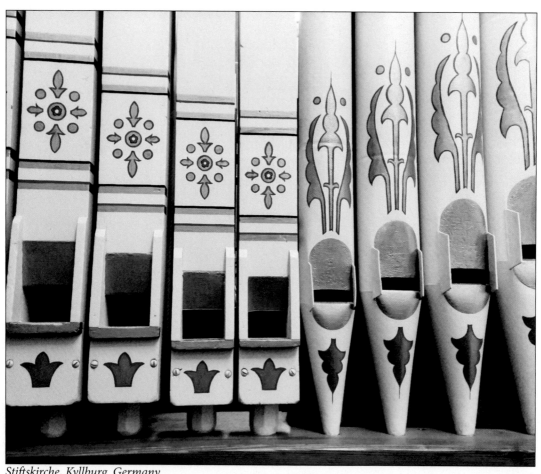

Stiftskirche, Kyllburg, Germany

Just any old pipes? Take one step to the right and . . .

. . . oh look! A mouse organ.

Stadtkirche, Celle, Germany

All pipes have mouths, some of which appear to have come
straight from a dentist's waiting room

Christ Church Cathedral, Newcastle, Australia

(Nice shade of lipstick, Miss)

Introducing the noise makers

RANK: A row of pipes usually controlled by one stop (See page 134 onwards for more about stops)

EIGHT FOOT (8'): Indicates that the middle C will sound the same pitch as middle C on a piano (and all the other notes will be accordingly the same relative pitch). The 8' length is the measure of the lowest open pipe.

FOUR FOOT (4'): Signifies that the middle C will sound an octave **higher** than on a piano (ditto the other pipes).

SIXTEEN FOOT (16'): Pipes similarly pitched one octave **lower** than an 8' pipe.

THIRTY-TWO FOOT (32'): Huge pipes that make handy steps for organ tuners.

SIXTY-FOUR FOOT (64'): Only two organs in the world boast a complete rank of such pipes. Use on audiences of nervous disposition at your own risk.

HUNDRED FOOT (100'): A centipede.

FLUES: (1) The sound is produced by wind forced through a narrow windway to strike the sharp upper lip of the pipe; very like a common whistle, and the size varies from a tiny pencil to a tube with the girth of a large tree trunk. (2) Typo for flute.

REEDS: Grunty, rasping, trumpety sounds, a staple particularly of French and Iberian organ literature. Usually the first to go out of tune and always before a crucial trumpet voluntary for a wedding.

STRINGS: Narrow pipes, which have a sharper tone and sound a little like violins, cellos, etc. Only a little.

PRINCIPALS: (diapasons, montre, prestant, etc.). This is what most people recognise as a pipe organ sound.

FOUNDATION STOPS: the basic family of diapason stops, known in French as the Fonds, and Prinzipal in German.

MIXTURES: A composite stop using more than one pipe for each note. Adds brightness and sparkle to the sound if well-tuned, or a ghastly clattering if not.

MUTATIONS: Stops which speak at a different pitch giving higher overtones. These are the ones with fractions after their names, such as $2^{2/3}$, $1^{3/5}$.

TREMULANT: (1) A device which can simulate a shaky vibrato sound of a warbling soprano or nervous violinist. (2) Novice registrant before a concert.

PIPES

Without the pipes, you have what looks like a 4-storey, million-dollar sewing machine crossed with fire bellows, made from Swiss cheese.

Pipes make the sound, and it is the length, shape, and material of which they are made that sets one apart from the other, and makes the unique pipe organ 'accent'.

Although it is the keyboards that organs have in common with the piano, the pipes are what relate it to flutes, recorders, clarinets, trumpets and even alpine horns.

CURIOUS VISITOR: *Is that all there are?*

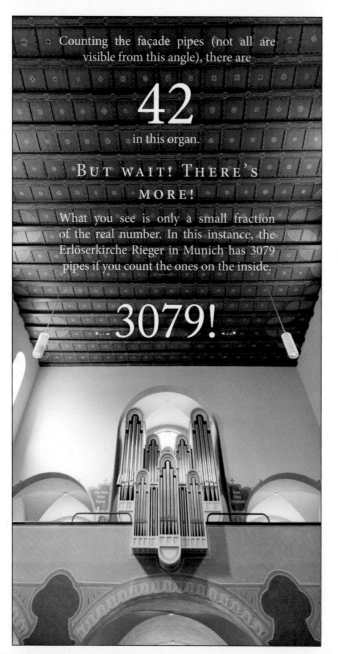

Counting the façade pipes (not all are visible from this angle), there are

42

in this organ.

BUT WAIT! THERE'S MORE!

What you see is only a small fraction of the real number. In this instance, the Erlöserkirche Rieger in Munich has 3079 pipes if you count the ones on the inside.

3079!

WYSINWYG

(WHAT YOU SEE IS NOT WHAT YOU GET)

Pipe organs are bigger on the inside than the outside. Think *Dr Who* and the Tardis.

Melbourne Town Hall, Australia

Melbourne Town Hall sports one of the largest organs in the world; but you would never guess it through a cursory count of the façade pipes. A mere 29 are on show, yet the organ boasts a whopping 9568 (or so) in total. Even some of those pipes that are visible may just be there for show, as 'dummy' or 'non-speaking' pipes.

Christ's College, Christchurch, New Zealand

Even relatively small organs are bigger on the inside than they appear on the outside. The organ of Christ's College in Christchurch, New Zealand, has 25 front pipes (all of which are speaking pipes) but take a look INSIDE the box:

Christ's College, Christchurch, New Zealand

A total of 2474 pipes, invisible from the outside, are meticulously
stacked, layered, lined up, and marshalled around to make them
fit into the tiny chambers behind.

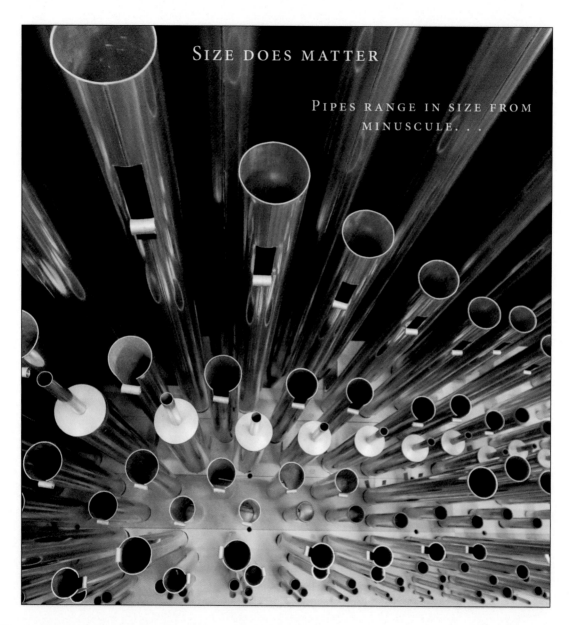

SIZE DOES MATTER

PIPES RANGE IN SIZE FROM
MINUSCULE. . .

. . . To massive

2 TYPES OF PIPES

FLUE PIPES

These are built on the same principle as a flute or recorder. Flues are the oldest type of organ pipe, and some of them are the ones you see at the front of the organ, in the façade. The wind pressure, the height and width of the mouth, the diameter of the pipe relative to its length, its shape, whether it has a stopper in the top, and the material used to make it, all determine how it sounds.

REED PIPES

Every reed pipe has a vibrating brass reed or tongue at the bottom (the boot) of the pipe. The 'beating' of the reed is amplified or modified by the pipe extending from it. The type of reed tongue, the pipe shape, its length and other tone-altering features all affect the timbre. The pressure of the wind pushed through the pipe is also important.

Stopped wooden pipes

Each pipe in a rank (see page 72) is a different length. The longer the pipe, the lower the pitch; the shorter it is, the higher it sounds. If a stop knob of an open pipe has 8 written on it, its longest pipe is 8 feet long, and it sounds C, 2 octaves below middle C (the same as that note on a piano); 4 sounds an octave higher, 2 sounds 2 octaves higher; 16 sounds an octave lower, and 32 sounds 2 octaves lower. Stops of pipes with pitches in between these basic sounds are called mutations and mixtures, and give the organ its rich sound.

Pipes are not only cylindrical. Square, squat, as long as 32ft (or even 64ft are found in two organs in the world) down to babies less than an inch tall. They can be tapered, stopped at the top, thin or thick, bent in the middle to fit the spaces, or bulge in the middle (very like organists, in fact). Shape, and the material they are made from, all make a difference to the sound.

With all these variables among the pipes, combined with different players, and the unique acoustics of every venue, the number of possible sounds is excitingly infinite.

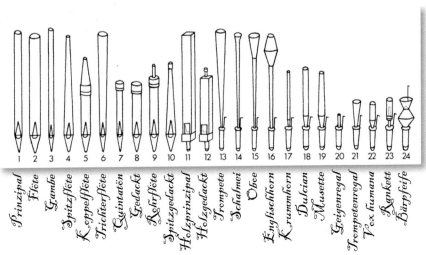

1 Prinzipal 2 Flöte 3 Gambe 4 Spitzflöte 5 Koppelflöte 6 Trichterflöte 7 Quintatön 8 Gedackt 9 Rohrflöte 10 Spitzgedackt 11 Holzprinzipal 12 Holzgedackt 13 Trompete 14 Schalmei 15 Oboe 16 Englischhorn 17 Krummhorn 18 Dulcian 19 Musette 20 Geigenregal 21 Trompetenregal 22 Vox humana 23 Rankett 24 Bärpfeife

Fat and thin

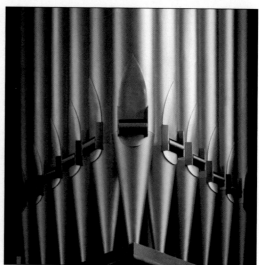

Key to organs page 402

Textured or plain

Or prettily painted

Key to organs page 402

Metal, bottles, bamboo, stone, wood, or glass, anyone?

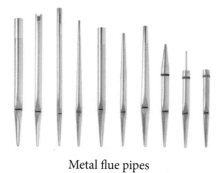

Metal flue pipes

Pipes are commonly made from wood and metal. Metal used for organ pipes consists of alloys of tin, lead, and zinc in different percentages.

More adventurous builders have experimented using bamboo (Las Piñas in the Philippines), porcelain (Dresden, using Meissen porcelain of course), bottles (which makes them technically bottle-organs, but who cares?). Ivan Larrea, of Alicante, Spain, specialises in building marble and stone organs.

Klais Organ Builders installed a rank of glass pipes called the Kōauau (Maori flute), in the Auckland Town Hall, and Xaver Wilhelmy's American Flag Sound Sculpture (opposite) is the first and only pipe organ in the world with pipes made entirely from glass.

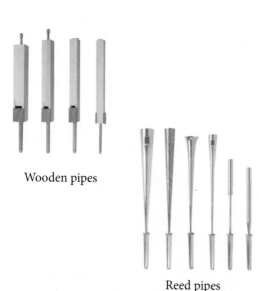

Wooden pipes

Reed pipes

Photo: Xaver Wilhelmy

American Flag Sound Sculpture by Xaver Wilhelmy [9]

THE CASE FOR CASES

Saint-Etienne Cathedral, Limoges, France

The housing for the pipes brings out the creativity and sense of humour in organ builders. In order to design a unique façade, while fighting limitations of the building, acoustics, budget, specifications of the organ, builders try almost anything when creating their masterpieces.

St Elisabeth, Augsburg, Germany

Organs can work without an enclosing case. Many extraordinary designs minus the restraints of wood or stone exist, such as the skew-whiff Disney Hall Rosales organ, (nicknamed French Fries[2]); or the organ in St Elizabeth, Augsburg (above) which masquerades as the popular pick-up sticks game.

Formerly the First Church of Christ, Scientist, Basel, Switzerland

Extreme precision.
Great for pipe-counting during sermons.

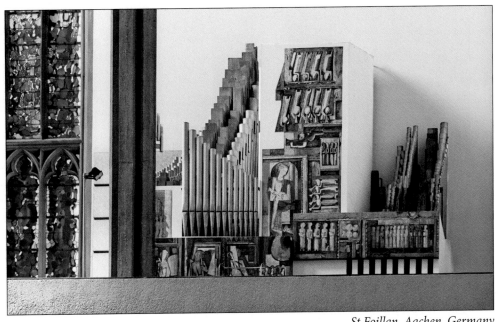

St Foillan, Aachen, Germany

Hedging their bets? Half encased. This is either the
organ or the parish jumble sale. Or both.

St Mariä Empfängnis, Monschau, Germany

Then there are the self-disciplined, serious, no-nonsense separate box arrangements.

St Matthew's, Hastings, New Zealand

Or, thinking (and playing) outside the box.

St Ulrich und St Afra, Augsburg, Germany

TAKING WING

Painted doors can be closed to protect the pipes from dust and debris; when open, they display the skills of the craftsmen.

Wollaton Hall, Nottingham, England

St Valentin und Dionysius, Kiedrich, Germany

Händel-Haus Museum, Halle [3]
Photo: Archiv Stiftung Händel-Haus

Breda Grote Kerk, Netherlands

Sion, Switzerland: An organ with painted wing shutters that was thought to be the oldest playable organ in the world.

BUT!

Notre-Dame-de-Valère in Sion is

THE OLDEST

in appearance

The organ in Notre-Dame-de-Valère Sion, Switzerland, vies with a German organ in Ostönnen, Westphalia, for the title of the oldest playable organ in the world. Sion's 'swallow's nest' case is probably older, dating back to 1435 (give or take a year or two) but only about half of the 376 pipes remain from the Gothic period.

Notre-Dame-de-Valère, Sion, Switzerland

St Andreas, Ostönnen, Germany

St Andreas in Ostönnen, Germany, is

THE OLDEST

in sound

The organ in St Andreas, Ostönnen, Germany, restored in 2003, has windchests and divisions dating from 1425-1430, and more than half of its pipes are original. But its newer case and keyboards are mere youths from the Baroque period.

SHY, OR BOLD AS BRASS?

St Wilhadi, Stade, Germany

*Some organs are discreetly
camouflaged*

A shy and retiring example of
a Positiv chamber organ. The
Hospitality Union for church
mice is negotiating shared rights
to use the pipes as nesting boxes.

Behind the 'brickwork' painted
onto the concealing canvas of the
San Francisco Legion of Honor
apse lie the 4526 pipes of the
symphonic organ.[4] A battery of
drums, gongs, castanets, triangle,
(and even a thunder pedal) clang
and clatter inside the chambers.
Without the tuner's light on behind
the canvas, no-one would know
this armoury of noise lay behind
the gallery 'stone' walls.

Legion of Honor, San Francisco, USA

Christchurch Cathedral, New Zealand   *Hong Kong Cultural Arts Centre*

Others have bold, sticky-out bits

Cautionary note for small boys: these are not rocket launchers, but reed pipes called *en chamade*. They began to appear in organ cases from about 1620, because it 1) improved sound projection where the organ did not face the congregation, 2) made them accessible for tuning, and 3) saved money by replacing cathedral trumpeters. Choristers (of all ages) regard them as potential pea shooters. They also scare the living daylights out of secret service agents. (See page 362)

Stiftskirche, Stuttgart, Germany

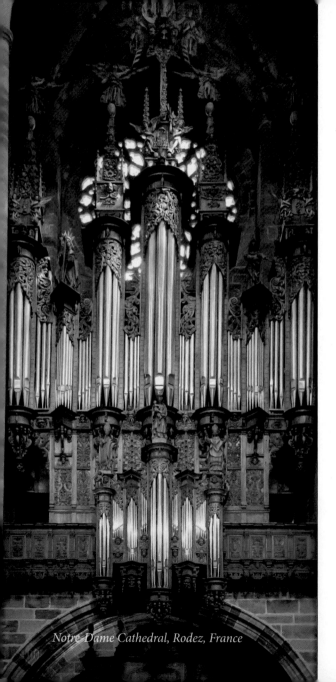

Notre-Dame Cathedral, Rodez, France

'I believe the right

question to ask,

respecting all ornament,

is simply this: Was it

done with enjoyment ~

was the carver happy

while he was about it?'

~ *John Ruskin*[4]

Notre-Dame Cathedral, Rodez, France

See a few faces here? If you include the nightmarish creatures, there are 39 in this view.
A true face-ade . . .

Wood carving schools from Renaissance France have given congregations untold hours of pleasure looking for faces in organ cases. One example, the Rodez Cathedral organ, is a monumental 16th-century masterpiece. The flamboyant organ case by Raymond Gusmond, a master sculptor from Périgueux, has had jaws dropping (and face-spotters counting) since 1629.

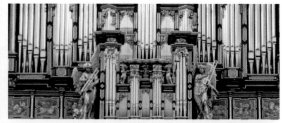

WHILE CHERUBS AND
ANGELS CAROUSE

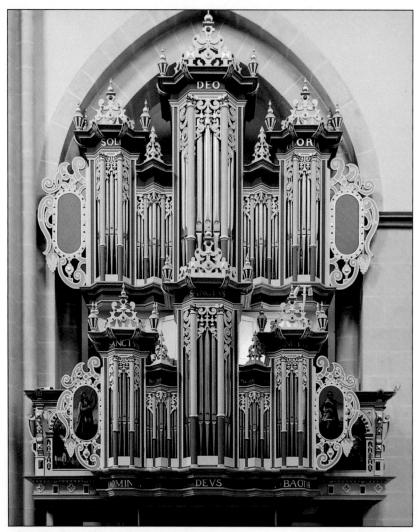

Klosterkirche, Riddagshausen, Germany

From delicious lollipop . . .

Marktkirche, Halle, Germany

. . . to lavish wedding cakes

Wieskirche, Germany

St Antonio di Padua, Bologna, Italy

Consoles

Musical cockpits

Manuals

MANUALS

Heavens! So many notes!
Must one play them all?

— Anon

VISITOR: *Why does the organ have two keyboards?*

ORGANIST (JOKING): *The top one is for the right hand, the bottom is for the left.*

VISITOR: *So what happens when there are five?*

ORGANIST: *Um. . .*

Some consol-ation

COUPLERS: Used for joining two or more divisions of an organ; the mechanism where the pipes of one division are made to sound on the keys of another keyboard or pedal.

DRAWSTOPS: The buttons, knobs, tabs, and levers on the console which control the kinds of noises the organist makes. (Grunts to the page turner are quite uncontrollable). Stop knob, stop-tablet, stop-key, stop-lever more or less do the same thing.

KEYBOARD: (1) another name for a manual. (2) Board used in a traditional game of 'Hide-Those-Keys', mainly by vergers and other church staff.

MANUAL: A keyboard or keyboards with keys (typically 61) which the organist plays. Keys can be short black, long white, or long black, short white (like coffee). The texture is defined by eraser rubbings, crumbs, sweat, sticky tape, and blood.

MEANTONE: One system of tuning the notes, which along with Werkmeister, equal, and well-tempered tuning systems involves lots of maths, arguments, and funny sounds. Best avoided for a quiet life.

ON/OFF SWITCH: (1) The most difficult switch to find on the organ, often deliberately placed somewhere inaccessible. Believed to be an early variation of an IQ test. (2) The one switch you can never be sure you have turned off, especially when you wake at 3am, and you live 25 kilometres away from the organ.

PEDALS: The notes below the console which organists play with their feet. Think bicycle, minus the headwind.

PISTONS: Buttons (usually found under the keyboards within easy reach of a thumb, or above the pedalboard to be operated by a toe) controlling combinations of stops, often called playing aids. Also known as playing hindrances when placed too far away to reach easily, or when pressed by accident.

RUBBISH: (1) Compulsory collection of decade-old detritus on the console comprising tissues, sweets, broken pencils, nail-clippings. (2) What organists sometimes think their clergy (bless 'em) choose for hymns.

STOPS: (1) A rank of pipes or group of ranks (speaking stops), the same as voice or register. (2) Other stop knobs when activated will operate couplers, wind valves, registration aids, and other gizmos. None yet function as annoying-people ejectors.

Keyboards: jaws of the crocodile

Manuals are keyboards for the hands, like a piano keyboard. Pianos sport a modest single keyboard, admittedly with 76 or 88 keys. On an organ, the compass (number of notes) differs from organ to organ, ranging from roughly 45 to 61 on the manuals. Pedals have a more alarming scope, from eight notes on early models to the more realistic standard of 30 to 32 on modern instruments.

The limited compass on some organs (usually earlier instruments) dictates the repertoire that can be played on the instrument. Virtuosic pieces with fistfuls of runny bits up in the top register are never quite so impressive if you suddenly find you have run out of keys.

Keys are the levers which activate the mechanism to make the noise. They are the contrasting toothy-looking chompers, made from wood (often grenadil), plastic, tortoiseshell (tsk-tsk), or ivory (louder tsk-tsk). Early organ keys were struck with whole hands or fists rather than by the fingers, a kind of primitive anger management course for those of choleric disposition.

Enthusiastic organs can have up to 4 or 5 manuals — and more. This appears to thrill people with gorilla-sized arm spans. Why are organists so greedy and want more than one manual?

The reason is that different ranks of pipes are connected to different manuals, allowing the performer greater flexibility, variety, and expression.

For example, you can solo an important melody on one manual using, say, a clarinet stop, while the accompaniment to the tune can be played using softer string stops on another. The pedals are just another manual, played by the feet and falling hymn books.

Usually manuals and pedals can be coupled together to produce greater diversity of sound, or to allow a non-gorilla to couple the sounds from a top-most manual down to a keyboard more comfortably close to hand.

With organs, bigger is not necessarily better, or more pleasant to play and listen to. Granted, the more buttons and levers confronting the player, theoretically the greater variety of sounds to be made.

But the downside of having a whopping goliath to command is that it is beyond the ability of any organist — no matter how accomplished — to explore and use all the possible combinations of sounds in the time that is usually available to them.

Even gorillas struggle.

Positiv organ, Marktkirche Unserer Lieben Frau, Halle, Germany

I MANUAL

Church of St Mary Magdalene, Castle Ashby Estate, England

2 MANUALS

St Katharinen, Oppenheim, Germany

3 MANUALS   *Going up . . .*

Weingarten Basilica, Germany

. . . and up . . .   4 MANUALS

Frombork Cathedral, Poland

5 MANUALS   *...and up...*

Mainz Cathedral, Germany

(We haven't finished yet) 6 MANUALS *...growing...*

Joseph Routon

In America, the Wanamaker organ in Macy's store, Philadelphia, and the Boardwalk Hall organ in Atlantic City fight for the crown as the largest working King of Instruments in the world. These jumbos have organ buffs dribbling with excitement at the very thought of stroking their starter buttons. The Wanamaker organ has 464 ranks, 28,750 pipes, and 6 manuals from which to pilot the thing.

6 MANUALS   ...*growing...*

Compared with the Wanamaker organ, the Boardwalk Hall giant has 7 manuals, and more pipes with roughly 33,112 (give or take a few). However, it has fewer voices, and has not fully functioned since a disaster flood in 1944 rendered about only 30% of it usable; systematic restoration is underway. Even so, they are both awe-inspiring beasts to meet. Sitting on the bench is like sitting in the jaws of a crocodile.

7 MANUALS   *Grown!*

The In-betweeners

Keyboards that are having a little trouble making up their minds . . .

Left: A parish organ in Alsace where the keys sitting lower than the others have not yet been connected to pipes, so have a limited compass. The patient organists have been waiting for these pipes only since about 1525, but good things take time. Likewise, the exposed mechanism at the back of the keyboard is meekly waiting for a replacement panel. It's no use rushing things.

*Sainte-Croix Kaysersberg,
Alsace, France*

Right: Confused? Don't be: the half-grown top keyboard (the Glockenspiel manual) in St Anna's, Limburg, is linked to a carillon rather than pipes, and is not the result of a mathematically challenged organ builder.

St Anna, Limburg, Germany

Memorial Chapel, Stanford University, USA

Equal temperament

Our modern ears think all semitones are created equal, but they are a compromise; although D# and Eb, and G# and Ab are strictly different pitches, on our normal keyboards they share the same key. The Fisk Op.85 organ (above and below) in Stanford University goes a little way to solving that by fixing the Brustpositive and the Brustpedalia in meantone, adding two sub-semitones, or split sharps, per octave. [10]

Photo: Ole Jacobsen

Photos: Huygens-Fokker Foundation

Microtones:
The Huygens-Fokker 31-tone organ

How to keep nervous performers awake at night: the Huygens-Fokker 31-tone organ, in the Muziekgebouw aan 't IJ, Amsterdam, is a unique creation for playing microtonal music fortunately not foisted upon everyday organists.

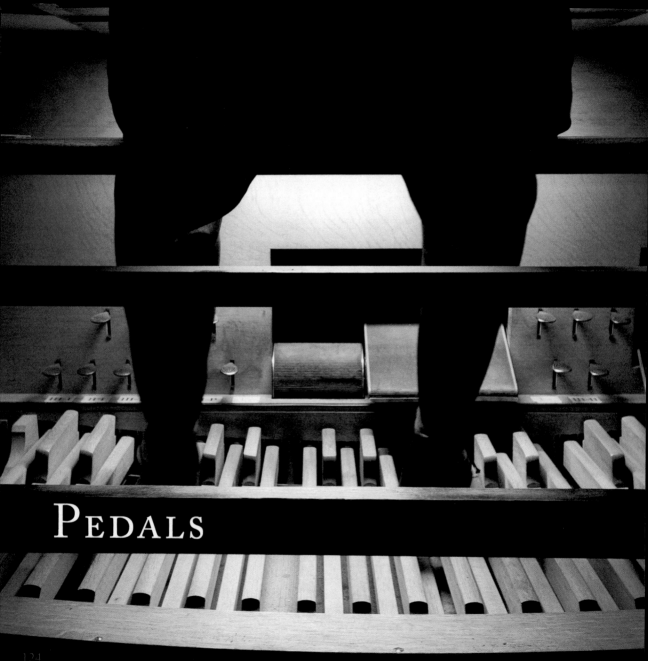

PEDALS

BELOW THE BELT

*My dear Sir, I never in my life played
upon a gridiron.*

— Sir George Smart, 1851 [11]

PARISHIONER 1: *Our organist played the pedals for the first time yesterday. He stood on them when the organ was turned on.*

PARISHIONER 2: *Ouch. I don't think ours makes that sort of racket. Horrid.*

PARISHIONER 1: *Exactly. We couldn't hear ourselves talking over the din.*

Toeing the lines

CONCAVE: Notes of the pedalboard are further off the floor at either end than in the middle.

COMPLEX: Everything, but everything, about the organ. Trust me.

EXPRESSION PEDAL: One or more treadles centred above the pedalboard. These control the volume by opening or closing shutters of some pipes enclosed in a box. Often referred to as a Swell pedal. Never, ever, ever, ever confuse it with a Crescendo pedal (See page 152). You will die.

RATCHET SWELL: a forerunner of the modern balanced Swell pedal, often positioned to the far right above the pedalboard. Also known as trigger, hitch-down, whizz-bang, nag's head, notch, jigger, the hernia machine, and other unmentionable terms, for obvious reasons.

KEYS: Precious objects belonging to organists for locking doors, houses, cars etc that have been dropped between pedals since the 14th century. Archaeological treasures.

RADIATING: Design of a pedalboard which has the notes splaying outwards for ease of playing; also often concave.

STRAIGHT (PARALLEL): the notes point directly ahead. This is bad news for splay-footed and pigeon-toed players.

PEDALBOARDS

While the organist is happily playing with notes and pulling the stops with their hands, their feet have a life of their own. They play solo melodies, fugue subjects, bass lines and even chords; they push pistons and coupler levers, kick inattentive registrants, and work the expression pedals that control the dynamics. Not a lot happening, then.

Like everything else to do with the organ, pedalboards vary widely. Take your pick: concave or flat, straight or radiating, thin or thick slats, or a mixture of the above. Some cook breakfast, others make beds or take you to the football. Life for the organist is rich with surprises.

Not all pedalboards are created equal. Although they all provide a keyboard for the feet to play, how they are designed, where all the knobs and assorted levers are placed, and how the touch feels to the player are different from one organ to the next. Organists are trained to use the pedals without looking at their feet, so adjusting to each layout and distance between pedals, rollschwellers (see page 152), pistons and expression pedals, is a critical job.

Pedals come in all sizes, degrees of dustiness, complexity and playability. Space between the notes is guaranteed large enough for pencils, sweets, money and car keys to fall between them, but too small to be retrieved.

(Key to organs page 404)

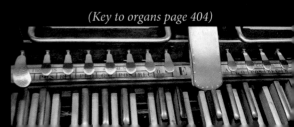

All breeds of organists are catered for, including five- and three-legged contortionists. The chubby rolling pin contraption (bottom right) is called a Rollschweller, and like the Expression Pedal it adjusts the volume by adding or removing stops, while giving the organist's calf muscles a decent working out.

DUAL CONTROL FOR THE LEARNER DRIVER

Stadtkirche, Bietigheim—Bissingen, Germany

An extra expression pedal is helpful when both of the organist's feet are already busy; the assistant can help control the shutters unobtrusively.

A SOLUTION FOR DRAGOONED PIANISTS

Castle Ashby, England

If the player does not wish to use the pedals, a handy (or 'footy'?) board prevents them standing on the pedals as they get on the bench

Soldiers Memorial Hall, Tanunda, Australia

The organist's view of a straight pedalboard.

Stops

STOPS THAT START

The paint of the musician's palette

When the organist pulls the 32' pedal reed, the clerks smile and say 'Ahhh, our organist plays splendidly'!

— Nicholas Gorenstein

THE REASON FOR STOPS?

Press a key on a piano, and you will hear a sound.

Press a key on an organ, and you will hear absolutely nothing (unless you use one or more stops).

Remy Mahler organ, Stadtkirche, Karlsruhe, Germany

What's in a stop name?

Stops look and feel different from one organ to another. From common white circular knobs, through coloured tabs, to long switches, or highly ornate and carved wooden levers, they provide hours of endless entertainment (read: frustration) as the organist tries to find which ones do what.

Since the organist must select which stops they want to colour the music on the page before any sound can be heard (just as a painter must first put paint on a brush before they can make any mark on a canvas) on the face of each stop are usually two bits of information to help:

- A name describing the pipe family to which the stop belongs such as Flute or Trumpet.
- The length of the pipes in that rank or ranks (8', 16', 32', 2 2/3 etc). See page 72.

Sometimes there is a number for each stop (useful for noting in a score when hand-registering). At least 16 different languages are used to name stops worldwide, with German the most common, followed by English, French, Italian, Latin, and Spanish, plus a variety of obscure or corrupted words.

Organ builders derive great joy from playing practical jokes on organists. To that end you can find stops that will release a foxtail instead of making a sound, or perhaps more usefully, one that opens a drinks cabinet such as in Ratzeburg Cathedral (see *"Wishful thinking"* page 311).

The stops on an organ are listed in groups such as Great, Swell, Positif, Choir, Solo, Pedal etc. Organists spend a lot of waiting-for-brides time by inventing fantasy stoplists, or inventing names that best describe their own sad calliope, as one anonymous dreamer did:

GRATE
16' Grunt
8' Scrape
8' Hoot
4' Hoot
2 2/3' Scratch
2' Scratch
IV Shriek 1 1/3'
IV Screech 2/3'
8' Blatt
Clanging

WIMPY
8' Chuff
8' Murmur
8' Mumble
4' Choof
2 2/3' Squeak
2' Squeak
8' Buzz
8' Noise (hideous)

SWILL
8' Moosh
8' Mooshier
8' Hoot
4' Scrape
4' Hoot
2' Squeak
VII Yell
16' Snort
8' Blare
8' Honk
4' Blatt
8' Blatt
4' Blare

LUMPY
32' Woof (wooly)
32' Woof (hooty)
16' Woof (scraping)
8' Scrape (scratchy)
8' Hoot
4' Scrape
2' 4' Moan
IV Scratch 'n' Sniff
32' Pain (frightful)
16' Ugly (downright)

Just kidding. . .

St John's, Kinlet, England

Steinmeyer organ, Erlöserkirche, Munich, Germany

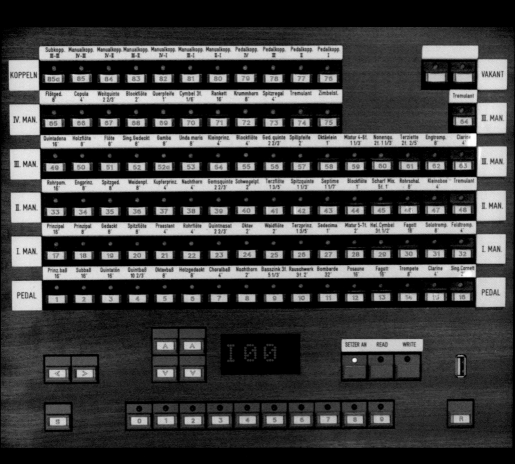

Steinmeyer organ, Stadtkirche, Karlsruhe, Germany

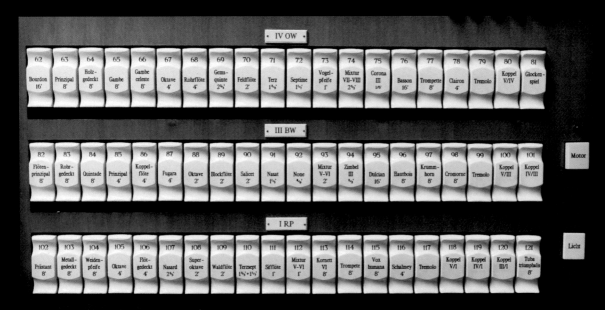

Ulm Munster, Germany

Casavant organ factory, Québec, Canada

Liebfrauen Cathedral, Munich, Germany

Privately owned Cavaillé-Coll, France

Weingarten Abbey, Germany   *St Katharinen, Oppenheim, Germany*

Stiftskirche, Stuttgart, Germany

Schnitger organ, St Nikolai, Flensburg, Germany

Scherer organ (1592), St Jacobi, Hamburg, Germany

Stumm organ (1778), Abbey church, Sayn, Germany

St Andreas (1430), Ostönnen, Germany

FROM AGE TO AGE, BUILDER
TO BUILDER, COUNTRY TO
COUNTRY, THE DIFFERENCE IN
STOP DESIGN IS ENORMOUS.

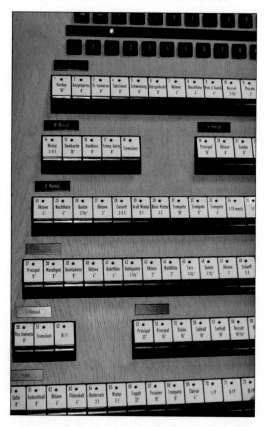

Dom St Marien, Erfurt, Germany, rebuilt in 2007

Oberlinger organ, Wiesbaden Marktkirche, Germany

St Leonhard, Basel, Switzerland

St Anna, Limburg, Germany

Kaiser Wilhelm Memorial Church, Berlin

YOU CAN NEVER BE SURE WHERE THE STOPS ARE.

'Hunt the stop' is the name of the game for organists registering a piece on an unfamiliar instrument. Is it above my head, to one side only, part of a huge semi-circle, or behind me? And can I even reach it without falling off the stool? Organs from the 17th and 18th century in Northern Germany and the Netherlands particularly rejoiced in wide-placed, far-reaching heavy wooden stops. Albatrosses with 8-foot wing spans were organists back then.

JUST FOR FUN

Photos:
John Mander

Photo: Andrew Bryden

The owner of a new organ in a private chapel wanted a bear, so the British firm of Mander Organs obliged with one that emits a growl and pops out of the organ case when the bear stop is pulled. It was inspired by the Gabler organ in Ochsenhausen where an ox emerges from its stable as the player draws the Cuckoo stop.

In Ripon Cathedral, choir conducting was aided by a spooky hand mounted on the organ screen, and operated with a foot pedal. Instigated by organist Charles Moody during his tenure at Ripon in the first half of the 20th century, the hand is still in place and is operated by a handle. Today it is used only to scare the tourists and other novelty purposes.

In the Pauluskirche, Ulm, the organist was uniquely prepared for emergencies. 'Notarzt' in German means emergency doctor. The stop set off an interesting array of sirens, but whether help was ever forthcoming probably depended if there was a doctor in the house. The stop has since been replaced by an unexciting tab that takes life more seriously.

Photo: Christian Boiseaux

Inset photo: Winterhalter

Saint-Savin in Lavedan, one of the oldest in France, built in 1557. It features bizarre masks with moving jaws and eyes, (manipulated by the organist) as well as a nightingale and a tremulant. The pipes of the Regal are made of bamboo.

A Krötenesel (a composite toad and hare fantasy creature) was incorporated into the organ in the Weingartenkirche, Offenburg. When the Krötenesel stop is drawn, its mouth moves and the little toad-hare goes "eeeuuu-quaaak". A riveting, even hair-raising, experience.

The world-famous Arp-Schnitger organ of 1693 in St Jacobi in Hamburg was rebuilt between 1959-61, but removed in the 1990s, and remains in the gallery. Human heads purportedly portray musicians and prominent Hamburg citizens.

With apologies to the organ console in the Oxford Town Hall, UK.

WM. HILL & SON
AND
NORMAN & BEARD LTD.
1929.

Playing
Aids

Playing Aids

The non-speaking cast members
of organ music

VISTOR: *What do all those little buttons and lights and switches do?*

ORGANIST: *Don't know. I never use them.*

Shortcuts for hands & feet

PISTONS: Buttons placed above or below manuals, and above the pedalboard which control preset groups of stops. Saves having to frantically grab handfuls of stops and risk getting the wrong ones. That's the theory. . .

COUPLER: The mechanism that allows the pipes of one manual to sound on another manual, or pedalboard. Can be a piston or stop knob, and it indicates which is being coupled to what.

CRESCENDO PEDAL: A foot-operated treadle designed to gradually bring on more and more stops until the organ is at full throttle. Accidental use of this is one of the main reasons for bad language in the loft.

ROLLSCHWELLER: A cousin of the crescendo pedal, where a foot operates a rotating drum to bring on, or take off, stops. The experience is akin to slipping on a banana skin.

SEQUENCER: A kind of on-board computer capture system which stores Stop changes (registrations) that are recalled in sequence during performance with the press of a single button. If you're lucky.

STEPPER: Like a sequencer, but it is limited to advancing general pistons in order.

WIND GAUGE: Dials with numbers and needles usually indicate wind pressure of the windchests. If they display altitude and figures in feet, you're in the wrong cockpit.

PLAYING AIDS

Playing aids are designed to help both player and registrant(s). Depending on the skilful (or otherwise) design of the console, they can be useful, or confusing and tricky to use. Confusing, because to the uninitiated these mute helpers resemble other buttons, tabs or stops which are connected to pipes and therefore make noises.

Playing aids are the strong, silent, non-speaking parts. As shortcuts to multiple actions they are extremely valuable to the player. For example, pistons control pre-set stop combinations, which enable registrations to be changed rapidly by the organist while playing.

Buttons range in size from teensy . . .
. . . to budding dinner plates

Tewkesbury Abbey, England

In case the fingers are already fully occupied flailing around in a furious flurry, and every other body part is otherwise engaged, the feet can press the pistons. Unless they, too, are rattling off a dance of their own. This is where the organist needs extra limbs (now is the time for them to be nice to their page turner/registrant. Really, very, extra nice).

St Andrew's, Hingham, Norfolk, UK

A 'horseshoe' reversible Great to Pedal coupler; press one side to bring on the coupler; press the other side to take it off.

Couplers

Couplers couple. Meaning that the pipes of one division are connected so they sound on the keys of another; hence Swell to Great, Solo to Great, Great to Pedal etc. Couplers can be operated by either the hands or feet, and although they look like speaking stops, whether tabs, knobs or levers, they don't give a hoot, or a boom, or whistle. They are strictly mute.

To tell them apart, these are the clues: couplers might be labelled in red lettering rather than black; they huddle together in an obliging heap, and can be recognised often by their abbreviated division labels, which sound like someone with ill-fitting dentures. Gt to Ped, Sw to Gt, Ch to Gt, Ch to Ped, and so on. Even, as in the Melbourne Town Hall organ below, a 'Bomb. to Pedal'. That'll wake them.

Shanghai Oriental Arts Centre, China

Melbourne Town Hall, Australia

ABOVE: A line-up of stops and couplers above unmarked pistons in De Montfort Hall, Leicester.
BELOW: a lonely minimalist and nameless button in Oxford Town Hall, England

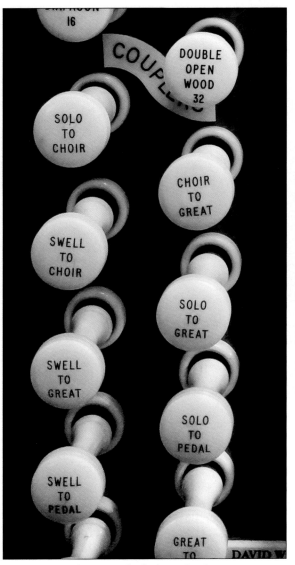

Chester Cathedral, England

Gillingham Methodist Church, Dorset, England

EXPRESSION PEDALS

The revolutionary idea of varying the volume in an organ was the inspiration of a Londoner, Abraham Jordan. In 1712 he thought it would be jolly to enclose the pipes of one section of the organ in a box, with a lid at the top which could be opened or closed to let more or less sound out.

So the Nag's-head Swell was born, and after a slight modification of changing the lid to a series of venetian blinds or shutters on the box front, enclosing the Swell pipes has remained an important part of organ construction ever since.

Larger organs can have other divisions enclosed, so the Solo, Choir or even the Great might also be enclosed, if you're lucky. Shame about the limit of only two feet to control them.

The original ratchet system used to control the shutters (also known as the whizz-bang and hernia gadget) at the extreme right above the pedals, consisted of a notched stick holding a lever in place, which the organist had to kick sideways to move between the notched positions. Prone to noisy mishaps and hardly subtle, it was a relief to all when the balanced swell mechanism was devised in the 1860s.

Modern systems show detailed gradations using a digital display above the manuals. (*See page 163*)

Marktkirche, Wiesbaden, Germany

Pull-down levers which bring on a pre-set group of pipes with one lunge of the foot.

Castle Ashby, England

Tanunda, Australia

LEFT & ABOVE: Ratchet swell levers, variously referred to as the whizz-bang, trigger, hitch-down, or Nag's head, which operate the shutters of the boxes enclosing certain pipes to make the sound louder or softer.

159

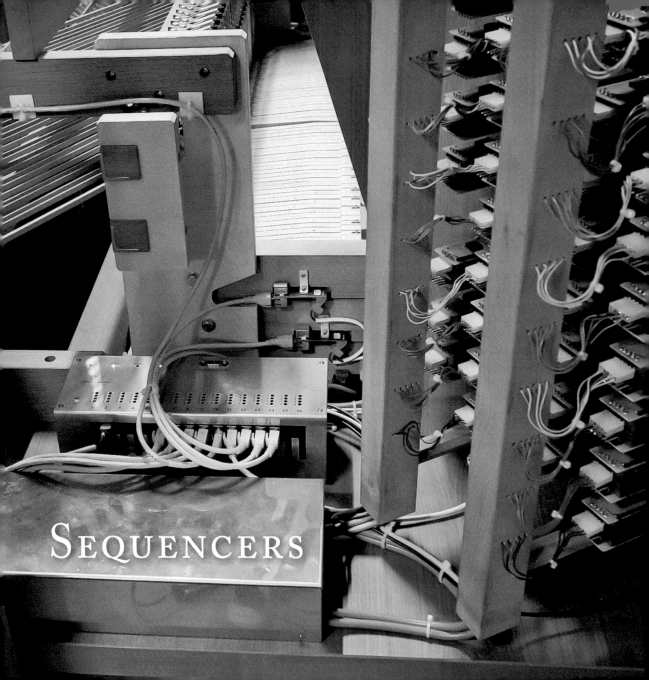

 SEQUENCERS

For some performers, sequencers (an on-board computer capture system that stores registrations. See page 152) are vital. These little modern additions to organs are as necessary to some organists as electricity, computers, or mobile phones. But not all agree. Like much new technology, sequencers and steppers are misunderstood, misused, abused, or adored, and are always the subject of lively debates wherever two or more organists are gathered together.

ORGANIST ONE: *I hate sequencers — terrified silly by the stupid things.*

ORGANIST TWO: *I love sequencers — best things ever invented. Can't live without them.*

[CUE FIST FIGHT]

Frombork Cathedral, Poland

The precursor of sequencers, called free combinations, filled the consoles with layers of knobs and buttons, most without names. But they look impressive and pretty.

Himmerod Abbey, Germany

St Nikolaus, Stuttgart, Germany

St Johannes, Arth-Goldau, Switzerland

Christchurch Town Hall, New Zealand

St Peter Basilica, Dillingen, Germany

Predigerkirche, Erfurt, Germany

Sequencers and steppers work by the
push of one button . . . sometimes . . .

Sequencer pads lurk in drawers or are embedded in the wood at the side of the console, where a page turner or registrant can access them discreetly and easily.

The symbols < and > indicate Back and Forward for the sequence. A warning to the over-eager: Do make sure you know which symbol you are pressing; severe organist grumpiness may result if incorrect buttons are pushed, or pushed twice by accident. Mea culpa — been there, done that.

OTHER CONSOLE GIZMOS

Organs that are stars of stage and screen as well as providing the usual sacred functions (such as in the Mormon Tabernacle and the Conference Center in Salt Lake City) are equipped with more lights, read-outs, buttons and technical wotsits than a space shuttle.

Mormon Tabernacle, Temple Square, Salt Lake City, Utah, USA

Mormon Convention Center, Salt Lake City, Utah, USA

These can be operated by the organist directly from a pull-out drawer under the organ bench. There the organist can: change the colours of the hall lights, use the intercom stations, the broadcast timer, and adjust the pedal light with a dimmer. He can also keep an eye on the special master indicator light, "Stand by", and "On the Air" signals, and, if all else fails, use a Technician call button (at the top of my Christmas wish-list for organs).

ALTERNATIVE TV

If the congregation/audience can't see the organist, the organist can't see them without using a large rear-vision mirror or closed circuit TV. Such monitors are an invaluable addition to the console, allowing the organist to follow the conductor, watch what happens when the groom faints at the altar, or check if the communion has finished. It would be a bonus if they occasionally included access to the Sports channel or a rollicking documentary or drama.

St John the Baptist, Montreal, Canada

Mainz Cathedral, Germany

Keeping an eye on everything: sport, movies, news and uh, perhaps the choir.

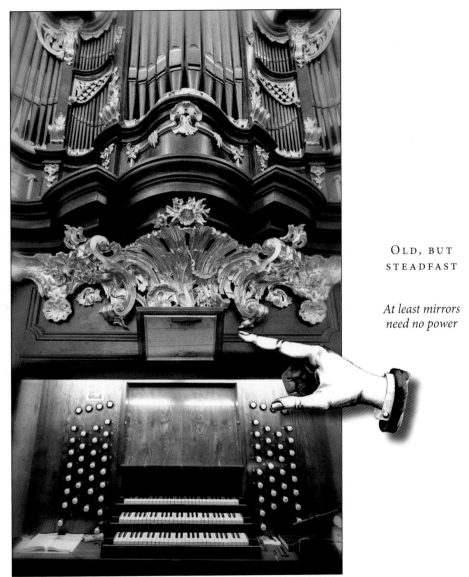

OLD, BUT
STEADFAST

*At least mirrors
need no power*

Bardo, Poland

167

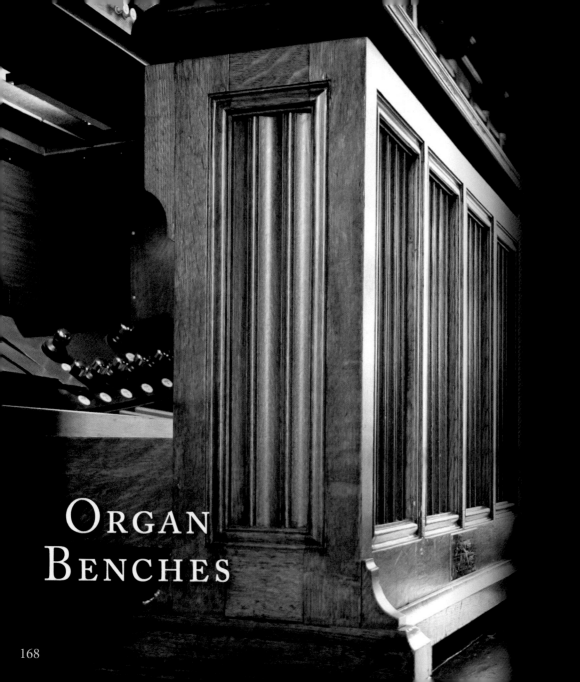

Organ
Benches

BENCHMARKS

"— in an American main-line Protestant church where I had been engaged to perform, the custodial staff had been given the green light to dust and polish the console and bench, the latter having been so diligently waxed and buffed that as I gently leapt onto the south end, I found my ample frame discharged as if shot from a cannon at the north. Only a manic, lucky grab to the hefty console frame prohibited my ending in a sultry heap on the terrazzo floor! Is it absolutely mandatory that cauldrons of commercially available sprays be incessantly lavished with such unbridled enthusiasm on proper wooden surfaces?"

— Carlo Curley 1952-2012

THE BOTTOM LINE

Be it ever so humble, this little French organ stool has a footrest at the back, and bull bars on the kickboard. There the organist can rest their feet, weary no doubt from the exertion of playing the entire octave of notes.

Was it borer worms dining in style or someone's bright idea to use this English organ seat as a colander? Perhaps they misunderstood the phrase 'strains of music'.

One of the most famous organs in the world still relies on an age-old, sophisticated height-adjustment mechanism.

Any similarity between this small English village church stool, and mediaeval punishment stocks, is possibly coincidental.

Organists in Harness & Other Quirks

What's a lad to do when all his limbs are already occupied, and he needs to open an enclosed division? Some organs have an extra expression pedal (see p. 132) for the registrant to operate, but why stop there? — just throw your whole body into playing expressively with a harness.

The harness contraption worn in a demonstration by Scott Farrell was designed and presented to Rock Church in the UK, by Holford Bosanquet of Rock Manor. The Squire was responsible for the system of operating the Swell shutters from the organist's backrest, the player being attached by an adjustable harness, leaning back and forward to open and close the slats. An organist with a severe coughing fit would enliven any regular church service, but the harness is unlikely to catch on as a fashion accessory.

Not a harness, but still quirky, is the split-seat Howard Organ Chair, spoken of in hushed (and quite possibly falsetto) tones by users who have survived the experience. Suffice it to quote a promotional note: 'male players will learn to sit a bit more cautiously than the ladies for reasons that become self-evident'.[12]

Photo: Sheila Hignett

Temple Church

Hanover Marktkirche

A TAIL OF ORGANISTS: HOW HIGH OR LOW CAN YOU GO?

Organists range in size from toddler to giant. So the height of the organ stool is far more critical than the minor adjustments required of a piano stool because of the need to reach up to several manuals and play with the feet. I have found myself dangling helplessly like a 4-year-old above the pedals, and seen lanky pine trees playing with their knees around their ears — all for want of an adjustable stool.

Players are resourceful when it comes to getting the distance perfect for practice, but how can you be sure that, come the concert, it will be the same as when you left it?

Hanover Marktkirche has a simple gradation method that at least gives the height, if not the position, from the manuals. Temple Church's

solution is a reliable little happy-crank system with a moving pointer. The snaggletoothed jaws of the bench at Welschensteinach probably need to be approached with caution unless you want to lose a few fingers.

St Peter and Paul, Welschensteinach

INNER WORKINGS

THE MECHANICAL MARVEL INSIDE

Inside the boxes that we know as organs lies a convoluted paradise, not unlike a child's toybox: Meccano mixed with bits of Lego, spiced with umpteen jigsaw puzzle pieces, flavoured with tubes, nuts, and whirligigs galore and connected by enough electrical spaghetti to power the world. A brief rummage inside the inner workings should arouse your curiosity about the miracle of how an organ — an instrument whose basic working principle has changed little in the past 600 years — speaks. Or should that be thunders? Whispers? It depends. . .

INCREDULOUS VISITOR: *WOW! WOW! But where are the speakers?*

Where the action is

BLOWER: Machine supplying the wind to the reservoir.

CIPHER: An organ pipe sounding without anyone touching a key. Can be due to damage or a fault. The sound no-one wants to hear — it's spooky and annoying, and can bring a concert to an abrupt and early end. Even worse, no-one is sure how to spell it. With an 'I'? Or a 'Y'?

ELECTRO-PNEUMATIC ACTION: The keyboards are connected to the windchest using electrical circuits. Electromagnets activate pneumatic motors that pull down the pallets under the pipes.

MECHANICAL (TRACKER) ACTION: Manuals are connected directly to windchests by trackers & rollers. Often preferred to more modern electrical action as many consider that it gives the player more direct control over the speech of the pipes.

PALLET: The valve which allows the wind into a pipe or a wind channel.

RANK: (1) A row of pipes usually controlled by one Stop (see page 134 onwards for stops). (2) The whiff of old organ shoes in lofts. (3) What the clergy pull when they want one hymn, and the organist wants another.

RESERVOIR: A box, like bellows, with a weighted lid regulating pressure and supply of air to windchests — the 'lungs' of the instrument.

ROLLERBOARD: The device in a mechanical action organ which allows the key action movement to be transferred laterally to the wider-spaced windchests.

STOP OR VOICE: A rank of specific pipes or a group of ranks. Several ranks can make up a single stop such as a Cornet or Mixture.

WINDCHEST: A box filled with air supplied by the windtrunks, on which ranks of pipes sits.

WINDTRUNKS: large tubing made of wood, metal, or plastic to carry wind to the windchests. (*See pages 178-179 for illustrations*)

The pipes sit in holes on the top of windchests through which air is pumped from the reservoir.

No sound is heard yet because 1) you've forgotten to turn the power on, dummy; 2) the holes are 'stopped' by sliders and 3) you have not touched any notes. When you choose the sound you want by pulling out the appropriate stop knob, (which moves the slider), it allows air to pass into the pipe. The only thing left is to press a note down.

By depressing a key on the manual, and by a series of tracker rods, rollerboards and varied fulcrum mechanical actions, the rods pull down the valve for that note. This allows the wind to pass through, and yes, finally, the pipe speaks. All this happens within a zilli-fraction of a second.

Imagine the whirring turbulence of activity when the organist plays a piece with thousands of notes, at break-neck speed; think of all those myriad rods and pallets all pushing, tracking, pulling, clacking, chiffing, and woofing inside the organ case.

With luck (and good construction) you won't hear any of this industrial clattering.

IT WORKS SOMETHING LIKE THIS, HUH?

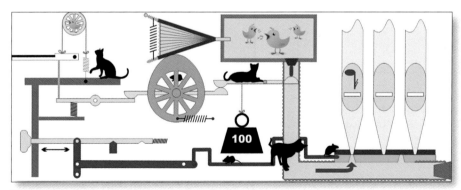

Illustration: Towser Burko

UM, WELL, NO, MORE LIKE THIS

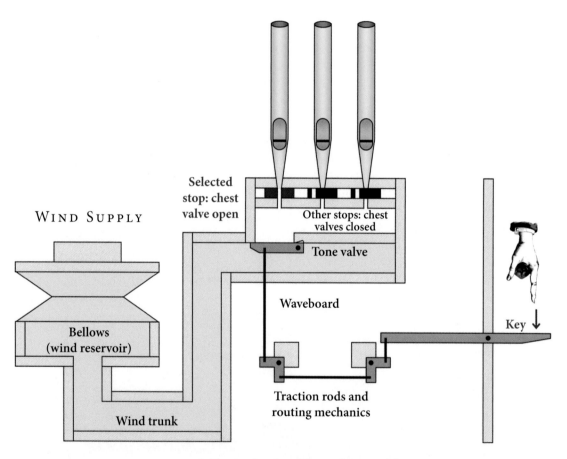

1. *The stop is selected but no key pressed*

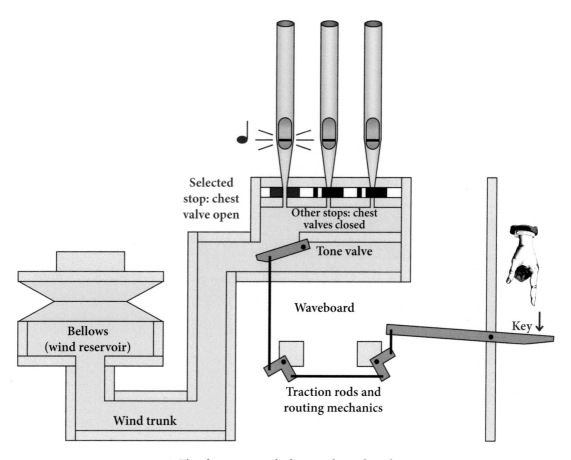

Selected stop: chest valve open

Other stops: chest valves closed

Tone valve

Bellows (wind reservoir)

Waveboard

Key ↓

Traction rods and routing mechanics

Wind trunk

2. The player presses the key to release the valve

Diagrams: Martin Doering ~ www.die-orgelseite.de

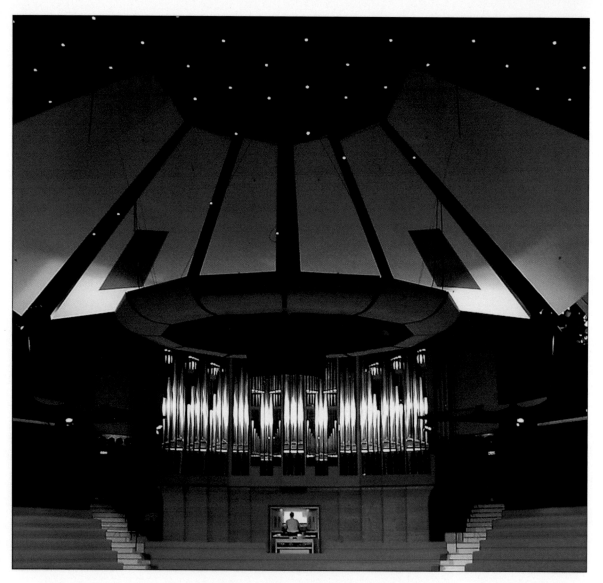

Of the 4314 pipes in the Christchurch Town Hall Rieger organ, only relatively few are visible. Most of them are distributed over several levels behind the façade pipes, in four main sections, called Divisions: Hauptwerk, Schwellwerk, Oberwerk and Pedal.

THE ORGAN IS A HUMAN BEING TOO

A pipe organ operates in some ways like our own bodies; it needs air under pressure in its lungs (windchests) which is then expelled from the appropriate pipes (mouths). As recorded by 18th century organ builder Dom Bedos, before electricity came to our aid, organ blowers slaved away behind the scenes to provide the puff. (See page 370)

FIRST, THE LUNGS TAKE A DEEP BREATH. . .

In Christchurch Town Hall the air reservoirs are regulated by bricks wrapped in tissue paper. In Tanunda Memorial Hall, South Australia, 90lb railway tracks weigh down the reservoirs.

Christchurch Town Hall reservoir

Tanunda Memorial Hall reservoir

Two Town Hall organs

Despite their visual, size and specification differences, organs work basically the same way. To show how relatively similar organs are in principle, follow this basic description of two large city organs in New Zealand.

Christchurch ~ Rieger ~ 1997

From the blowers and through the wind reservoirs, the air is directed via 46.5 metres of trunking to the windchests on which the pipes are sitting — all within a millisecond of the notes being played. Windchests and their pipes are grouped into divisions and stacked throughout the organ case, giving the best chance for every pipe to make itself heard. The tight fit is a challenge for chubby organ builders, and as for cat swinging? Forget it.

Tracker action exposed

Rollerboards

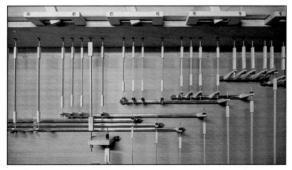

Rollerboards

THE BRAIN SENDS INSTRUCTIONS...

As the player, you choose which sounds you want by pulling out the appropriate stop knobs. The knobs open sliders to the chests holding the pipes so the wind can blow through. Wake your page turner, and begin playing.

VIA THE NERVOUS SYSTEM. . .

Playing the notes activates tracker rods throughout the organ, passing the message along sideways, so to speak, to the windchests of the required pipes. As the notes are played, the pallets below the pipes open, letting the wind in and the sound out. Once your fingers leave the notes, the pallet closes, and the note stops immediately. Unless, that is, one of the pallets jams open and you get a cipher. Lucky you! (Ciphers are like death; everyone has to cope with one eventually. See page 176)

Top level: Schwellwerk (Swell)

2nd level: Hauptwerk (Great)

Bottom level: The action behind the console

The pipes are organised into divisions, in stacks, layers, and levels. The Christchurch organ has three main levels, with walkways between pipes allowing tuners and builders easier access for tuning.

The four divisions of this organ are the Hauptwerk, Schwellwerk, Oberwerk, and Pedal

(English organ equivalent divisions would be Great, Swell, Solo, Pedal)

With the appropriate sliders open to the chosen ranks of pipes, the message gets through to the mouths of the pipes; and the organ speaks.

Hauptwerk division of the pre-earthquake 1997 Rieger

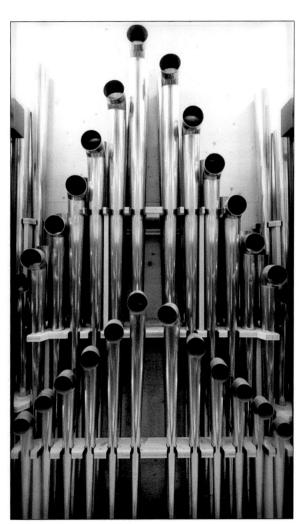

Bombardes

Different sizes, builders, ages, looks, specifications, layout, but the process of making music is the same. Again, in the Auckland Town Hall, the Klais organ starts with the wind supply, which goes to the windchests; the chosen stops operate the sliders to open the ranks, and the pallets for specific pipes are operated by the notes which the organist plays. Easy when you know how.

Auckland Town Hall, New Zealand

Three electric blowers provide the wind for 23 bellows (left, loaded with 4 tonnes of weights) which in turn supply the 5291 pipes of the Auckland Town Hall organ through 320 metres of wooden trunking.

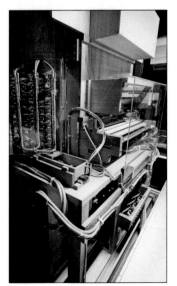

Some of the 68km of electrical umbilical cords

'Oh. Santa! Hi! Stuck again?'

A family of submarines gathering for a conference

Looking out to the Auckland Town Hall auditorium from behind the pipes. . .

. . . and what the audience sees

The Organs — Grandest instrument the hand
Of man has placed in Music's galaxy;
In which all Nature's wondrous sounds are linked
In golden chains of countless harmonies.
Responsive to the touch of man's weak hands
As if a giant's fingers swept its keys
And called concordant voices from the depths,
The diapason of the storm-struck sea,
The thunder's peal, the wind's wild whistling wail,
The songs of swift-winged warblers in the air,
And the soft sighing of the ambient breeze
Temple of Tone art thou! The shrine supreme
Of Sound's mysterious powers and richest gifts,
God-given thought alone could have inspired
The human mind to frame so grand a work;
Great Organ — Monarch of all Instruments!

~ George Ashdown Audsley

Strasbourg Cathedral, France

ORGANIST ON
THE LOOSE

PART TWO

ORGANIST ON THE LOOSE

~ Martin Setchell ~
On the road with a
free-range concert
organist

Up-close and personal snapshots of
life behind the scenes by his itinerant
registrant - groupie - chauffeur - PA -
photographer - wife

ORGANIST ON THE LOOSE

On the road with a free-range concert organist

KITCHEN SINK, PLUS PLUG

Touring the world, giving concerts in famous cathedrals, visiting exciting new cities — is it as much fun as it sounds? Yes. And no. A thrilling privilege, but it's no holiday. Hundreds of organists travel long distances and work hard to bring music to organ lovers, and all our stories are different. What follows are some of my own personal — and occasionally very odd — experiences

Symbiosis is the key here: my husband Martin is the performer, but I prefer to be a silent partner. Martin meticulously plans concerts, choosing his repertoire, establishing programmes, researching the organs and organising travel up to three years ahead; I am in charge of last-minute packing and panicking. Here are a few basic items that are priority baggage in case of famine, fire, plague, and clergy attack.

My essential travel equipment comprises: a Canon 7D camera, lenses, laptop, two-way radios, batteries, universal adaptor plugs, a digital recorder, mobile phones (with SIM cards of assorted countries), baby tripod which looks like a thumb-screw, a fully grown tripod, memory drives and cards, three external storage drives, SatNavs (x2 so we can enjoy them arguing whether to send us directly into a canal, or to Iceland via the Nile), chargers for all of the above; a portable LED

lighting source.

I carry enough dangly stuff in the form of cables and cords to start a bungy jumping business, plus a large bag, inside which I throw all of the above. This mélange of circuitry excites airport security people and guarantees I will be treated as a person of interest at airline departure gates.

Clothes are also useful.

HUNTING ORGANS

Since we are not long-distance swimmers, we must fly from New Zealand to reach most of our concert venues. The best we can hope for is a trance-like coma until the awful reality of modern air travel is finished. Our nearest neighbour is a little island to the west of us called Australia, but if we stay on a plane long enough (13 to 24 hours or worse), we find other signs of musical life and an abundance of instruments to unearth. Organs flourish everywhere (a rough guess as to the number of organs worldwide is in the hundreds of thousands) but getting to them can be a challenge. Tracking down instruments, whether to play or pay homage, we have:

- strolled along the top of a Swiss mountain, awe-struck by the view.
- taken a gondola, a cog-wheel railway, and a bus all to the same venue.
- hopped on a passing ferry.
- trained — the ironhorse variety.
- driven, guided somewhat erratically by an elderly GPS system having an emotional meltdown.
- ridden on the back of a farm trailer in the company of hay and party goers en route to a wine and music festival.

- played sardines in a bus containing the entire population of Turin, during rush-hour, in a heat wave, sitting on a motor seemingly about to burst into flames.
- bounced around in jalopies driven by any number of wannabe rally drivers.
- huddled nervously in a train compartment between Germany and Poland, hiding from robbers.
- and always, walked, and walked. And walked. Exercise regarded as warm-up sessions for those tricky pedal solos.

Getting in: the key to it all

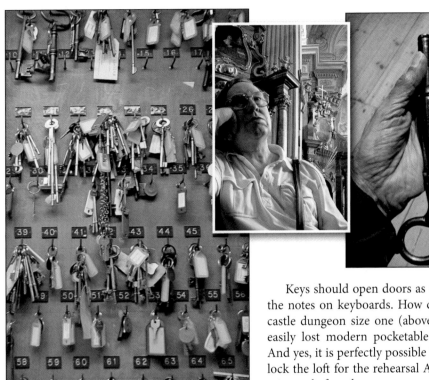

Keys should open doors as well as playing the notes on keyboards. How do you fancy a castle dungeon size one (above) or the more easily lost modern pocketable variety (left)? And yes, it is perfectly possible for a church to lock the loft for the rehearsal AND until only minutes before the concert starts (centre).

Try this game today:

The "Muggins' Boardgame" is a charming little game that church authorities play with visiting organists. It starts with the verger pointing to a board like the one above and saying: "The organ key is on the board. So is the toilet key. Not sure which ones they are." Then it's your turn. Thanks a bunch. Of keys.

Mountaineering gear optional

Lofts (or galleries) are where organs like to roost. Lofts are also simply that: lofty. Translated, this means high, or really, really high, with lots of steps of varying degrees of precariousness to get there.

Loft access is ideal for weeding out the weak and infirm — stout hearts and bodies are vital prerequisites for organists (although some take the term stout a little too literally, and more than one person has become firmly wedged on the way up or down a stairwell). Surprisingly, the longevity of organists is legendary, with many playing into their 80s and still able to climb the umpteen, sometimes perilous, steps to their driving seats.

Spare a thought for the young J.S.Bach, who, in the early 1700s, trudged for 450km from Arnstadt to Lübeck to listen to his hero, Dietrich Buxtehude. Having finally arrived at the Marienkirche, his heart must have sunk to the bottom of his battered boots to see the last remaining hurdle: a zillion steps to the loft (opposite, left).

The access to Regensburg and Magdeburg Cathedrals in Germany obligingly have lifts but there is a catch. The Regensburg Rieger lift to the organ, suspended 8.2metres from the ground, provides a two-minute sedate levitation experience so the occupant must be in no hurry to get there.

In Magdeburg (opposite, right), where the organ gallery is even higher, the elevator is a great help — except there are no labels on the buttons. Unless you can remember which level your organ console is on, you can be unavoidably detained with a Grande Tour of the tower, courtesy of the lift, as Martin discovered before his concert in Magdeburg.

Making what was meant to be a simple journey from ground floor to the loft, he paid unscheduled visits to the soft furnishings level, via the menswear and shoe departments. After an impressive but brief stop at the top of the tower, he arrived breathless at the organ with seconds to spare as I cowered in the gallery with the terrifying prospect of filling in for him. But aching muscles and pounding heart rate were a small price to pay for the privacy and quiet of the loft in which to practice. And think of the gym fees we save.

Kemper organ (1968), Marienkirche, Lübeck, Germany

A. Schuke organ (2008), Cathedral of Saints Catherine and Maurice, Magdeburg, Germany

The stairway to
heaven is strewn
with grunts,
moans, gasps,
puffs and curses.
Be prepared to
climb. Or abseil,
whichever works
for you.

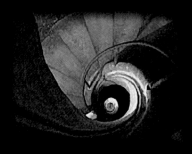

Don't
look up,
either

*Consider handrails
a luxury item*

Oh, the joys of being the only musicians who can climb
up inside the instrument in order to play it.

Paris

Béziers

The thrill of making it to the console despite crumbling stones or missing floorboards is tempered by some of the traditional accessories that adorn organ lofts. As organists tunnel their way to the console through the innards of the instrument, they may occasionally trip over bodies of trapped birds and bats. The journey is more often garnished with inedible trash left by organists, choirs, and other guests (i.e. anything that moves and has two or more legs).

Visitors have reported finding old books, music, robes, 30-year-old service sheets, broken electricals, tools, magazines, ashtrays, cobwebs and dust galore, broken plates, glasses, a frying pan, a novel; prizes retrieved from under pedalboards have included a child's baby tooth, pieces from a plastic Batman cloak, melting sweets, and tissues.

Building materials, nativity play sets, and pretty much anything that church members have no room for anywhere else also end up in lofts. Surprisingly, a crate of beer found tucked in one dark corner is still looking for its owner.

London

Made it.

HOT TIP: Sleeping organists should never be disturbed. Drink the wine instead.

210

One feature of nearly all organ lofts: organists' shoes. Tatty, worn, and smelly, but greatly loved. Only by the owner, of course. Touch them at your peril. Special organ shoes need to be pliable and just slippery enough for swift foot movement, with a higher heel so the organist can use both heels and toes on the pedals, and long enough so they can play two (or more) notes at once. Shoes are to the feet of an organist as gloves are to the hand: the fit is vital.

An extra dimension creeps in for the fashion conscious. Organist Jeannine Jordan writes: 'You can always tell an organist by our shoes. Our footwear makes us distinctive. Rarely does anyone over four years old wear black patent leather shoes with perky ribbon laces other than an organist. At times my feet have been shod in classy silver tie-up shoes or gold-dusted shoes in a stunning strap style. These 'magic shoes' help an ordinary person become someone different, someone special, someone unlike others — an organist.'

NOW PEEK OVER THE GALLERY:

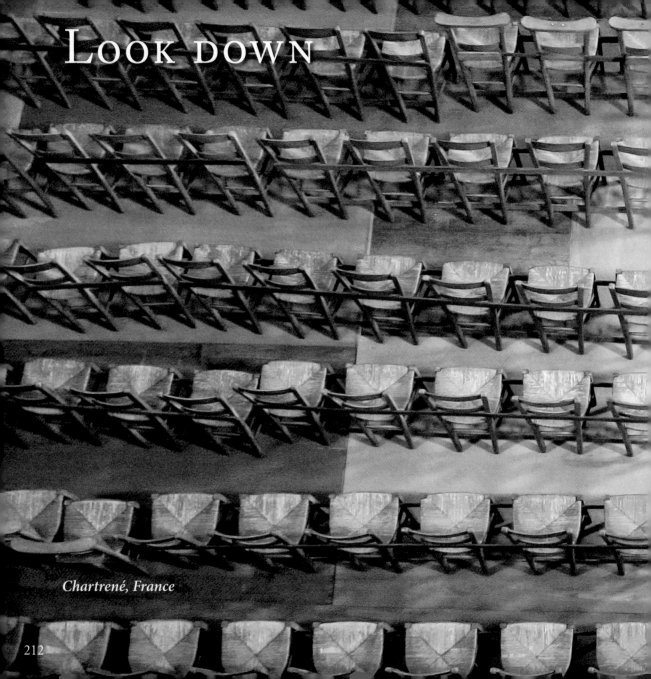

LOOK DOWN

Chartrené, France

LOOK UP

Münster, Ulm, Germany

Weingarten Basilica of St Martin, Germany

Only from the organ loft is it possible to see some of the typical organ builders' word play; for example, in Weingarten (wine garden) the Glocken (bells) are hung as a bunch of grapes. [13]

Sydney Town Hall, Australia

Sitting at the Sydney Town Hall organ under some of the largest pipes in the world, the organist can only hope that the subterranean rumbling he can hear is the 64' and not an earthquake. [14]

LOOK AROUND

Fulda Cathedral, Germany

Once aloft, unless you suffer from vertigo (in which case, what are you doing here?), take a good look overboard; over the gallery, around the walls and up at the ceiling. Organists are privy to a magical and exclusive world.

In rare idle moments, people-watching makes an entertaining hobby for loft dwellers. A favourite trick is to let rip with a sudden loud chord from the pipes directly above the audience. Now, that's fun.

Bamberg Cathedral, Germany

'Yoo-hoo, sleepy audience man in the fourth pew from the front. We are armed with hymns books and other heavy weaponry in case you nod off. Just letting you know —'

Meanwhile, what happens to me, the assistant, registrant, page-turner, wife, with all my paraphernalia?

For the first few hours, I sit where the audience will sit, making myself oxymoronically comfortable in a pew, with my gadgets. Visitors see me, hush their children, stop running, taking selfies, eating or whatever other intrusive activity they usually enjoy, and begin to show the space they are ogling the respect it is due.

Such is the policing effect I and my little two-way radio have on people. That, and the laptop and occasional flak vest I wear to carry multiple lenses and spare batteries. Mistakenly looking like the Pope's personal security guard, my mission is much simpler, but still vital to the success of an organ concert: I am Martin's ears, seated where the audience will sit, to listen, to follow the music score on my laptop, and to record. I do this because, ironically, the organist has the worst seat in the house to hear what he is playing. To the performer, the music can range from deafening to inaudible.

Imagine sitting inside a jet engine, and you will get the idea. The console may be stationed almost inside the case, or at least intimately close

Working in Oliwa Cathedral, Poland. The distant white dot under the pipes in the marked orange circle is Martin at the console.

to the pipes. Organs with one division behind the organist's back (the Rückpositiv) make it especially difficult for the organist to hear the total sound as a perfect balance; it may sound completely unbalanced to the audience far away.

Just as every organ is unique, so is every acoustic. The reverberation will vary between a cavernous 9-second echo to none at all. That affects how the music is heard. So my role, using the 2-way radios, is to let Martin (up in his console nest) know of a potential problem for the listeners. For example if an accompaniment is over-powering a beautiful solo, or he is playing too fast or too legato for the sound to be heard clearly in the nave below. If we get it right, the audience doesn't have to suffer a whirl of nonsensical jangling noise, or muffled incoherent rumbling. An organist who has registered solely according to what he hears at the console, without knowing how this sounds to the audience in the nave, is asking for trouble.

A note to confused taxi drivers everywhere: Now you know — the unidentified caller who told you to *'bring up the strings and get rid of the mixtures'* and similar, was probably me straying onto your bandwidth. Sorry.

Fulda Cathedral: The organist is up there among those pipes, somewhere, I think. I can hear him. Just.

At Speed Dating Central, Freda and Harold found the organs more difficult to get to know than the other participants

HOW LONG DO YOU NEED?

Lose no opportunity of practising on the organ; there is no other instrument which takes a swifter revenge on anything unclear or sloppy in composition or playing.

— Robert Schumann

NICE BUT CLUELESS ORGANISER:	*Would an hour be enough?*
VISITING ORGANIST:	*Ah — no.*
NBCO:	*Oh. A couple of hours?*
VO:	*Ah — no.*
NBCO:	*Oh. Three then?*
VO:	*Keep going —*
NBCO:	*How about 10 hours?*
VO:	*Yes, please.*
NBCO:	*Wow. Don't you know the pieces well enough?*
VO:	*NO. I don't know the ORGAN.*

Time, time, and more time, gentlemen, please!

Let me in. Preferably before my concert

What's the difference between organists and all other instrumentalists? All members of an orchestra have their own carefully treasured and maintained instruments which they guard zealously. Cellists pay for airline seats for their cellos to sit quietly alongside them as a member of the family when they fly.

Organists cannot (usually) take their instruments with them, and every organ they play is unfamiliar. If they are wise, they will have researched its specifications and console layout well beforehand. It does not matter if the venue is a church or a concert hall, every organ is a new revelation for the performer.

As a rough estimate, for every 10 minutes of recital running time, a minimum of one hour is needed to explore the organ, make friends with it, and set registrations of the pieces. It is not a matter of rehearsing or learning the notes — the organist has already done that long ago. So every second, every minute that the player is delayed from figuring out how these unique contraptions work adds stress and does not provide the best conditions for ensuring they can give their best in the concert to come.

Once chosen, registrations then have to be preserved. If the organ has some technical means of storing the stop changes (e.g. sequencer) it can take a seeming epoch to figure how that system works; there is no industry standard for sequencers, and some of them compete with Mensa intelligence workouts for mind-warping difficulty. Before one concert on a 4-manual organ, an assistant organist struggled for 90 minutes to prepare the extraordinarily flaky sequencer system (taking up crucial rehearsal time) before Martin could set his registrations.

If there is no such modern capture system, then every stop change has to be laboriously written on the music to be executed by hand(s). Extra time is needed to double check that nothing has been missed, and to rehearse the registration changes.

If you prevent your organists from having enough time to prepare in this way, it's like asking a pilot to take off before having run a full safety check of his aircraft. Expect a crash.

"So every two hours you have to turn it off and wait for half an hour for the motor to cool down. . ."

How to make a chappy happy

Give them aeons of time, and then some, so that they can get to know the instrument and register their programme properly. A locked-out, delayed organist is not happy (and no, these pictures are not posed. This is a reality show).

'I CAN SEE YOU'RE NOT BUSY'

BACK TO EARTH WITH DETACHED CONSOLES

Detached organ consoles in a nave might be easier to get to, but that's exactly the problem; if the player has no difficulty with access, then neither do inquisitive visitors.

As an educational exercise, this is a Good Thing; except when time is tight, minutes are racing by, and precious practice seconds are lost with constant interruptions.

Altenberg Cathedral, Germany

Friendly visitors readily grab the chance to watch an organist rehearse. Sometimes they offer genial advice, occasionally requesting a particular tune that they can sing along to (because, as they point out, they 'can see you're not busy'). For some, it is a fortuitous moment to ferret through the organist's music.

The closer a tourist can get to the console, the better — for the tourist. What a perfect time to share this experience with their friends, the visitors in the next aisle, or the entire bus group at the back of the church. Aloud! For extra effect, stand just behind the organist! Such fun! Tell all the world! Take selfies! (But push the page turner out of the way first — yes, it really happened).

'I can see you're not busy — '

'— so can you play "Happy Birthday" for my friend?'

Polite solution: Improper use of a hotel **Do Not Disturb** *sign*

So you think you're going to practise?

(Hysterical laughter offstage)

They promised you a six-hour rehearsal slot, right? But when you arrive you are cheerfully told that this minimum time has been eroded because there is an unexpected meeting, a baptism, a funeral, a guided tour, or a wedding (how can a wedding be unexpected?). Every interruption, no matter how fleeting or minor, disturbs concentration and can turn already pressured schedules into tourniquets of stress for performers.

With only a few more hours to set the registrations, the fire/smoke/burglar alarm will go off. This allows 20 minutes of downtime during which the emergency crews discover there was no fire/smoke/or burglar, and in which we consider changing jobs.

Workers reinstalling seating, resealing floors, or hammering back the church roof, LOVE hearing you play! They whistle out of tune, and hammer out of time — it's such jolly fun. As a gentle hint, ask if there is too much noise and (continuing to shoot nails like bullets) they'll reassure you that everything is "just fine, mate; you carry on with your songs. We don't mind a bit."

Sufficiently powerful VIPs can stop anything in their tracks, including rehearsing organists. Needing every second in the lead up to a concert in an English church, Martin's precisely honed practice schedule vanished when the Archbishop of Canterbury and his entourage arrived to halt proceedings.

And he didn't even stay for the concert.

DUETS

As every organist knows, the organ is hot-wired to all earsplitting machinery within a 1km radius. Press the console starter switch, and watch as rabid vacuum cleaners, floor polishers, and even forklifts delivering chairs gravitate lovingly as close as they can to the object of their affection. Yes, vacuum cleaners really do suck.

Instead of competing with a noisy accompaniment, all you can do is give up and instead watch in wonder as lustrous, highly polished surfaces are transformed into even more lustrous, highly polished surfaces.

*'Oh, hello Health and Safety Police.
Where have you been all these years?
Why now? Oh, tower renovation. Not
the loft stairs then? Pity.'*

Above is a unique variation on *Organists'
Strip Poker* that was necessitated by a
sudden cloudburst en route to the church,
and the urgent need to dry sodden
trousers in the fortunately secluded loft.
Those of sensitive natures will be relieved
it was only the rehearsal. We were glad it
was Summer.

Cameras and other contraptions

Cameras that project video images of the performers hidden in a loft to the audience below are popular, and rightly so. However, setting up projection equipment can erode vital rehearsal and registration time, and create challenging hurdles for page-turners. If the concert is also lucky enough to attract local press coverage, the photographer will arrive two minutes before the recital starts, and settle down for a chatty interview.

My job as bouncer begins here.

In sickness and in health

When sickness strikes (as rare as that is) during a tour, it will happen at the worst possible time. Illness during rehearsals is annoying, and it delays preparation, to say nothing of the worry that it will carry over to the concert. Like ciphers and earthquake aftershocks, knowing that something can happen any time is enough to set your nerves jangling like chimes. We wouldn't be the first to carry a precautionary bucket or watertight plastic bag to the console; but concentrating on the niceties of Bach Trio Sonatas is a daunting exercise when eyeing an expectant receptacle, hopefully within reach. Luckily not many organists expire at the helm apart from famous examples such as Louis Vierne, who died at the console of Notre-Dame de Paris.

Castle Ashby cricket ground and pavillion
(A.K.A church conveniences)

For several years I waged war with a persistent and loyal diverticular disease. It followed me everywhere and knew exactly when to wake up and cause trouble. The best venues for it to flourish were:

• Places that had no handy lavatories. These are usually the prettiest and most historic, such as the utterly charming church on the Castle Ashby estate owned by the Marquess of Northampton. The ancient church humbly possesses bathroom facilities only in the nearby cricket pavilion; this lies on the other side of the cricket field and is a good 10-minute walk (or a frantic four-minute gallop if necessary) away. It brought new meaning to the game's "getting the runs".

• Mediaeval cathedrals run by authorities who delight in locking people inside the building until released at a vaguely prearranged time. Any toilets in such buildings are usually barred, somewhere through a million doors and down a trillion stairs in the darkness, or so camouflaged that they are unrecognisable as such; which contributes towards needlessly interrupted or delayed rehearsals. Thankfully the era of mobile phones has removed much of the worry about being forgotten (yes, it has happened) but being imprisoned in an emergency — of any kind — is not my idea of fun.

Cancellation of a concert for illness is something we resist at all costs, and that cost can be high. I once watched anxiously as the disgustingly healthy Martin, fighting a high fever from 'flu and with sweat pouring down him even before playing a note, insisted on going ahead with a programme that featured his energetic transcription of Mussorgsky's *Pictures at an Exhibition*. Both clothes and man had to be wrung out afterwards, but no-one had any idea why the performer looked as if he had just swum the Rhine to get to the cathedral.

It's not always possible to carry on. Once Martin was struck by a violent stomach bug that confined him to a wheelchair. The concert was postponed until the following evening. It was left to me to sit alone on the church steps to explain in my kindergarten-level German to the arriving audience that Herr Setchell war sehr, sehr krank und could not play, but would they come back tomorrow?

Apparently, my garbled efforts coupled with those of Google's translation service told bewildered punters that he had been run over by a hedgehog and was going to sing a song at midnight. I stepped up my efforts to learn German. Or sign language. Anything.

OTHER METHODS OF SELF-HARM ON TOUR

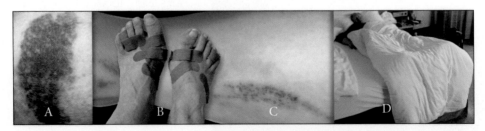

A: Falling down church steps; B: Post-tour, too much running up loft stairs & catching trains; C: Falling into manhole; D: vicious stomach bug (concert postponed 24 hours).

Four Rehearsal rules
for the Organ

Rule #1:

Make sure you break down or refuse to start when (a) there is an important concert that day, (b) the organ builder or anyone who can get you working again lives more than three hours away by road. Or is ill.

Rule #2:

At least one (preferably more) of your reed pipes must go out of tune, even though you were tuned the day before. A Trumpet stop that was intended to be used as the solo voice in one of the pieces is an excellent choice. Nothing makes an organist madder.

Develop a cipher or two. Or three. The more the merrier!

A cipher (keeping a random note sounding after the key has been released) is your best way of letting the organist know who is boss. Make it the loudest one you have! Even if the organist can trace which delinquent refuses to stop screeching, they will be unlikely to fix it quickly. They might think of stuffing the mouth of the wayward pipe with an item of clothing, or perhaps extract the pipe altogether (ouch). Failing that, they will usually abandon ship and swim to the safety of the nearest pub.

So a little reminder like this during the rehearsal is a cunning way to put the organist on edge — your victim can never be certain that you intend to behave during the concert.

Immediately the concert is over, fix your faults before the tuner arrives, then pretend that nothing was wrong and hint that the organist must be delusional. Works every time.

WHAT COULD POSSIBLY GO WRONG? GO WRONG? GO WRO. . .

Well, the wardrobe, for a start. Especially if you have a change of costume after the interval. In the Concert Hall in Fukuoka, Japan, Martin played the first half dressed as Bach, complete with lacy 18th-century shirt and wig. At half-time, he could not change into his concert shirt because I had helpfully washed and ironed, and then left it, at the hotel, which was miles away from the Concert Hall. Undeterred, he sported it beneath his tailcoat, spiffy cuffs, frilly ruff and all, for the second half. The Japanese were intrigued, but a little nervous about our fashion sense.

Extreme heat is bad news for performers; organs go out of tune, and sweaty fingers have a good chance of slipping onto wrong notes, to say nothing of the discomfort of playing in blistering temperatures. A heatwave in Germany was so intense that Martin was inspired to make a tiny adjustment to his normal formal concert dress. To the audience seated below the organ gallery, there was nothing amiss as he took his bow; but the camera reveals the solution: his lower half was clad in old-fashioned, cool, ever-so casual, kiwi-style shorts.

Bride's, groom's or organist's side?

Busy venues — both concert halls and churches — have to juggle the time allowed for performers who need to set up, rehearse, perform, and pack out their respective shows; mass-appeal teeny-boppers or populist crooners who attract more people, therefore more money, are likely to be given priority over humble organists. When events overlap, the organisers sit back and hope everyone plays nicely.

We have been scheduled back-to-back with church weddings, Masses or Evensongs that precede or follow the concert. When three such events (wedding-concert-Mass) run hard up against each other, such as here (right) in Montpellier, the resulting jam is like the meeting of two major motorways. The only way to avoid colliding with the next Mass (and priestly wrath) is to omit from the programme the pieces that have been so carefully timed, balanced and registered for hours beforehand.

Roll on the day when an orchestra or rock band is prepared to do the same.

Photographing the organ is one way to pass the time before or during your concert.

Waiting, waiting, waiting

Some apparently imperturbable organists, especially in the hospitable Parisian churches, encourage onlookers in the loft while a service is in progress. During a concert, it is less conducive to a good performance to have visitors up close who are prone to fidget, natter, take selfies, and can't help but distract the player from the task at hand. But it happens.

The crowds gathered for a concert on a steaming hot night in Limone-Piemonte, Italy. The Good News was that the church was packed, with two to a chair in some parts. The Bad News was that one of the audience chose to park himself in the loft. On the organ bench. Beside Martin. His chatty comments (in Italian) were well-intentioned, but I had to remove him pronto. At least he left obligingly enough.

By contrast, a total stranger materialised in an organ gallery in Germany (below) after Martin had begun his concert. The intruder ignored my efforts (in between flipping pages and pulling stops) to signal for him to leave. He edged closer to the console, and things turned nasty with a tug-of-war between him and me. I pulled. He stayed put. I yanked harder. He struck back. I was concerned about the chance of him having a weapon and becoming violent, so dragging him over to the gallery edge, I shouted for help from the audience (oblivious to the drama upstairs). The intruder was promptly removed by more brawny beings than me. Martin played stoically on.

Organists keep going, at all costs.

'Yes, I know I'm gorgeous, but I am 247 years old, and my feet are killing me, so if you don't mind, I'll finish right now and go to bed. I know you are in the middle of your concert but I'll leave on just one nice loud stop so you don't forget me. Good night.'

If the organ hasn't practised ciphering during rehearsal, it might save the surprise for the concert, bringing the organist — and the concert — to its knees.

At least if the console view is projected onto a screen, the audience will understand something is wrong if they see hands frantically trying to jiggle keys to free the jammed mechanism while a note or two keeps sounding. Usually, the organist gives up the fight, and everyone trudges home, programme unfinished, souls destroyed.

A cipher can happen to any organ, anytime, and is no fault of the organist. It has happened to us during a concert twice in three decades. That's more than enough.

The organist has played his heart out, thrown all his soul, mind and movable bits into awe-inspiring music for the past hour, and sweated enough fluids to have refloated the Titanic. This, surely, must have transported the masses into paradise. So what do people say as they leave? Here are a few post-recital critiques organists have heard:

- *Do you know XXX ? Now, (s)he's a REALLY good organist*
- *I have no idea how you do it.*
- *You're very small — how do you make it so loud?*
- *Aren't those 4-year-old pianists on Facebook the best?*
- *My second cousin comes from XXX. Do you know her?*
- *I watched a great version of that piece on YouTube.*
- *A lot of people seemed to like it.*
- *Do you take your own organ with you?*
- *Your playing was wonderful. Particularly for a young lady.*
- *Can you play any Heavy Metal stuff?*
- *Your performance was remarkable.*
- *I don't want to buy any CDs. Just sign the programme.*
- *Now that WAS interesting.*
- *Well, that was more than we expected.*

- *I actually enjoyed it.*
- *Where do you buy your shirts?*
- *We hope you didn't hear Sam throwing his little tantrum.*
- *I have never heard you do better.*
- *Amazing. I had an auntie who played the harmonium too. Perhaps you know her?*
- *I loved it when your music fell down.*
- *We're thinking of buying an organ. What do you recommend?*
- *Boy, I'll bet you're glad it's over.*
- *I'm hungry.*
- *I knew some of the songs! It was great!*
- *Oh, you're a woman?*
- *I knew a musician once.*
- *Your shoes looked really shiny in the video.*
- *I was thinking we should get one for home.*
- *Here, this good luck charm is for you.*

'Ah, music,' he said, wiping his eyes.
'A magic beyond all we do here!'

~ Dumbledore in
Harry Potter and the
Philosopher's Stone

St Gregory, Ribeauvillé, France

ORGANIST AT
YOUR SERVICE

PART THREE

THE DAILY
ORGAN GRINDER

*Organist and choirmaster Adrian Marple reveals that life in the
English church scene is not all cute, cassock-coated choirboys.*

A 'REAL LIFE DIPLOMA' FOR ORGANISTS

If I am honest, part of my early fascination with the whole organ mystique was the elaborate garb that organists ponced about in. My parents had just about got over the shock of seeing me as a young chorister in a red cassock and ruff, but when I got presented with my white surplice, there was a tearful Mum and a fearful Dad present. For Dad, the natural progression from this would be to ballet lessons, embroidery classes, and then who knows where it would end?

I remember that it took several hours to prize the surplice off me that day, and then naturally I set my sights on more decorative bling — there were medals with different coloured ribbons, light blue, dark blue, red, and even purple for the really good choristers. The organist and choirmaster had a special cut-away surplice and A HOOD.

So began my life-quest for one of my own.

There are many varied colours and patterns of hoods available, and I know several people who even chose their university on this fact. Yes, the suitability of the course and the geography of the campus played a little part, but careful attention was paid to the prospect of graduating with a long black gown and a swanky hood. After all, no-one wants to slog away for three years, only to be presented with a limp polyester rag in bright orange (apologies to you if you own one like this).

There are many laudable organists' diplomas out there, and the world is a better place for the people who put themselves through the rigorous tests to achieve them. I have had a bash at a few, and one particularly tortuous diploma, the FRCO (Fellow of the Royal College of Organists), well and truly deserves (and receives) worldwide acclaim.

From my memory of the requirements, I had to sight-read a piece of music in four different clefs and key signatures while being poked by a large stick, in front of a jury of what seemed like 15 people, where at even a hint of a mistake, a trap-door under the organ stool would be opened, and I would disappear down a chute and hurtle towards a dungeon full of other mere mortals.

Having escaped the dungeon, and returning to my everyday console, I thought we should have a diploma fine-tuned to the real-life drudgery of a church organist.

So with much pride, I exclusively reveal to you in this book, the launch of my all-new diploma for Church Organists:

S.O.D.

(SPECIAL ORGANISTS' DIPLOMA)

Syllabus:

PERFORMANCE SKILLS

The candidate must:

i) Present three hastily-chosen and fearsomely under-rehearsed pieces to be played to a gathering of disinterested chattering people. The performance should compete with the audience/congregation noise, and the candidate will be expected to continue playing, even unheard, while remaining calm.

ii) While playing the above, the candidate will be required to recite the hymn numbers for a future service from memory to one of the examiners.

iii) Play over the first line-and-a-half of a hymn before changing it to a different hymn when told that they are playing the wrong one.

iv) Play a hymn in time, with a thunderous bass standing and singing behind them, at a speed of his choosing.

v) Play, transpose, conduct, and sing the tenor part of a psalm simultaneously, as on a typical Sunday Evensong.

SCALES

vi) Manual Scales (in all keys), at a temperature of either -30°C or 360°C (the examiner's choice). There will be two 'out of tune notes' on the organ which must be avoided at all costs.

vii) Pedal scales — C major. To be played with the heel coming off one shoe (candidate's choice).

At all times during the performance examination, the music desk shall be full of hymn books, old music, church magazines, and service books. At the discretion of the examiner, s/he may knock any of these onto the manuals below. All piston settings shall be changed by a churchwarden, just before the examination. The transpose button on the console may be activated by a small child at any time during the examination.

PAPERWORK

(90 minutes — or the length of a sermon, whichever is longer)

i) Without manuscript paper or the aid of a keyboard, on the back of a hymn list, prepare an arrangement of a well-known pop song, for a wedding next week. You must use a white-board marker for this exercise.

ii) Secretly prepare next month's hymn/ music list during a sermon while maintaining a 'pious listening' face to all around you.

iii) Prepare your accounts for how much you earn from your church job, without crying.

Any successful applicants will receive the entitlement to be called SODs and to wear the academic dress associated with the diploma.

Now it only remains for me to decide on a suitably tasteful hood.

MY DAUGHTER'S GETTING MARRIED AND SHE WANTS THE 'STACCATO'

(THE PHONE RINGS. I STUMBLE OUT OF THE SHOWER, MY MODESTY INEFFECTIVELY BEING COVERED BY A SMALL HAND-TOWEL).

'Hello?'

'Is that the organist?'

'Well I am AN organist, yes'

'This is Mrs Sternly-Bustling. My daughter Brünhilde is getting married, and she wants the "Staccato" by "The V Doors". The wedding is only three-and-a-half years away, at St Kessogs Church, Lower Uffern – do you know it?'

'I have to say, I haven't yet had the pleasure — '

'They have got an organ there, although I don't think it's used that often'.

(I reach for laptop, and look up said church organ on the National Pipe Organ Register. It is a single manual, hand-pumped Crappitt & Sons of 1834; unaltered since then, and unvisited by a tuner, with a total of 4 stops and no pedals.)

'I can well imagine'.

'They're not a musical couple, so I thought of the "Trumpet Volunteer" to come in to, and Brünhilde's sister Fortuna is going to sing during the signing of the register. She hasn't done much singing on her own in public since she was at school, but she used to be very good, she got a merit on her Grade 2'.

'And what will she be treating us to?'

' "Memory", but the tune is all wrong — she can't reach the notes in the high bit, and the low bit is too low for her'.

'Leaving not too many options in between?'

'Can you do the high bit a bit lower, and the low bit a bit higher for her?'

' — so that they meet in the middle, you mean? Well that certainly would be a challenge for both me and the listeners — '

'Or the other idea is to walk in to "Lara's theme" from "Gone with the wind" — '

'I need to get a pen.'

(I REACH FOR THE PEN, LOSE THE TOWEL, AND FRIGHTEN THE WINDOW CLEANER, WHO RUNS AWAY).

' — she wants to walk in at the loud bit, so we'll need to rehearse with you a couple of times before, to make sure you get it right.'

'I don't usually rehearse the entry music with the bride that often, but I can make sure that the music reaches a suitably majestic climax when she appears — I'll pull out the 4-foot flute, and the effect will be theatrically stunning, I'm sure'.

'So you'll be at the three rehearsals at the church, then?'

'Did you say 'three rehearsals?' That would mean a round trip of 115 miles to Lower Uffern and back, each time.'

'Well the vicar there said that five rehearsals were too many, but it has to be right, hasn't it? I mean, the dress is costing us £35,000. It's being specially hand-stitched by nuns from Norway. And we've had to pay out for the 'Hotel Louche' which is the best part of £100,000, then there's the 'Kajagoogoo' tribute band, another £5,000 and the cake, the bridesmaid's dresses, the vintage cars, not to mention the honeymoon, suits, rings, flowers, stag night, hen night, chocolate fountain, photographers. . .

'We'll pay you for playing of course — only the best for Brünhilde. Shall we say £25? — hello? — hello? — '

'Are you still there?'

[DIAL TONE]

WILL NO-ONE RID ME OF THIS MEDDLESOME PRIEST?

No organist would ever seriously consider the sentiments of what King Henry II was traditionally heard to say in exasperation at the constant bickering between him and his Archbishop of Canterbury, Thomas Becket. Reputedly, he was overheard by four of his knights and in one of the grossest misinterpretations of an eavesdrop in history, they travelled to Canterbury and on December 29, 1170, murdered him in his own cathedral.

That is a harsh result of a disagreement between a member of the clergy and Royalty; I know many organists that would gladly crown their vicars, but most would draw the line at actually bumping them off — particularly in their own church. For one thing, if it was in the Church of England, you couldn't do it without several meetings, minutes taken, a rota being drawn up, and tea and biscuits served afterwards.

So what of the 'special relationship' between a vicar and an organist? Tales abound of two people who work together in these roles not speaking to each other, or being at constant loggerheads. Stories of noisy blowers and tremulant motors being switched on during sermons, and car tyres being let down, have been told. The first cause of potential problems between the throne and the noise-maker behind it is money and how much to pay the organ-grinder. Most of us know it is a vocation and feel drawn towards the windy bag of whistles often from an early age. Years of practice, studying how to play, and putting ourselves through exams leads us to present ourselves to a church and their interviewing panel in the hope of getting access to a decent organ. The panel will probably consist of the churchwarden, a couple of members of the choir and a flower lady (the real power-hub of the church).

A few pieces played to the panel, maybe a choir practice taken, and an interview, will seal the organist's fate. Often it may just be a cosy fireside chat at a vicarage, over a bottle of red. Either method is followed by the thorny issue of how much you'll be paid. This is a good time to check out your shoes, not making too much eye contact, while the Reverend wails about the church roof costing hundreds of thousands, and the price of heating the building, the new set of hymn books bought 20 years ago, and the number of weddings and funerals. Then the figure is mentioned. You do some quick calculations and decide that should just about get you through the month, before it becomes painfully obvious: this is the Annual Salary.

The choice of music is central to the healthy relationship between cleric and the minstrel, and it helps if you share common ground here. Nothing is more likely to bring the organist out in a rash than being presented with a copy of "Kool Songz 4 the Kidz 4 2dayz worship zones (choonz edition with chordz in both eazy keyz)". Organists: beware when the vicar goes to a conference and returns with IDEAS! It could result in having to learn new songs not written with your skills in mind. If he has bought a didgeridoo or a set of bagpipes, leave instantly.

The vicar sometimes chooses the hymns, or an influential person who makes all the important decisions in the running of the church, for example, the vicar's spouse. If you are lucky enough to have some influence on the hymn choice, then you face hours poring over church lectionaries, finding the appointed bible readings and theme for the service, taking into consideration the congregation's penchant for familiar hymns, together with the choir's need for new challenges, and the church's desperation to attract youngsters. This will leave you with a list of three hymns which fits all categories, and you go for *Praise, my Soul* instead.

I am a fan of all kinds of worship music serving the needs of the worshippers and suiting the style of worship. But my sympathies go to those who have to make their centuries-old pipe organ with a leaky wind-chest sound like a worship band with guitar, drums, and a funky Hammond.

'What to do about the organ' is a painful recurring subject involving profound moral and ethical questions, priorities of the church's future vision, the preferences of the churchwarden, Diocesan organ adviser, the PCC and of course, the organist's spouse. It has been known for the organist to be consulted too, but usually this is just about the 'choice of a really good organist to give the opening recital'. Much blood has been spilt in the war between *Ancient & Modern*, preservation or innovation, digital (electronic) or pipe organ but that is an entire book on its own.

To train as an organist takes a great deal of dedication, but so does foaling a vicar. It is always a pleasure to watch young curates find their feet, but I feel duty-bound to test the 'sense of humour' aspect of their training — hence the curate-spoof. I try things like:

- Hide sermon notes or Banns of Marriage book.
- "Yes, it's usual for the curate to always sing the responses at evensong" (give them a variety of high-pitched notes just out of their normal vocal range).
- "I believe the vicar wants to include some interpretative dance into the services. How are you at leading the congregation in the paso doble?"
- Invent a 'long-cherished tradition' for your church: "Are you doing the early

morning dawn-rising top-of-the-tower service on New Years' Day?"

- The following is my favourite, which works particularly well if the organ is at the back of the church: Just as the procession starts at the beginning of the service call out *'Did you get the message from Hilda about her jam stall? Could you remember to announce it is next Thursday at the church centre from 10 until 4 in aid of the roof, and there is Brenda's 'bring and buy' at the library on Wednesday at 10.45 — 12.55 in aid of the Organ Fund, and Claire, Connie, and Cathy's coffee and cake morning on Tuesday from 11 to 3 here at church, and we're leaving out verses 3, 4, 7, 8 & 12 in hymn 436, and we're swapping hymns 454 (leaving out verse 4) and 445 (leaving out verse 5). Psalm 54 has been changed to 45 starting at verse 5, not verse 4. Don't forget.'*

Through all this, though, a positive working relationship based on mutual trust and respect is one to be worked at and to be treasured, if you are to avoid anything like the murder of Thomas Becket. Compromise, a sense of humour, and a common goal has to be achieved. So if you ever find a CD of "New Christian rap classics arranged for organ" left casually as a hint on your organ stool, simply return the compliment by leaving a Messiaen organ CD on the pulpit, with a poster proclaiming:

"A series of weekly organ recitals of the complete organ music of Olivier Messiaen, with an appreciative talk given before each one by the vicar".

You may just get your own way — for once.

Why organists prefer lofts

[IT IS SATURDAY MORNING, THE CHURCH IS FREE, THE ORGAN IS FREE.]

Most importantly, Mr Organist has a spare half hour while Mrs Organist minds the children. Just enough time to get to grips with that tricky bit in the G minor Fugue (where all fingers, thumbs, toes, ankles, legs, and arms are spinning in opposite directions). Where the whole body relies on the gluteus maximus doing a job it wasn't designed for. The church is open to the public. What could possibly go wrong?

[POM DIDDLE-DIDDLE-DEE POM DIDDLE-DIDDLE-DEE DOODLE DUM DUM POM DIDDLE]

'Practising are you?'

'Yes. Are you visiting?' asked in a charming-organist-of-church-not-wanting-to-offend-anyone kind of way.

'Yes, we've not been to this church before. It's so nice to come into a church and hear the organ being played. I'm Ernest Lee-Blathering and this is my wife, Constance. That piece sounds difficult. Having some trouble are you?'

'Well, yes. It's Bach's G minor Fugue—a magnificent piece and needs a lot of pract. . .'

'Ah well, we've got a FANTASTIC organist at our church.'

[ORGANIST, KEEPING CALM, FEIGNS INTEREST]

'Oh really, and where's that?'

'St Bunion's in Whiplash. We've got an 1850 Father Willis, untouched, 3 manual. The organist is a very young man, Peter Overly-Brill. Have you heard of him? No? Well, HE's very talented. Do you know, he got his FRCO when he was just 12? Blindfolded, won all the prizes. He can play that 'Staccato' piece by Vee Door from memory, with his eyes shut. He practises all the time, night and day.'

'Gosh, how lucky for you, and him. It is difficult finding the time to practise. This is my monthly half-hour slot. So, it's been really interesting talking to you, and I'd love to keep listening to you, but I really must —'

'This is a very big church. Do you get many in your congregation?'

'Yes, actually we do. We have several services each Sunday and during the week. There is an 8.30 early morning service, and a 9.30 which is a family service, more suited to people with young children. We also have a traditional service at 11 where our boys' and men's choir—'

'— *you see, at St Bunion's they queue outside half an hour before the services, just to hear Peter play. Do they do that here?*'

'Err . . . not every week, no. But it's been lovely listening to you, you'll have to excuse me, I have to do my practice. Please come again.'

[ADRIAN RESTARTS THE FUGUE]

Pom diddle-diddle-dee, Pom diddle-diddle-dee, doodle dum dum dum. . .

'Beautiful'

doodle dum dum dum diddle. . .

'Just beautiful.'

Dum dum dum —

[ADRIAN TURNS ROUND, SEES AN
ELDERLY, EXCESSIVELY FRAIL WOMAN,
VISIBLY AND TEARFULLY MOVED]

'Are you alright? Can I get you a drink of water, or a chair, perhaps?'

(Gasping for breath) *'Can — you — play 'The Old — Rugged — Cross?'*

'Err. . . well, I could do. Are you alright? You look a bit—'

'I've walked from the station to see this church . . . (gasp) I haven't been here . . . since I was a girl, and my grandmother got married here, and had "The Old Rugged Cross" at her wedding. It is my dying wish to hear it played one... last... time... at the place... she got married.'

'It sounds like I'd better hurry up then.'

(ADRIAN HASTILY FINDS ANCIENT HYMN
BOOK AND DULY OBLIGES)

Now, which other musical instruments can grant you the public scrutiny of your technical failings coupled with a discussion of your inadequacies? There you are, at peak concentration trying to master the intricacies of the King of Instruments while holding a conversation with a visitor, during which if you even hint at irritation, you know that a complaining email will zing its way to your vicar before you have even had time to switch the blower off.

During one practice session when I was blissfully hacking my way through Widor's 6th, I casually looked in my mirror to see about 200 students who had noiselessly visited St M's, most of whom were recording my practice on their iPhones. So, somewhere on YouTube, I'm sure there is a hilarious video of an organist turning around and jumping three feet in the air with a startled yelp. That's me.

At times, my frenetic fumblings have been accompanied by vacuum cleaners, wedding rehearsals, a visit by the fire brigade, many talkative visitors, and on a couple of occasions some famous cathedral organists on holiday.

So: those organists who are in the stratosphere, in a loft — I envy you. Spare a thought for those of us at ground level. It may be a hefty and dizzying climb to your eyrie, but at least you have a fighting chance of getting the G minor nailed.

[POM DIDDLE-DIDDLE-DEE,
POM DIDDLE-DIDDLE-DEE. . .]

An ideal sanctuary for organists, a thousand metres above interruptions, in Ulm Münster.

Every week comes a new challenge for the church organist: that of setting the right mood for the congregation as we prepare for worship at the beginning of the service. Most of us arrive at church having travelled by foot, car, bike, bus, train, boat or plane (some may even use all of these methods, especially in Scotland). Some of us have had to frog-march a family with all of its forms of travel delays. Small children with lost shoes is a particular Sunday morning tradition in our house, coupled with errant dummies and missing car keys.

So what goes through your mind on your home-to-church journey? Mine goes something like this:

'Locked front door timer's on for chicken wife both children seatbelts four shoes dummy Bach G minor would be nice afterwards nappies wipes keys going to be late no we ARE late don't get caught speeding have we got enough tenors for the anthem left the bathroom window open what shall I play before the service the opening hymn's in G must fix that timer on the cooker and it's the 22nd Sunday after Trinity the fuel gauge is on 'empty' the pedals are tricky in the Bach so. . .'

'Are you listening to me? '

'Yes, dear. *Rhosymedre* would do nicely, or something more rousing that ends on the dominant.'

'Pardon?'

'What?'

'I said we must have my family for lunch soon.'

'I'd prefer chicken, or I could just improvise on the first hymn?'

(Confused silence in car).

I have developed a 'Sunday morning apology face' for my regular late arrival, to greet the understanding nods and barely disguised frowns from the patiently waiting choir and already-seated congregation. So, with moments to spare, I don my special organ shoes, angelic robes, grab my choice of voluntaries, and alight the slippery stool.

Setting the mood and calling the congregation to worship is something over which organists take great care. Composers have written some wonderful stuff, designed to transport people from their pre-service nattering to preparing themselves (which

the power of music to express the inexpressible with the spoken word which speaks directly to the heart.

The version we have this morning is the combination of *Schmücke dich, o liebe Seele* — J. S. Bach, BWV 654 (**Performer**: organist) and *Can you hear me at the back?* (**Performer**: Sound desk operator testing the microphones). Bach knew a thing or two about how to write music suitable for services; after all, he had enough practice. But I am sure he would have been delighted to know how well his serene chorale preludes could have been enhanced with prose such as this:

Organ: Chorale preluding begins (pianissimo and suitably unobtrusive).

Sound Operator: (hitting microphone) 'boom. . . boom. . .' (mezzo-forte, crescendoing to chest-thumping volume) 'Testing, testing, 1, 2, 3, 1, 2, 3.'

Organ: Continues (mezzo-forte and slightly more obtrusive).

Sound Operator: 'Is it on? Boom, BOOM. Stan, can you hear me at the back? Stan? Staaan?'

Organ: Continues (forte, and getting molto exasperato).

Sound Operator: 'Can you hear me above the noise of the organ?'

[Cue microphone feedback, rapidly gaining volume from inaudible to way beyond pain threshold, continuing until Sound Operator runs to the desk at the back of the church, finds the right knob and duly turns it fully up, then fully down]

means sitting down with a hymn book and reading the notices on the service sheet, while mouthing 'hello' to their friends across the aisle.) Many people find this a rare oasis of peace in their busy week, and so close their eyes as they contemplate and meditate on whether they left the bathroom window open, and how they can fix the timer on the cooker.

What happens next is a beautiful duet, heard in churches around Christendom throughout the world in various versions. It is the synthesis of music and speech, a performance that marries

The members of the congregation slowly get up off the floor and return nervously to their pews. One elderly gentleman thinks it is an air-raid warning and is bustling towards the exit, some of those with hearing aids are still visibly shaking.

Organ: (now playing with shoulders up, trying to protect ears) plays perfect cadence, then stops to wipe away the tears. Starts again.

After a couple of minutes, the two elderly clergy are fitted, rather reluctantly, with 'new-fangled' radio microphones, which causes them and the operator untold stress. Each device is fitted with two minuscule buttons, virtually invisible to anyone without 20/20 vision; to these two severely myopic gentlemen, they may as well not exist. Sadly, one of the buttons is 'mute' rendering the microphone silent; useful if you want a private conversation, but perilously close to the on/off button. The resulting confusion is inevitable:

Organ: (quiet improvisation on the opening hymn)

Clergy 1: Is this on? Which button did he say? I can't see the blasted thing.

Clergy 2: I don't see why we need these mikes anyway.

Clergy 1: There aren't many here this morning, are there?

Organ: (plays subtle reference to *Where, oh where has my little dog gone?*)

Clergy 1: Have I got time to go to the loo?

Clergy 2: If you're quick.

[BELL SOUNDS FOR THE BEGINNING OF THE SERVICE]

Clergy 2: Too late, off we go. . .

[MICROPHONE CLIP FAILS, MICROPHONE FALLS TO THE GROUND]

Organ: (Plays Handel's *Water Music*, now accompanied by a rhythmic rasping as the mic gets dragged behind the slightly worried clergyman.)

[THE SERVICE BEGINS WITH THE NOTICES, UNHEARD AS THE 'MUTE' BUTTON GETS PRESSED]

Can you play for our *Messiah?*

(with the emphasis on mess)

ACT I

[A Saturday in early December, England. 1.55pm. Somewhere bleak. Adrian has arrived at his rehearsal and parked in a muddy field next to a sign proclaiming CAR PARK written in ballpoint on a sheet of cardboard, attached to a broom handle.
It starts to rain.]

I squelch my way to the nearby church, armed with a Watkins Shaw and a Prout edition of the *Messiah*, my organ shoes, and a pencil.

These, of course, are fairly standard accessories for an organist accompanying a choral society or a 'scratch choir', as we gather to attempt another complete performance of this mammoth work, with an afternoon rehearsal (including tea, biscuits, and expenses).

The church and organ are this time, however, new to me. I am greeted warmly by the choir's concert manager. ('concert manager' sounds impressively efficient. Things are looking good.)

'Hello, Adam', (not so good, since my name is Adrian) *'glad you found us alright. I'm afraid the heating hasn't been working lately, it's a bit chilly, isn't it?'*

'Yes' (heart sinks).

'Come and see the organ. I hope you know how to get it working, they haven't had a regular organist here for years.'

'I can imagine,' as I spy in the distance the nightmare box that I shall be spending the rest of the day and night with. 'Blimey! Err — there must be some mistake; have I come to the right church? We are doing the *Messiah*?'

'Yes.'

'On this? On my own? Without an orchestra — just me?'

'Yes. Is anything wrong?'

'No, no, not at all' (heart plummets further). 'But before we start the rehearsal, I wonder if I could use the toil . . .'

'. . . *try the organ? Yes, of course. We've had to build a stage in the chancel for the choir, so you can get to the organ only by going along this plank and climbing over the choir stalls. You'd better get in quick; we're starting in two minutes.'*

The 'stage' is a mighty impressive collection of pallets, crates and boxes, perched on an odd assortment of doors, loft boards, and any choir cast-offs up to the job.

As I clamber over my assault course, I am followed by the massed assortment of singers, who wrestle their way into their seats and gingerly balance like novice surfboarders on a choppy sea.

Then there follows a heated discussion among the assembled throng, as most of them complain they can't see the conductor, even though they have no intention of looking at him once the music begins anyway. I have to focus on my own problems.

[ADRIAN LOOKS IN DESPERATION FOR ANY REGISTRATION AIDS, MAYBE A PISTON — EVEN A KICK-SWELL — BUT FINDS NONE.]

So it is just the one manual, six stops, a candle for the light, a row of straight pieces of rotting wood which used to be pedals and a small circular convex driver's mirror, the sort to enable you to see a wide area. This is positioned to give a perfect view, not of the conductor, but of a over-magnified, bloated, frozen, slightly-scared organist with large cheeks and bulging eyes. Just behind my back, I am joined by four enormous basses, who prevent me from seeing anything apart from the backs of four enormous basses when they stand.

'AARON — CAN YOU SEE ME?'

(I assume this must be the conductor, shouting to me.)

'Only if I stand on the pedals, I can just about see your head'.

'That'll have to do. Let's begin with "And the Glory", three in a bar.'

And so it begins.

I realise within a bar-and-a-half of the opening that Handel's masterfully crafted work may well have to be hastily adapted if I and this organ are going to survive the next seven hours together with any sense of dignity. The uplifting majesty of the opening organ passage of *And the Glory* is muted by desperate clunkings from the organ, and a medley of notes not working. Instead it offers a hiss of escaping wind where once was a pipe. The pedals that work are next to ones that stick on (cipher), and can be released only with a clearly audible stamping on the pedal.

Never in my playing days have 10 bars of music created such a bad impression in such a short space of time. The altos, who by now should be launching into their opening salvo, are looking at each other and their music, puzzled. The rehearsal continues, as we go through every chorus. The enormous basses, (whom I now imagine as Posh Bass, Sporty Bass, Scary Bass and Baby Bass), seem to have been to all the rehearsals, but in shifts, and spend the rehearsal vaguely rumbling the soprano part down two octaves. After an extended eternity, we finally have the break, but my hope of investigating the toilets is dashed by the concert manager screaming:

'*CAN YOU ALL KEEP THE NOISE DOWN DURING THE BREAK, BECAUSE THE SOLOISTS NEED TO REHEARSE WITH THE ORGANIST.*'

The Spice Basses have left for their tea and biscuits, and have been replaced by a quartet of smiling soloists, who tell me the speeds for their arias. The tea and biscuit break is taken up with rattling through and 'top-and-tailing' the solos. Ted Drags (Bass), lives up to his name and proceeds to shake uncontrollably through *Why do the nations*. He complains about no trumpet sounding in his big show-stopper. I sympathise with him.

[ADRIAN GOES INTO A BRIEF DREAM]

I am woken by the contralto who wants to rehearse every note of *He was despised* with all the repeats. She indicates a speed to me. I follow it. She then slows it down. And so it continues until the chorus reappears, suitably tea'd and biscuited, and ready for *Part the Third*. I manage this cross-legged and with ever-increasing tempi until the conductor declares the rehearsal over, and I fight back the tears. The concert manager runs over to me and grabs my arm, in apologetic mood.

'*I am SO sorry that we have got your name wrong during the rehearsal — I don't know how it happened. It's most embarrassing. Please forgive us? But may I say how much we are REALLY enjoying your playing, Andrew.*'

It is now 7.05pm. I excuse myself from all conversations and hastily make an exit. There is no convenient convenience in the church, as the nearest facility is across a couple of fields, down a path, over a sty, catching a bus —

[IT IS NOW DARK OUTSIDE]

263

In desperation, I choose a basic but ancient solution, and subtly sidle my inconspicuous way towards a darkened corner of the church, behind a gravestone.

This next moment I can only describe as being on a par with the joy of being at the birth of my firstborn. Words cannot adequately express the feeling of relieved exhilaration.

[ADRIAN IS BLINDED AS THE CHURCH'S FLOOD-LIGHTS CLICK ON AND CAST HIS 60FT SHADOW ONTO THE SIDE OF THE CHURCH TOWER]

Now in abject shock and fully illuminated as I am, in the dazzling glare of the floodlights, I swear I hear voices:

'Deirdre, isn't that the organist over there?'
'Keep walking, Enid, just keep walking.'

[ACT II AND III CONTINUED]

"The previous organist complained about the lack of facilities"

264

ACT II

[We return to the scene of a small, English country church in sub-zero December, for a performance of *Messiah*, which is not billed as a 'Come and Sing' scratch performance, but might as well be. Adrian is going into battle armed with a 1-manual nightmare wheeze box]

I am squashed onto an organ bench next to a pile of hymn books to my left, and my copy of the *Messiah* on my right, due to a music desk that fails miserably with its sole function of being a desk for holding music.

[The chorus now rise, like a court jury, to tackle *For unto us*.]

The four enormous 'Spice' basses behind me also rise, not as confidently, but more like the accused, to accept their fate, having not attended as many rehearsals as they should have.

I strike up optimistically with the six-bar intro and off go the 20-plus sopranos with *Four Runtoussachild is born*, answered rather feebly by the tenors (both of them). When they get to the 'born-hrn-hrn-hrn' semiquaver runs, the ladies show how it ought to be done. It is a demonstration of a confidence and agility of which they can be justifiably proud. After all, they've been to ALL the rehearsals and they know their stuff. This only serves to scare the basses, who soon realise it is

their turn for public exposure, and off they go on a muddled mixture of muffled and approximate wandering groans.

A collective uncertainty spreads through the choir, and their tuneful notes gradually peter out to a puzzled silence, until we gird our loins at full throttle for *WON-der-ful! COUN-se-llor*.

I too get rather excited at this moment, and reach for the 4' Principal, giving it a confident tug. The stop knob has not been treated like this for years, and breaks off in my hand, leaving me in a slight one-handed pickle.

A quick assessment of my situation ('*I have practiced hard for this, but I have already upset Deirdre and Enid, we have another 250 pages to go, and I have just broken their organ*'). I decide that there is no escape; I shall have to use the remaining stalk in my hand to bodge the 4' Principal back every time the music goes quiet. This is not going well.

The *Pifa* (Pastoral Symphony), thankfully allows me some brief respite, as my feet get to rest for a while with a few long notes; thank you, Mr Handel.

[The soprano rises]

But then, up gets soprano Verity Trilling, for her BIG moment. She has brought with her a huge support team of relatives and university friends, filling the front five rows of pews.

Her singing teacher has already lectured me intensely on the exact metronome marking for her optimum performance, where to let her breathe, and the notes to play loudly for her. She

now sits on the front row animatedly conducting, breathing every breath and singing every note with her protégé.

Verity's performance is worthy of YouTube but alas mine struggles, as I can smell burning from the back of the asthmatic windbox at my disposal. The poor old girl was not designed for this many semiquavers in one evening, and the Handel is pushing her beyond her limits.

The next selection of choruses, recitatives and arias are somewhat of a blur, as I reconsider my options regarding the burning smell.

'Could I possibly go home during the interval? Where is the fire extinguisher? Do I really need the expenses cheque?'

The contralto performs *He was despised* suitably laconically, and we all share her pain. Then she treats us to a much more exciting bit, which sounds from where I am seated like *He gave his bag to the spiders.*

After many more choruses and solos, we arrive at *Why do the nations* by bass Ted Drags.

[THE BASS RISES]

I have spent weeks at the gym training for this and confidently set about the semiquaver pedal bit. It is like running on the spot on a treadmill.

The bottom C on the pedals has no desire to respond to my weeks of training. Instead, it decides to rest and stubbornly hold on to its note (rather like a drone on a bagpipe) throughout the piece.

Ted casts many desperate and threatening looks at me as he launches into 'so furiously rage together'. I resolve to avoid Ted during the interval, to prevent my fingers getting broken. The churchwarden-bouncer becomes my saviour unexpectedly, and with no pretence of ceremony, strides over to the organ, yanks the offending pipe out of its hole, and the drone stops.

The heart-throb tenor rises to do some breaking and dashing, but is joined in an unrehearsed, unscheduled duet by one of the over-enthusiastic chorus tenors, who confidently launches into *Let us break their bonds*, before realising that it had been cut.

[DURING THIS, 12 OF THE SOPRANOS DISAPPEAR TO THE BACK OF THE CHURCH]

The sopranos go to supervise the urn and collectively peel back the cling film from the five plates of rich tea biscuits in time for the interval.

The *Hallelujah Chorus* has the congregation rising to its feet in a cherished tradition, probably arising from the need to allow a supply of blood to the hinder parts of His Majesty King George II, back in 1743.

Finally, we clamber our way into:

[THE INTERVAL]

As the final chord of the *Hallelujah* reaches its dying twitches, the Concert Manager leaps to his feet to announce 'Ladies and Gentlemen, refreshments will now be served at the back'. The remaining sopranos do not need a starting gun. They sprint away with a start that Usain Bolt would envy; nothing and nobody is going to get in the way of their desire for a cuppa.

Alas, they had been standing on one end of a section of staging, the middle of which was resting on a fulcrum, rather like a see-saw. The effect of six sopranos rapidly exiting one end en masse only serves to catapult the tenors on the other end into the air.

For those who survive the elbow-assisted dash to the West end, the prize is a boiling cup of brown liquid, vaguely resembling tea, served in a flimsy plastic cup.

This type of cup has several unique design features including:

- Auto-scald (simply squeeze the sides)
- Easy-spill (one nudge of your elbow and the contents cascade over your wrist)
- Universal finger-burner (wherever you try to hold it, the result is the same)

Then there is the Rich Tea: a biscuit of utter disappointment, well-known worldwide as delivering little to entice the taste buds.

But right now, for an organist who has been at the rehearsal since 1.55pm, it is a prize worth fighting for. Posh Bass clearly thinks so as he swipes a mighty handful, leaving a forlorn pile of crumbs for me to pick through.

It is then that I spy HER (Verity Trilling's singing teacher), who has a look that could freeze my tea. She is heading in my direction, armed with her cup of scalding tea-style drink, a biscuit in her mouth, 'Prout' under her arm and waving a metronome in the air, hoping to attract my attention. By now I have not got the mental stamina to have an argument, listen to a complaint or even string two intelligible thoughts together, so I do the brave thing: look at the floor and run away.

For the remainder of the interval, she stalks me. As she heads Westwards down the South aisle, I hastily head Eastward up the North one, and vice versa. We spend the next few minutes doing circular laps of the church, like those track cyclists who hover on their bicycles at opposite sides of the track, waiting for their opponents to twitch before launching off at great speed.

The Concert Manager decides enough is enough and screams that it is now time for the raffle. Conversations continue unabated as he calls out several colours and numbers and no-one takes any notice.

'Blue 36? no?' 'Pink 12 — anyone? Please?'

It continues like this as the choir push and shove their way back into their seats, and I tiptoe over my plank and launch over the choir stalls ready for the final part.

'Blue — 45? Someone must have it?'

ACT III

[IT IS THE SECOND HALF OF THE PERFORMANCE OF THE 'MESSIAH', FOR SATB SOLOISTS, SATBBBBBBB CHORUS, ACCOMPANIED BY ADRIAN ON A SINGLE-DECKER BRONCHIAL SQUEEZE BOX, WITH AN EVER-DECREASING SPECIFICATION AS BITS DROP OFF OR STICK ON.]

The conductor returns to his podium (an upturned beer crate), picks up his baton, has a final check of his raffle tickets, and dramatically gets the chorus to stand.

He then meekly sits them down again as the soprano's singing teacher gives him a withering look, and we start Verity's *I know that my redeemer liveth*. I am sure I can hear the faint ticking of a metronome in the distance.

Part the third is a welcome sight, indicating we are nearing home. There are some hairy moments as the chorus is caught out by the sudden change of pace and dynamics in *Since by man*. It even wakes Sporty Bass behind me, who was enjoying a quiet nap.

The Trumpet shall sound has no trumpet available, so we must use our imagination.

A couple of cuts later, and we arrive at

Verity's final display. This time I definitely hear clicking, and try to decide if it is the urn cooling or a demand from Verity's teacher. Against my better judgement, I assume the latter and proceed with her aria at that tempo. It quickly becomes apparent that poor Verity is not going to survive those long notes and runs without either a major accelerando or by giving her an oxygen mask. I choose the former and inwardly resolve to hide in the organ until long after the concert has finished.

[Clattering noises off]

The aria seems to be a new arrangement, previously unknown to me, as it contains an obbligato part for percussion — namely the folding and putting away of trestle tables, and the squeaking of the urn trolley. Personally, I prefer the version without added percussion, but if that is what the public wants, they get it.

Tears of joy and exhilaration fill my eyes with the words and music of the final *Worthy is the Lamb*. The *Amen* fugue, with its single iteration of the word 'amen' never ceases to amaze me with the depth and complexity of its superb polyphonic writing. If you composed only that in your lifetime, never mind all the rest of this great work, you would die happy.

One of the Spice Basses, Baby Bass, apparently shares my enthusiasm for it, as he leans over to his mate and whispers loudly '*I like this one, it's got good words*'.

The applause at the end is generous and sympathetic, and the soloists are given gifts. Marjorie was recently elected Soloists' Gift Coordinator by the rest of the choir, but she has forgotten to coordinate the flowers and bottles of wine as gifts for the soloists.

Instead, Verity is given talcum powder; the contralto receives a chocolate orange; the heart-throb tenor is handed a calendar with pictures of cute kittens, and bass Ted Drags is delighted by the gift of a colouring book with attached crayon set.

Each gift is tastefully adorned with a blue or pink raffle ticket.

'*Blue 36, Pink 12, Blue 45 —* '

ELSEWHERE
IN THE ORGAN
UNIVERSE. . .

Saint-Hyacinthe Cathedral, Quebec, Canada

PART FOUR

LIFE ALOFT AROUND
THE WORLD AS SEEN
THROUGH THE EYES
OF ORGANISTS OF ALL
VARIETIES ~ AND THEIR
HELPERS

Church musician code words

ACCOMPANIMENT: Bells, loud speakers, vacuum cleaners, floor polishers, sirens, tourists; anything making a louder noise than the organist who is trying to practise.

COFFEE: Person whose mission in life is to store enough phlegm and throat gunk to let loose loudly at the quietest moment in a service or concert.

DEPS: Similar to substitutes but are called deputy as a nod to Wild West fans. Deps fill in for absent regular organists and are always told they are 'much better' than the usual one, to ensure they return.

DoM: Director of Music; posh name for Jack of All Trades which is meant to compensate for a risible salary and appalling work hours.

FIGURED BASS: (1) Early musical shorthand, representing intervals above a written bass note. (2) Opposite of a disfigured bass, ostensibly a soloist who has upset the organist.

HSC AND TSG: Short for Here She Comes and There She Goes, the 'usual' music organists play during the entry and exit of the bride.

MAJOR: (1) Happy music. (2) member of the congregation who really runs the parish.

MINOR: (1) Sad Music. (2) member of the congregation who must be pandered to as the future of the parish.

OFFERTORY: The piece of music played by the organist to disguise the sound of no money dropping in collection plates.

SIGN: The sign (known as a sharp) is used to indicate that the pitch of a note is raised by half a tone. (Note for nerds: it was around for centuries before Twitter and hashtags.)

SUB: Either a Substitute Organist (as in 'There's a cricket match that I want to go to on Sunday') or a pretend 16' stop.

SURPLICE: A loose white overgarment worn by choristers and organists to hide phones and sweets.

VOLUNTARY: Is anything but voluntary. The obligatory piece of music before and after services during which congregations discuss the weather, the vicar's wife, and their latest illness.

LIFE ALOFT AROUND THE WORLD

We are the music makers,
And we are the dreamers of dreams. . .
— Arthur O'Shaughnessy (from *Ode*)

Organists are:

Organists:

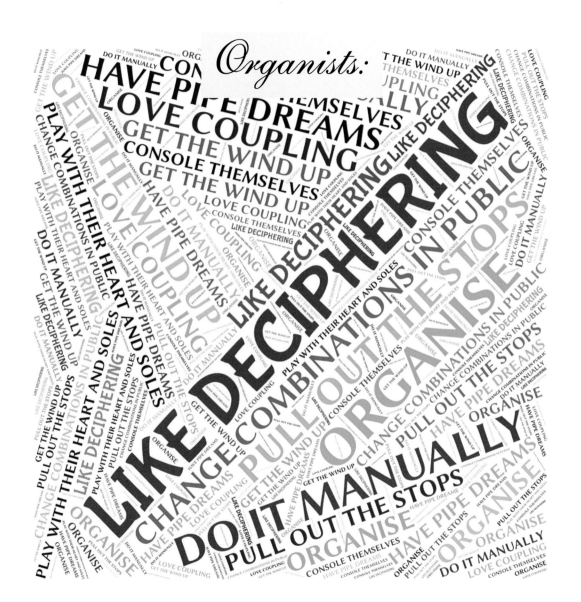

HAVE PIPE DREAMS · LOVE COUPLING · GET THE WIND UP · CONSOLE THEMSELVES · LIKE DECIPHERING · ORGANISE · DO IT MANUALLY · PULL OUT THE STOPS · CHANGE COMBINATIONS IN PUBLIC · PLAY WITH THEIR HEART AND SOLES

The bewildering vocation of the liturgical organist defies explanation. Why would any normal person skulk around dark, dusty buildings for hours on end, year after year, receiving more criticism and thoughtless comments than financial reward?

Worst of all, organists can never lie in bed on a Sunday. This daft lifestyle is the chosen path for thousands. What attracts them to life at the console, day-by-day, and what really do they do?

'*Don't forget to release the brake pedal . . .*'

Marktkirche, Wiesbaden, Germany

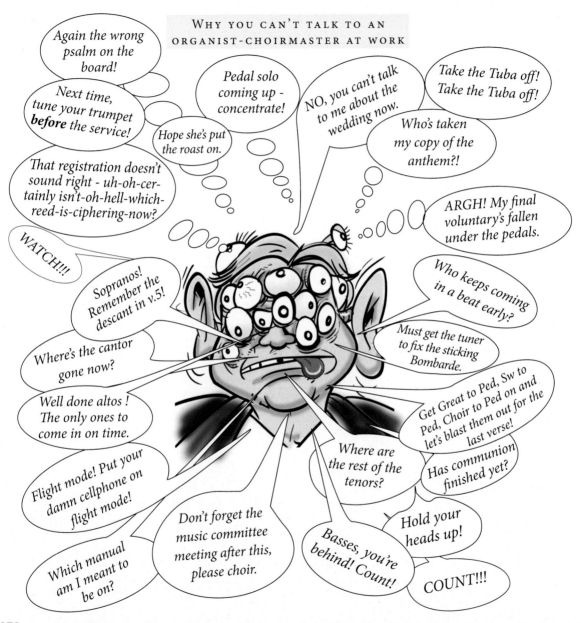

Multitaskers extraordinaire

Welcome to the giddy, lofty world of the manually labouring, day-to-day church organist. If you think playing pedals with your feet while playing keyboards with your hands is tricky, fasten your seatbelt and learn what else the average liturgical organist does at the same time. Expert head-patters-tummy-rubbers by nature, they are multitaskers supreme. While in command of this musical Airbus 380, an organist constantly watches the two hands on any number of manuals from 1 to 5; while pummelling out pedal parts with their feet.

Add to this: checking stops, pistons and other gadgets which need to be adjusted according to the singing of the choir, congregation, or soloists; this is done 'on the fly' as the whim of the assorted participants alters and falters. Without a co-pilot to flap at singers or orchestra, the organist uses their fourth arm to coax musicians into beginning and ending roughly at the same time.

Church authorities, ever with an eye for saving money, devised yet another way for the organist to use their fifth arm while 120% occupied: they ditched hymn books (or burned their illegal photocopies) and replaced them with a button-gadget-thing to flash up hymn numbers, and even more fun, another remote control to project the hymn verses onto a screen. Here the organist must use precision timing with their button to switch to the correct verse in a quadrillionth of a second. Traps for the unwary include non-continuous verses, so don't forget omitted verses 2, 4, 9 and half of 10 with a repeat of 1, (on days with an 'R' in them).

Sometimes the organist is both cantor and choir. A bulbous microphone attached to the console enables the organist to provide a croonful lead of the congregational singing during Mass. This one-person orchestra also copes with any misbehaviour from the organ such as ciphers. Retrieving music scores (which have a penchant for sliding off the music desk during tricky prestissimo passages) adds a frisson of novelty should boredom set in.

The organist must be on the alert for potential interruptions from playmates such as clergy, church council members, organ builders, choristers, wedding couples (i.e. mother of the bride), sacristans, vergers, orchestra members, soloists, cleaners, church secretaries, and curious tourists (sometimes all at once). That an organist produces anything resembling music is a small wonder; that they don't become mass murderers and locked away is the greatest miracle of all.

HALLMARKS OF A REAL ORGANIST

Forget all those fancy initials like FRCO, ATCL, ARCM, Dip.ORG,
BMus, Ass. Mechanic (Hons) after your name. As Morwenna Brett writes,
you're still not fully qualified for real organist pro status until:

- Your organ shoes look like they've been in a tussle with an enthusiastic puppy and lost.
- You have a few improvisation tricks, which although they wouldn't get you a job at Saint-Sulpice, get you through service moments.
- You have learned to ask *Crimond* or *Brother James' Air*? *Love Divine* or *Blaenwern*? as soon as you arrive at a new church.
- You can survive for 24 hours on the broken biscuits lurking in the bottom of your music bag.
- You can choke up at a funeral but still carry on playing.
- You can book the departing sopranos for next week while simultaneously smashing through a Bach prelude and fugue at the end of a service.

- You always visit the bathroom before leaving the house, as you know that where you are going does not have any facilities, or they are behind three sets of locked doors to which you have no access.
- You have perfected a withering stare for people who insist on having a chatter during your precious practice hour.
- Your home is full of cardboard boxes of old organ music wished onto you by dead organists' friends and relatives.
- You always carry a miscellaneous selection of harmless music for when they suddenly announce, 'The organist will now play something —'
- Your Satnav Favourites list is full of destinations starting with the word "Saint —"

Another peaceful Saturday morning practice time for the organist, while engaged in meaningful dialogue about the merits of organ music versus vacuum cleaners and assorted chatterings.

HITCHES WHEN GETTING HITCHED

A wedding is a big day for the bridal couple. To an organist it is just another job, when they might prefer to be fishing, watching cricket, ironing the cat, or simply anywhere other than a church. Only once have I played for a ceremony where the pair seemed equally keen to be done with the whole business. It was a couple already married in Japan who wanted a special short blessing ceremony in New Zealand — short being the operative word. When I played them in, the groom and his bride galloped up the aisle, screeching to a halt in front of the waiting celebrant, the semi-retired Bishop. He beamed at them in his usual benign way:

'Welcome to this House of Go —' he began.

'I will,' interjected the panting groom. The Bishop, a little miffed at this unseemly interruption, dug his heels in and continued in even more measured tones. The bridal pair, champing at the bit, cantered out again in under five minutes, rushing off to wherever they were so keen to go. I barely finished the first four bars of the *Wedding March*.

So although most couples could never forget their day of matrimonial manacling, examples of organists forgetting the time, date or place are surprisingly common. In such cases, panicking clergy pluck last-minute substitutes from wherever they can find them. Lynley Clarke began her life-long organ-playing vocation aged 16 after being hoicked out of a warm bath.

'I must have been going out to a dance in the evening and had opted for a luxurious mid-afternoon bath. My mother answered the front door to find a flustered church caretaker. He had made a bride and attendants drive around to kill time while he went in search of an organist. The incumbent had gone on holiday and forgotten about this wedding. "Could Lynley please come and play the organ?"

'I have vivid memories, as I hurriedly dried myself, of my mother desperately rummaging through my bedroom drawers and throwing garments onto the bed, to aid my swift departure to the church. The rest is a merciful blur. I can only guess that I did my best, but goodness knows how it sounded. I would have been terrified.'

Sometimes, although the organist has arrived, the circumstances (such as a one-day international cricket match) can outrank even the most forthright bride. Many years ago, both vicar and organist were passionate cricket fans caught with the dilemma of having to attend a wedding service at the same time as a deciding major cricket match. Kept up to progress by the crackling wisps of match commentary on a little radio, the pair hovered in a conspiratorial huddle in the vestry to wait for the final ball. With the game poised on a possible home team win only minutes away, the organist reluctantly left the broadcast to play pre-service voluntaries while the vicar stalled the bridal party with instructions to drive around the block for five minutes.

The game finished, and the bride finally marched up the aisle to join her groom at the chancel, at which point the vicar substituted the standard wedding service greetings of "Dearly beloved, we are gathered here —" with "I thought you would all like to know: we won!" The congregation, composed of many disgruntled cricket fans deprived of any news, erupted into cheers. A wedding guest later reported he had never before heard an organ console apparently whooping with joy.

Not all such spontaneous announcements are appreciated. A deputy filling in at a memorable English wedding on Cup Final Saturday relates with a degree of relish that the parish priest disappeared towards the end of the ceremony, returning to the church just before the happy couple walked back down the aisle.

'For those of you that are interested in the football, X won,' he announced.

A voice from the congregation shouted out, 'You bastard!! I was videoing that!'

Bruce Steele played as the wedding party assembled 10 minutes before the ceremony was due to start at 2pm. The kick-off time came and went, no sign of anything remotely bridal and the

minutes ticked by. Bruce played stoically on.

'I was running out of music, wondering what to repeat. Someone came up to say that the bridegroom's mother carrying the heirloom ring had not arrived from another state. At 2.35 the minister borrowed a ring from a lady in the front row, and the bridal procession, at last, took place. I was ready to play the outgoing *Wedding March* when there was a flutter of activity at the door. Hot and breathless, Mother stormed in bearing "the ring". Blow me down; we had to go through the whole ceremony over again. Only one fee was forthcoming.'

Like all organists, Stephen Best always has a stack of prelude music ready in case weddings get delayed.

'Only once have I run out and had to start through the stack again. The best man and groom thought it would be fun to take the car through a car wash on the way to the church.

'You guessed it. The car wash malfunctioned, and the car got stuck. It wasn't until the owner of the car wash was summoned that the water could be turned off and the car extricated. Meanwhile, I just kept playing. Seemingly forever.'

Bruce Steele's first job as an organist in his teens was at a small inner suburban church with a fine harmonium, placed at the front near the communion table.

'At my first wedding, I played the bride in to Wagner on the old squeeze-box. The happy couple and the minister were perhaps two metres away from me.'

As the minister was enlightening the couple as to the origin and meaning of matrimony, it all became too much for the bride. She leant forward, pulled at the minister's gown and said in a loud voice: "Hey! When do I get to kiss 'im"?

During Colin Jenkins' 14 years at Wesley Church Melbourne, he, like most organists, endured some interesting wedding soloists.

'One of the most memorable was the guy who came up into the gallery, flung his music at me and informed me that he did not need a run-through as he had sung it dozens of times. It was an easy accompaniment; however, I asked him to do it — for my benefit. Rhythmically and tempo-wise what issued from his mouth bore virtually no relationship to the printed score so I asked him to do it again, which he did, but not with good grace. This rendering differed greatly but

was still no more accurate. When he came to sing it during the wedding it was different again, but I merely followed him, leaving out beats and bars as necessary.

Afterwards, the soloist told Colin: "You know, you're not bad! You're the only person who's been able to play it properly."

Barry Holdstock's first stipendiary post as an organist and choirmaster was in the heart of East London. He arrived to play for the first of the weddings there dressed in a cassock, and was greeted by two fully armed police officers with the words: "It's OK, Farver, the church is surrounded by armed men."

'I told them I was the organist and they "escorted" me to the console. The groom was out on licence for two hours for his wedding, handcuffed to a warder. His crime? Double murder.'

It always surprises me how few organists, clergy and mothers-of-the-bride don't murder each other in the search for suitable organ music — the crucial word here being 'suitable'. I am still not sure why we agreed to let a pianist cheerfully crash through *Let's Make Whoopee* for the entry of a bride, but it must have been out of sheer devilment to see what would happen.

In the choice of music for both weddings and funerals, poor taste and ignorance combine to make unbelievable selections — unless the organist is brave enough to stand up for decorum.

Alas, poor Charles-Marie Widor (for those who don't know, Widor is pronounced Veedor). Little did he realise how much people would massacre the Toccata from his *Fifth Organ Symphony*, both playing it and referring to it. Spelling it is only the start of the trouble. Kevin Bowyer once had a request from a wedding couple for Widor's *Tocata*.

'Being a pedant, I wrote back: "It should be *Widor's Toccata* (2 cs)". It appeared on the order of service as *Widor's Toccata (2 cs)*.'

Other mangled variations on Widor's piece that had to be deciphered:
- *Widow's Toccata* (hopefully not prophetic)
- *Vidor Stacatta*
- *The Toe Cutter*

Organists need great imagination when asked for specific pieces for both weddings and funerals. (Although when one widow asked Lyn Bromage for *I don't know how to love him* it was obvious, given it was for her 4th husband.)

"The sheep song" (*Sheep May Safely Graze*), "Packerbell's Cannon", as well as music featuring in advertisement soundtracks such as "Lloyds Bank", "Hamlet Cigars", and the distinctly unhelpful simply listed as "Track 16". Then there was the couple who fancied a "Wedding Day in Troll Town" (*Wedding Day in Troldhaugen*), and one bride was particular in her request for a piece to be played while the mothers of the bride and groom were seated: none other than "Jesus' Desiring For a Man". Then there is the perennial favourite 'The Trumpet Volunteer', by Persil.

And what would anyone make of this request: 'You know, that nice one that they always play at weddings? You know, you MUST know it? It goes la-la-la-la. You must know it? No? Perhaps you haven't been to many weddings?'

[Organist abruptly looks for a bus to throw herself under.]

When a wedding is a second time around for both parties a delicious extra dimension of possible tunes arises. In Aldrington, Philip Bailey was asked to do the honours for one such, which had strong naval links on the groom's side.

'They wanted me to play *A life on the ocean wave* and other such, before the service. They also asked for *Fight the good Fight* as a hymn (the previous divorces had been not without incident, apparently). I managed to dissuade them.'

'Another couple wanted "that tune from *Romeo and Juliet*" until I pointed out that the tune they were humming was the Prokofiev theme for the two warring families. They eventually decided on *O fortuna* from Carmina Burana, played on a CD player after I threatened them with a new music surcharge.'

As organist at a Lutheran church in Southern California Aram Basmadjian was occasionally asked for nonstandard music, which he was always willing to honour; but once he was left speechless and had to refuse when requested by a wedding couple to play *Another One Bites the Dust* for their recessional.

Colin Jenkins has had many strange requests for wedding music but two of his favourites were for 'The Strumpet Voluntary' and 'The Trumpet Vol-au-vent'.

Outrageous choices are nothing new; an organist in the 1920s nearly had a fit of the vapours when a wedding guest asked her to play the devilishly naughty *Just One Kiss*. It's not known if she obliged.

Mark Quarmby was booked to play for a wedding in a parish church where the organ had just been rebuilt and enlarged by a less-than-reputable builder who had replaced the electrical action with his own system. The organist warned Mark that there were some teething problems with the action, but they occurred only spasmodically.

The bride had requested the Lemmens *Fanfare* as the recessional and had a string quartet playing the other parts of the service apart from the hymns. Mark mused about what the organist had meant by "teething problems" as he sat at the console during the wedding.

Nothing had gone wrong so far. Famous last thoughts.

It wasn't until Mark launched into the recessional and the bridal party began their walk down the aisle that the fireworks started. As they passed the organ, the key action suddenly reversed.

'Every note I was playing didn't play and every note I was not playing DID play! You can just imagine the cacophonous sound and the shock the bridal party got, not to mention me. I jumped up to the Swell and found that only the Great was affected so continued until the end playing only on the Swell.'

Mark had a different skirmish with an organ (this time electronic) that was loaned to a parish while its historic pipe organ was being restored. The first week the digital organ arrived, there was a large "High Society" wedding. The organist of the church, one of the country's leading teachers and players, was reluctant to play it for such a momentous occasion, so he asked Mark, who was familiar with electronic appliances, to play for the wedding instead.

When Mark arrived, he found a super-duper, all playing, all singing theatre-type model with more flashing lights and buttons than traditional organ stops, placed by the chancel steps in front of the congregation.

The wedding was going fine until the *Bridal March*. The music took a sudden dive down a semitone and then came back up again; the blushing young organist almost fell off the stool with embarrassment and hoped the congregation had not noticed. It was a bit hard to miss. On close inspection, Mark found a button beside the Swell pedal which was easily bumped when moving the pedal, and which gave a Hawaiian guitar effect to the pitch.

Keeping his foot well away from the Swell pedal, the organist manoeuvred his way through the rest of the service without incident. For the moment.

The wedding was being video recorded, and the photographer had set up large lights to illuminate the bridal party standing by the organ console across the front.

The organist launched into the Mendelssohn *Wedding March*, and as soon as the bridal party passed the console on their way to the west door, the photographer switched off the camera lights. Immediately the organ stopped, and the bridal party left the church in total silence.

Later Mark found that the photographer had unplugged the organ before the service and put in a double adaptor for his lights and the organ. Unaware that the other plug on the adaptor was for the organ, the photographer had flicked the switch off as soon as he was finished with the lights. As you do.

After years of dealing with lunatic brides, Carol Dziuba thought she had seen it all. That is — until Jaclyn.

'Talk about nutcase. First, she said "I don't want *Here Comes The Bride*. I don't know how it goes, but I don't want it". Then she said, "I insist on sending you a deposit". I told her it wasn't necessary; I've never taken a deposit in 40 years and 1000+ weddings. She said, "But how do I know you'll show up?"

'In discussing her music, she said she wanted the *Ave Maria*. When I asked her which one she wanted, she replied, "The slow one". She told me that her Uncle Tony would be singing the *Ave Maria*.

'The day of the wedding, Uncle Tony showed up, all 350lbs of him, huffing and puffing up the choir loft stairs. His first words to me: "Hey Baby, I'm here to sing the Ave".

He was right out of Central Casting for The Godfather, with his shirt halfway unbuttoned, revealing his hairy bloated chest and numerous gold chains. We had a few minutes to rehearse, so I gave him the intro to the Bach/Gounod Ave in F, since he didn't have music and didn't know which key he sang it in. Well, F was too high, as were E Flat and D, so I settled on C. Two lines into the song, he stopped because he didn't know the words, and said "Hey Toots, do you have the music ?"

'To cap off this fiasco of a wedding, Jaclyn had ordered butterflies to be released by her guests after the marriage ceremony, and the butterflies were in small aerated boxes. Well, it was a hot day, and the butterflies were dead and dying, so Jaclyn had a meltdown.

'Perhaps the most fun I had that day was reading Jaclyn's wedding programme, which was filled with many misspellings: "Pacobel's Cannon", "Ava Maria", "Father of the Brid", and "Motzart" will remain etched in my brain forever.'

KITSCH KRISTMAS WEDDING

Weddings and Funerals are meat and drink for organists.
DAVID YEARSLEY, a Cornell University music professor (and author of
"Bach's Feet"), received a frantic email request for an organist at a wedding
to take place five days later. These nuptials had one of the most unusual
request lists David had seen in all his years "on the bench."

There is no better place from which to judge the folly of human desire and ritual than from the organ console.

Many, if not most, "serious" organists have standards when it comes to weddings. They will not play pop and steadfastly refuse such humiliations as Andrew Lloyd Webber's *All I Ask of You* from the Phantom of the Opera.

Whereas the arbitrary divide between high and low culture is breached with increasing ease and fervour, many a church organist continues to retreat to higher ground, however soggy it may already be. Not so the Musical Patriot, who happily rolls up his trousers to run barefoot through the surging surf of schlock!

Besides, the current standards of "serious" organ music for weddings are pretty appalling, with any musical value of this core repertory of modern nuptials utterly depleted by overuse. An historical study of this "traditional" music would doubtless show that this hodgepodge is mostly of recent origins. The default recessional, the Wedding March from Mendelssohn's *Midsummer Night's Dream*, is probably the oldest pillar of the wedding pergola, having become a mainstay a century-and-a-half ago, when it ushered newlyweds Princess Victoria and the future Emperor Frederick III of Prussia out of St James' Palace. Wagner's Wedding March from *Lohengrin* is as overbearing a bit of bombast as one is ever likely to be subjected to, even when it's shorn to the short time it takes the bride and her father to get down the aisle.

A good enough piece when allowed its natural verve, Pachelbel's *Canon* inevitably gets mired in glacial tempos for weddings. It was in this mangled form that the piece rose to prominence after the 1980 film *Ordinary People* gave it a dreadful boost. Since

Cecily decided that if Algernon wouldn't let her have "She loves you, yeah, yeah, yeah" while she walked down the aisle, she was just going to have to marry her more trendy IT adviser.

then countless are the number of Unity Candles that have been lit to this maudlin soundtrack, the vitality of the original music converted into dreary sentimentality.

The High Horse of the serious wedding organist is really a maudlin old nag.

So when the frantic email with its eclectic musical requests came in, I immediately declared myself ready to enlist: "The bride would like to walk in to *Palladio* by Karl Jenkins." The groom's mother wrote this as if referring to a classic, but I admitted my ignorance.

She referred me to YouTube. I had a look at what turned out to be part of an old DeBeers campaign for their 25th Anniversary Diamond. The ad chronicles in black-and-white the first 25 years of a storybook marriage in 30 powerhouse seconds, moving from the carrying-over-the-threshold moment, through the kids being born, raised and graduated from college, and then, in the last 10 seconds, races down the homestretch of the 25th-year and thunders past the post to claim the prize of a diamond-laden necklace.

This segment is part of what purports to be a famous series of commercials accompanied by Jenkins' music, neo-baroque strings that are all frantic energy: sawing violins and pounding basses, that for the most part mimics the simplest harmonic syntax of early 18th-century composers but then flails wildly at ungrammatical chords that give the piece its modern sound, its hyper-intense, amphetamine-addled character. It sounds like Corelli on Benzedrine.

The tub-thumping pedal points, the full-throttle strings and oddly barren harmony all give this 30-second spot an impressive epic reach, like shoving the 15 minutes of the first movement of Brahms' First Symphony into a trash compactor and transposing it up a half-step. The ad is not a honeymoon, it's a nightmare. But like most bad dreams it has real energy, and that makes it better than the Bridal Chorus. My enthusiasm for this gig was growing.

At 30 seconds, the ad's length is just about perfect for a walk down the aisle, and could be augmented in the necessary moments with a loop or two through one of its many careening patterns. In all my years as a wedding organist it's the only piece in a minor key I've ever played for the processional.

Powered by full organ, and as the lovely bride progressed down the aisle, I too saw the milestones of married life screened in the congregation's collective imaginations, mine included — another Madison-Avenue miracle of mass manipulation.

The bride wanted what she called "mingle" music before the start of the service, to begin with *The Heart Asks Pleasure First.*

This was another title I didn't recognise, but it turned out to be Michael Nyman's theme to Jane Campion's film, *The Piano*. This is another bit of apparently aimless high-energy oscillating meant to suggest, in the context of the movie, release from confining Victorian ladies' garments and an embrace of the heroine's unconstricted sexuality. I loved the illogic of playing *The Piano* on the organ.

After *The Piano*, the "mingle music" stuck to the classical Top 40: "Other than that, can you do Nutcracker Sugarplum suite, bolero and fleur de lis?" You bet I can! — assuming that "fleur de lis" was, in fact, Beethoven's music-box favourite *Für Elise*, another piano piece. I like the idea, too, of this halting and chaste theme rubbing shoulders with Bizet's tarty heroine, *Carmen*, and the effervescent tiptoeing of gay Tchaikovsky's fairies. Does this all sound condescending on my part? I don't mean it to be. This was fun stuff to play, not only as a salute to classical music's commando survivors in the jungle of pop culture, but also because people like it. And the tableau vivant of Carmen, Elise, and those ballerinas marching down the aisle and prancing around the tree is itself a classic.

I have to admit — and not just as a defence tactic — that I suspected healthy doses of irony behind this foray beyond the confines of the basic wedding playbook on the part of the couple. A bit of tongue-in-cheek for the wedding kiss.

Before the bride and her father were to march down the aisle, the groom asked to process with his grandmother to:

'A fancy-fied version of the *Imperial March* from *Star Wars*. Can you play this? Can you make it flowery versus hard and deep?'

The idea of making Darth Vader's menacing theme flowery seemed to challenge not only the intrinsic quality of John William's fascist anthem but also my meagre if oft-deployed, abilities for adaptation and distortion. The thing doesn't work by switching the mode to major, and would be unrecognisable to the listeners and therefore lose its impact. At the rehearsal the couple and I discussed what to do about this problem. The groom came up with the brilliant idea to play the opening of *Für Elise* on full organ, letting Beethoven's maiden let down her hair and loosen her corset, and then segue directly into the *Imperial March*.

At the ceremony, this got a huge laugh out of the entire congregation and proved the fundamental truth about weddings and Christmas: never take them too seriously.

CONFESSION TIME

Organists are no different from other people in that they have done things they would prefer to keep secret. So, as a licenced blabbermouth, I am making sure everyone can read all about these loft misdemeanours. Often they show quickness of mind and an admirably rebellious spirit.

Tales of organists smoking at the console are common from days of yore when it was considered a healthy habit. While rehearsing a long work, such as an anthem or canticle-setting, one English parish organist puffed away during choir practice, leaving burn marks on the ivories at the top of the manual. For hymns and psalms, he worked with the untipped butt drooping from his lower lip. All Hallows by the Tower in London even had an ashtray in situ in the 1980s. French organists happily smoked at work, notably among the offenders being blind organist Louis Vierne. The authorities at Notre Dame put a sign on the console with "Défense de fumer" written in large letters. Vierne replaced it with an ashtray.

Ian Macdonald confesses to sneaking unseen down from the organ loft and out through the vestry back door for a smoke during the sermon (he's not the only one). The puffing plot came unstuck when the vestry door slammed shut, and he couldn't return the same way.

'I had to go back in via the main doors and walk the length of the church to get back to the organ loft. On the way back in I grabbed some papers and a hymn book from the back of the church and clutching them purposefully, made my way innocently back to the organ.'

Hymn books can be the cause of grief in unintended ways. At St John the Baptist Church in Holland Road, Kensington, London where Gordon Atkinson was organist and choirmaster, the organ and choir were in a loft about 25 feet above the chancel floor. There was a low stone wall behind the organist, handy for placing books and music.

'One Sunday we had a visit from the Bishop

who preached, then returned to his place in the stalls. I moved to pick up a hymn book, it slipped from my hand and crashed into the stalls, just missing the Bishop. After Mass, I was asked to the vicarage to have sherry with the Bishop and others. The Bishop, with a slight smile, said to me, "You may not have agreed with my sermon, but your reaction was somewhat exaggerated". '

Some organists do anything to impress their needs upon the church authorities. Dr Gordon Slater, an 'Old School' character, was organist and choirmaster of Lincoln Cathedral from 1930 to 1966, and he had problems with an ageing instrument. By the late 50s, the cathedral organ had been used every day for nearly 60 years, which had taken a considerable toll on its pneumatic action. To impress upon the Dean and Chapter the need for a complete rebuild, Dr Slater resorted to unethical tactics.

One of the Choir organ pistons emitted a loud hiss if depressed half way, so he deployed this during sermons, sometimes for the whole sermon if the Dean was preaching.

Another little trick he indulged in concerned an old metal fire bucket in the organ loft, which no longer contained any sand. Dr Slater used to position this at one end of the pedalboard and kick it over while playing during the service, often in a quiet verse of a psalm.

An organist aged about 12 was among those taking organ lessons at an Evangelical Anglican Seminary.

'One organist playing for services always used the most dreadful registration to play a particular set of responses (it was probably an 8' string with a Tierce and tremulant, or a mixture). We decided that we should do something and probably with gunpowder.

'The organ worked on something like 25V DC so we jumped wired the stop combination, and ran a wire to the large central display diapason. We lowered into the pipe a coffee can full of gunpowder which I had made. Into that, we placed the filament of a light bulb that we broke and inserted into the powder. The

certain combination of stops came on, the circuit closed, the organ played, the filament in the gunpowder heated and ignited, and there was much billowing of smoke.

'The theological students, all wearing gowns, were on their knees. The faculty, dressed in their academic regalia sat elevated at the back. The Dean of the College ran down the aisle and tossed his robes over several students still in prayer on their knees as he sprinted to the front. What he expected to do we don't know. Evensong was cancelled ("Good Lord Deliver us") and that organist never used those stops again.'

At least someone was listening to what he played. James Henderson-Holloway admitted to having played the same postlude for six months straight just to see if anybody noticed.

'I simply listed a different title each week. Nobody commented.'

Occasionally organists are thankful that no-one does hear the noises emanating from the loft. Take the problem that faced Bruce Fletcher in the week before Christmas. Bruce had been at work where the tradition was that employees gave each other small amusing gifts. Bruce received a pair of musical socks; you put them on, clicked your heels together and a jangly version of *Jingle Bells* played for about three minutes. In accordance with the tradition, he took off his normal socks and put on the musical ones. So far, so good. But Bruce

was also the organist at a small, medieval church near Tewkesbury, Gloucestershire.

'After lunch that same day I had to play for a funeral, still wearing my socks. I didn't think any more about it until just as the vicar was midway through his homily about the deceased I heard the tinny rendition of *Jingle Bells* emanating from the depths of the pedalboard.

'I quickly took off my shoes and socks, wrapped the socks in my overcoat to muffle the sound, and stuffed the overcoat and socks down the side of the console. Fortunately, there was a very small congregation for the funeral and I don't think anyone heard my unintentional voluntary.'

Soon after his arrival at St Luke's, Old Street, London, in 1844 Henry Smart played the Fugue in C minor by Mendelssohn.

'This was objected to by an officious churchwarden as being altogether too secular and 'jiggy' as a postlude for divine service.

So the next Sunday, after playing a particularly lugubrious out-going voluntary, Smart asked the churchwarden if that was better suited to his taste.

'Yes, Mr Smart, I consider the piece we have just heard much more appropriate. May I ask what it was that you played?' 'That, Sir,' replied Smart, 'was an improvisation of mine

on the popular melody, *Jump, Jim Crow*.

Outfoxing the critics can be something of a sport for some organists. Timothy Tikker once worked with a priest who forbad him to play any Bach (she said it was because she once worked at a church where their organist celebrated the composer's tricentennial by playing his music exclusively the entire year, and that was enough for her).

'But since, as one parishioner put it, our priest "couldn't tell Bach from Al Jolson," I decided to work around this simply by programming Bach whenever I wanted, but camouflaging his name in the bulletin music listings by translating it into other languages: John S. Brook, Jean-Sébastien Ruisseau, Juan Sebastián Arroyo, Giovanni Sebastiano Ruscello (I may have even used Esperanto: Johano Sebastiano Rivereto).

'It succeeded: my priest never had a clue she was hearing Bach.'

Malcolm Boyle, the former organist of Chester Cathedral from 1932 to 1949 told his pupil, John Keys, the following story:

At Matins one Sunday, Bishop Fisher (later Archbishop of Canterbury) looked into the organ loft. The Bishop told Malcolm that he knew the preacher that day and suggested Malcolm could come over to Bishop's House for a couple of sherries during the sermon.

Unknown to the Bishop, the preacher was not feeling well, and drastically cut short the length of his address. Upon Malcolm's return, from the north transept he noticed the tail end of the procession leaving the nave stalls, and of course there was no-one there to play the organ. In a flash of inspiration, he quickly went up the organ loft steps, donned the tuner's boiler suit, and put some dust and grime on his face and hands. After the vestry prayer, he said to the Dean, 'I'm sorry about the silence Mr Dean, but I think I've found the problem and have managed to get the organ working again for the Eucharist'.

Maintaining an approved level of sobriety appears to have been a struggle for many church musicians over the centuries. In

Norwich Cathedral in the mid-1600s, the organist Richard Gibbs had to shoulder the blame for the wayward behaviour of his deputy organist Peter Sandley. Admonished for his 'malpertness [sic] and sauciness in his carriage by words towards Mr Dean that he shall henceforth demean himself as is fitting in his place'.

Sandley still did not improve. In 1639 he was rebuked 'upon his fault of distemper in drink when he undertook to play on the organ in the absence of the organist, from henceforth to carry himself with more sobriety.' Thomas Weelkes at Chichester Cathedral in 1616 was noted for being a 'common drunkard and notorious swearer and blasphemer', causing many ripples among the 'quire' and his superiors. Three years later he again came under fire for drunkenness and often came 'so disguised either from the tavern or ale house into the quire as is much to be lamented, for in these humours he will both curse and swear most dreadfully'.[15]

Moving along a couple of centuries but still in the dark ages before people realised

that drinking and driving (whether car or organ) did not mix, no-one worried about going to the pub after a choir session before wobbling home. The laws and ideas about imbibing were so lax they were nonexistent.

Colin Jenkins recalls that many years ago at the end of term or the tertiary academic year he and other staff members, plus students, would go to a pub for lunch.

'I was well lubricated by the time I left for my in-laws' home where we always dined on Fridays. One time a phone call came in from a clergyman trying to find me, since his organist could not make it for a wedding due to start within the hour. I was more than happy to play but obviously not competent to do so. I somehow managed the clutch, brake and accelerator in the car but simply could not find anything accurately on the pedalboard. Goodness knows what the Mendelssohn *Wedding March* sounded like manuals only, no doubt played 'Allegro Molto Blotto'.

'After dinner I cheerfully drove to the

other side of the city to play for a rehearsal of a boys' choir. Early into the rehearsal the conductor had to stop to tell me that I was playing the wrong piece. This was a learning experience. Since then I have always avoided alcohol before playing the organ and would never drive in that state nowadays.'

During World War I, a well-known organist in London used to take a little, ah, liquid, refreshment during the sermon (to sustain his strength until supper time, naturally). Owing to air raid regulations the church lights were reduced to the minimum, with the organ loft in darkness except for the pedal light.

Relating the tale, W.G. Webber noted that to his great discomfort, and to the immense amusement of the congregation who could see it, the organist discovered that his massively enlarged silhouette was cast by the light of the pedals onto the north wall of the church. The fascinated onlookers were treated to a little shadow play: first the uncorking of a flask, then the drinking of the cup's contents.

The organist protested to Webber that it was milk in the flask, but others were not so sure; some of the congregation on the following Sunday 'had to be restrained from entering the organ loft on the chance of being offered a little something to keep out the cold.'

Fondness for the odd tipple to while away the interminable hours spent in an organ loft has led many an organist into trouble, rightly or wrongly. Ronald Perrin left Ripon Cathedral after a long and acrimonious disagreement with the clergy about his drinking. Never incapable because of this, there was no ground for his sacking. Perrin quite brazenly kept a bottle of wine in the organ loft to "ameliorate the suffering of listening to innumerable incompetent preachers."

In 1997 he was buried in his academic robes; it is believed that he held his conductor's baton in his right hand and a bottle of claret in the left.

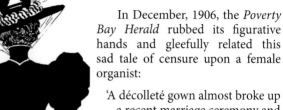

Organist Mariea Black and her church choir 'gown up' on Sundays, except for the hot months of July and August. Mariea thought the Church service was most uplifting on one such day.

'That was until I was told off by the 'auntie' at the end of the service. As I expected, I got spoken to about my attire, especially my 5-inch wedge sandals which I was delighted to discover let me play the organ as normal. Then it was my low-necked top. (*Ye Gods, lighten up woman, it's summer!*)

'I came home and about 15 minutes later, the phone rang. (*Ding-ding, round 2*) "Hello dear, I was just wondering if you were having an off-day today, or perhaps you are getting bored with your job as organist? Did you forget to play for the choir's anthem then?" (*No you daft old bat, it was unaccompanied, and I was singing.*)

"That's OK then dear, I worry about you. Remember to be properly dressed next week, even if you are going out afterwards, go home, and get changed first."

In December, 1906, the *Poverty Bay Herald* rubbed its figurative hands and gleefully related this sad tale of censure upon a female organist:

'A décolleté gown almost broke up a recent marriage ceremony and has separated a charming organist from the organ in the Church of the Atonement in Evanston, Chicago. Miss Lina May Haines, a statuesque beauty, was the organist, and appeared in the traditional Evanston society costume, at which the wedding party gasped.

'The rector was summoned and he explained to his organist as delicately as possible that her gown was rather scant. Likewise, the rules of the church required women to wear hats. Miss Haines blushed, then grew white. A friend threw a filmy evening shawl over her shoulders, but there was no hat. The sexton's skull cap was put in commission and, crushing it down on her brown hair, Miss Haines played as never before.

Then she resigned.

You know you're a woman organist when:

- You are told by a professor that your goal should be to 'play the organ not like a woman.'
- You're told by a senior colleague a week after getting married that you should give up work to support your first husband 'because he's really talented, and your career should come second.'
- Your recital is cancelled by the venue because you are pregnant.
- You're told: 'I can't believe you're strong enough'
- When auditioning for a place in a university music department performance degree, you are asked: 'But — are you planning to have a family?'

All this really happened. . .

A Mrs Thorp, writing in the 1920s for Tales of Organists indignantly noted 'I was frequently accused of playing the hymns too high, and was told more than once that it was not possible for a lady organist to play as loudly as a man.

In the early part of the 20th century, Annie Patterson (Mus. D., BA no less) had earned an organ scholarship and gold medal in organ playing from the Royal Irish Academy of Music, Dublin, and was blessed with a warm recommendation for her skills as a church organist by Sir Robert Stewart. Then when she was 18 she applied for a job in a Dublin church and went for the interview with a vestryman who was the registrar of candidates.

'I was curtly informed by this elderly Christian that a large number of ladies had sent in names as applicants for the position and that he had drawn his pen through the list.'

The passing of the years has not improved the attitudes as much as you might hope. With the announcement in 1999 that a woman was to be the head of an English Cathedral choir school for the first time in its history, a concerned chorister's parent reputedly posed the serious question:

"But does she play cricket?"

Advertisement for an organist at St John's, Southwark, in the Musical Standard, 1865

TO ORGANISTS.—The Vestry of the Parish of SAINT JOHN, SOUTHWARK, will meet on TUESDAY, the 11th day of APRIL, 1865, for the purpose of receiving applications from Gentlemen desirous of becoming Candidates for the office of ORGANIST. Ladies, and persons afflicted with blindness, will not be eligible. Salary £40 per annum. The person appointed will have to perform duty at all Sunday Services, as well as once in each week, and to instruct the children in singing.

Applications and testimonials to be sent to me, on or before the 10th day of April, indorsed "Application for the Office of Organist." Personal attendance not necessary unless requested.

By Order of the Vestry,

March 30th, 1865.   ROBERT SLEE, Vestry Clerk.

N.B. The candidates will be required to perform before a musical referee

THOSE NAUGHTY LITTLE HIDDEN TUNES

Nothing amuses an organist more than disguising familiar, raunchy secular tunes and dressing them up as an academic fugue or a typical Solemn-Melody-style of service piece. Using a camouflaged *Ride of the Valkyries* as the bride's mother trots down the aisle is a delicious way to ward off boredom behind the console as wedding season peaks with seemingly nonstop hitchings.

How many organists, I wonder, have extemporised on the tune *Adeste Fidelis* (*O come all ye faithful*, and often sung to the mock words *Why are we Waiting?*) when a bride has failed to appear. It would probably be faster to ask how many organists have not played it. Go on, own up —.

Philip Bailey admits it.

'My habit of improvising on *Adeste Fidelis* and other tunes at weddings when the bride is more than five minutes late has been noticed by various choirs, who play Spot The Tune. Once they spotted one more than I had put in. One time, a chorally inclined groom brought along a large choir of friends and family, for whom I worked in the openings of Evening Canticles by Howells, Stanford, Sumsion et al.'

In the much-maligned Victorian era, it was not all corsets and pursed-lips either. Even the highly respected and famous scholarly teacher, composer, and theorist Professor Ebenezer Prout was known for his sense of fun. Playing the organ for a wedding in the mid-19th-century he reportedly played the bride in to *Wretched Lovers*, and out with *Father forgive them for they know not what they do.*

An organist in a Roman Catholic Church attended a wedding rehearsal. The groom was being bossed around by his mother, his future mother-in-law, and his bride. His bride especially was telling everyone what to do.

The next day, the wedding day, for a postlude, the organist played a stylised version of *Who's Sorry Now?* The priest got the joke; no-one else did.

In one of his church posts, Peter Averi had to fill a gap between the blessing and the final voluntary with hymn tunes of suitable length.

'On one occasion a guest preacher had delivered an exceptionally long sermon which had some of the congregation almost asleep. At the appropriate moment, I thumbed through the hymn book and started to play a well-known tune. After the first line, I realised I was playing *Art thou weary, art thou languid* to the amusement of the choir.'

Earlier in Peter's career, he was also in the local Bible Class, whose members often indulged in challenges.

'I was dared to play a pop song as the voluntary during the offering. With teenage audacity I took up the dare and improvised on a current hit tune, *Put another nickel in the nickelodeon*. I played at a slow tempo with modulations between major and minor, so I got away with it undetected. It was worth the prize of an ice-cream sundae after the service.'

Many years ago, James Lally was organist in a church close to an army barracks.

'I had a military wedding to play for and a couple of weeks before, the bride and groom visited me at the church to discuss music. The two families and many friends were Gilbert and Sullivan fans. The music chosen was all in that genre, and I was sworn to secrecy and was not to tell anyone what I was going to play.

'It was a lovely service, good humour and lots of smiles, especially during the music. The happy couple left the Church to *Never*

mind the why and wherefore (from *HMS Pinafore*) which is about an officer's daughter marrying a rating. The congregation erupted with laughter at this music. I did not know that the bride was the daughter of a Captain and the groom was a lowly Private.'

One Sunday, at a suburban Methodist Church where Colin Jenkins played, a high-profile guest minister who was known as an advocate for temperance was the preacher.

'I was dared by one of the tenors to play the '*Drinking Song*' from the '*Student Prince*'. I did. No-one complained.'

Not all temperance preachers realised

what they had chosen. A visiting preacher innocently chose one particular hymn for Temperance Sunday extremely carefully, to the delight of the organist. *How bright those glorious spirits shine* would never seem the same.

A survey from Christian Research found

that half of churchgoers have heard of an organist slipping unexpected melodies into a service, wrote Madeleine Davies in the Church Times in 2013.

'From sneaking Bon Jovi's *Livin' on a prayer* into a sung eucharist to playing *Money, money, money* during the collection, instrumentalists appear to combine the topical with the irreverent. One of the 2250 respondents recalled hearing *Roll out the barrel* during the funeral of an alcoholic. One organist was reported as mixing the tunes of *Raindrops keep falling on my head* with *Make me a channel of your peace* before church one Sunday — the former music also having been played during a wet wedding.

'Organists are not above using their instrument to exact revenge. Stephen Goddard, who carried out the research, said that one organist, when asked to play at a former boyfriend's wedding, segued into *Can't help loving dat man*, as the couple processed back down the aisle. At one church in Glasgow, an organist bearing a grudge against the choirmaster opted for *Send in the clowns* as the choir took their places.'

Life in the antipodes is no less prone to tomfoolery from the organists. I learned of one rural player in a New South Wales town who had played *You gotta pick a pocket or two* during the collection using a solemn pedal line to intone the melody; and again in Australia a clergyman reports seeing *Ding Dong, the witch is dead* on a list of unusual themes requested of a funeral director.

Kevin Bowyer, on his last Sunday at St Mary's, Warwick, as the priest was ascending the steps of the pulpit for the sermon, played the theme to *Mastermind*. Presumably he then packed his bags and ran for his life.

It is not always the fault of the organist; occasionally it's the clergy (or more particularly their impish spouses) who goad musicians into pranks. David Scott was dared by the minister's wife to play particular pieces apt for the parish's Harvest Festival. So the resulting voluntary at the offering was based on *I've got a lovely bunch of coconuts* and postlude based on *Yes, we have no bananas*.

Appropriate pieces can happen by accident too. David was once asked to play for a funeral at the undertaker's request, which is why he did not know the person.

'As the coffin was entering the chapel I played Bach's *Sheep may safely graze* then found out to my horror in the eulogy that the deceased was a butcher.'

Richard Elliott was accompanying the great Mormon Tabernacle Choir during a rehearsal in a hall when without warning, a curtain behind the choir slowly peeled away from the velcro attachment and slunk to the ground. As it was being replaced, Richard quietly extemporised the theme *The Stripper* on the piano. What else?

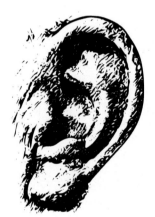

In equally playful mood, Stuart Palmer wove *Afton Water* into the pre-service music one Burns' Night, then the *Star Trek* theme in the week that actor Leonard Nimoy died, and the chord sequence from *Bat out of hell* on the occasion of the Harley-Davidson "Thunder in the glens" rally. Oh, and in anticipation of the afternoon's TV movie there was just a touch of *Jurassic Park* from him on Christmas morning.

Films, cult ones especially, have a lot to answer for. The *Star Wars Imperial March* has now infiltrated many a wedding music list. For one organist it began humbly as a bet at a stag party, but for Adrian Marple it moved on to featuring in the UK media when he was 'commanded' to play the theme for a wedding of ardent Stars Wars fans; others seemed to be following suit in Poland, the USA, and as far south as you can go in the Southern Hemisphere. It appears everyone is playing it. Move over Mendelssohn and Wagner — you have competition.

Continuing the movie theme, but in highly illustrious circles, Philip Bailey ushered in a royal party when he was assistant organist at the prestigious Royal Military Chapel (the Guard's Chapel). The trumpets with full organ heralded royalty with *Close Encounters of the Third Kind* as they took their seats.

And what do you play for a Mother's Day postlude? Why, just follow the lead of the wag who slipped a bit of *The Old Gray Mare Ain't What She Used to Be* into proceedings. Then make a quick getaway.

Music makes such sweet weaponry. After one organist had fallen out with his pompous headmaster over his dislike of final verse reharmonisations, it was only natural that he played the *Wedding March* as the headmaster and the equally pompous deputy paraded side-by-side down the aisle. The connection was not lost on the pupils who erupted with laughter as the pair left the building.

Early in the 20th century an organist at an elite private school in New Zealand was irked by the interfering (but musically ignorant) headmaster constantly trying to find fault.

So one chapel service he played Edwin Lemare's *Andantino* and waited for the inevitable reprimand from the headmaster who knew the andantino melody only as the popular secular song *Moonlight and Roses.* The gleeful headmaster seized his chance to expose the culprit in full view of the pupils and gave him a Force 10 dressing down in public.

'Sorry mate,' replied the organist sweetly, 'it is an original, serious organ piece.' Organist 1, Headmaster 0.

The right spontaneous touch can lighten an awkward moment too. When Thomas Murray was scheduled to play the Longwood Gardens organ during a regional convention of the American Guild of Organists, he slid onto the bench, pressed his pistons and hit the first chord with both hands. Immediately he stopped, examined the registration, checked some pistons. He explained to the puzzled audience that the couplers were not working.

After an organ technician had fixed the problem, Thomas explained to the gathering that a mouse had been busily chewing the wires, but the instrument was repaired, and the recital would continue.

In a token gesture to the cause of all the mischief, he began a slightly revised programme by pulling out a few stops and giving an impromptu rendition of the Mickey Mouse song.

Musicians don't always have the luxury of a page-turner, or perhaps have not been blessed with Herculean biceps necessary to tote a vast library of printed scores around with them on tour. Cue the brave new world of digital music storage and display. It can be via a phone, or a more practical tablet at score size, or on any of the specialist devices designed for musicians.

The bonus of these displays is that they can be used either as a 'score' sitting on a conventional music desk, operated by the feet (if idle at the time) or by blowing an apparatus to trigger the turn response. The advantages are numerous, but the potential pitfalls are easy to imagine. Batteries die at the worst of times, or the digital gizmo can behave the way computers always seem to: indulging in random acts of vicious revenge and going bananas for no good reason. Machines will be machines.

Jonathan Dimmock uses, and has a harmonious relationship with, his iPad; but he has had some issues with the ForScore program and with the AirTurn Bluetooth device used for turning pages. He learned the hard way.

'Last summer, I was playing a concert at Montpellier Cathedral. I was on a video screen. When I turned on the iPad and checked the page turner device, the page turner didn't work. So, in front of the cathedral audience, I rebooted and fished around in the settings until I got it running again. The issue, it turns out, is that I'm not supposed to close the settings when the AirTurn is functioning. (Too bad they didn't tell me that beforehand.) I had assumed the more windows that were closed, the longer the battery life.'

Jonathan adds that human page turners using this technology can mess up. 'One assistant I had couldn't get the page turner mechanism to work and made quite a to-do in the recital about getting the first several pages turned. As it happens, it would have helped if she had pushed the right end of the device.'

Ah. Good point.

Yet another toe-tapping gadgety thing to add to the foot controls

Technology was invented to embarrass us. Mark Quarmby rues the day a new gadget ambushed him.

'It was the early days of smartphones, GPS, and Bluetooth. I had just bought my first iPhone and had recently installed a GPS app with turn-by-turn verbal instructions. I was asked to play for a funeral in a distant suburb so used my new GPS app for the first time. With Bluetooth on, all the instructions came through my car's radio speakers. I made it to the church with no problems at all. I pushed the button at the bottom of the iPhone to close the GPS app and made my way to the organ loft where I played for 20 minutes. After the first hymn, there was nothing more for me to do for at least half an hour while the congregation listened to the eulogies and spoken parts of the service.

'Since I was hidden in the organ loft and being a typical 21st-century organist, this was my cue to pick up my phone to open FaceBook, and to my horror, the GPS app was still running in the background. Somehow, the phone's Bluetooth paired with the church's PA system and the GPS voice boomed over the speakers: "*In 100 metres, please turn left and you will reach your destination. Please mind your speed.*"

'Fortunately, nobody could see that my face had turned bright red as I grappled with the switch to turn the iPhone off. I still don't know if anyone there had any idea where that GPS voice came from.'

Tim Howard was in a school choir that visited cathedrals as a guest choir during holidays.

'I will never forget processing into choral evensong when the organ 'filler' music was interrupted by the theme tune to a radio sports show, and the entire evensong was spent fighting against the reading of all four divisions football scores. The new PA system had some teething problems, and was picking up Radio 4 when any microphone was turned on. It was proving difficult to solve.'

Technical glitches have been around to humiliate us all ever since the first Neanderthal attempted a DIY job of motorising his clubs.

The Lady's Newspaper of August 16, 1862, was as bemused as any of the participants by the tale from a small church in a little village near Brighton.

'The congregation recently bought a self-acting organ, a compact and convenient instrument, playing 40 tunes. The sexton had instructions how to set it going, and how to stop it, but, unfortunately, he forgot the latter part of his business. After singing the first four verses of a hymn before the sermon, the organ could not be stopped, and it continued playing two verses more, then stopped a little; but just as the clergyman completed the words, "Let us pray," the organ clicked and started a fresh tune. The minister sat it out patiently, and, on its stopping, once more repeated, "Let us pray," when click went the organ again, and started off on another tune.

'The sexton and others continued their exertions to find out the proper spring, but no one could stop it. So four stout men were got to shoulder the perverse instrument, and they carried it down the centre aisle of the church, playing away all the while, into the churchyard, where it continued clicking and playing until the whole 40 tunes were finished.'

When it works, technology is great. Erik Cannell harnessed the power of the modern cell phone when St Martin's, Brighton, hosted the annual diocesan Assumption festival, called *Merrily on High*. On one occasion, the service included a grand procession around the streets (it's said that people sitting outside a pub stood to attention as it went past) singing the 37-verse hymn telling the history of Walsingham as they went.

Being stationed at the organ in the church, and with no way of knowing what would happen when the procession arrived back 10 minutes later, Erik Cannell hatched a plan with some friends in the congregation and his assistant in the galley.

'We silently rang our friends downstairs as the procession began so they could hear the organ over the phone and keep the singers in tune, and we could listen to the singing over the phone and maintain the tempo. The result was that when the procession got back, everyone was on pitch and singing the right verse.'

James Lally was fortunate enough to be present during the following famous incident involving that notoriously temperamental tool, the microphone:

'It was back in the 1990s, and our priest had preached an exceptionally long sermon. During the following hymn, he had to answer a call of nature. Unfortunately for him, he forgot to switch off his radio microphone. The rustling of his attire followed by various indications of relief was clearly audible in the church. The congregation of between 80 to 100 began to wobble a bit with their singing until one person could control themselves no longer and laughed out loud and long.

'That was it, despite my efforts to drown the lavatorial grunts, the whole congregation had a fit of the giggles ending in peels of laughter. The

sounds from the loudspeakers ended with the passing of wind which any organ voicer would be proud to have extracted from a high pressure 16' reed. On his return to the church during the last verse, the priest looked mystified as many were wiping tears of laughter from their faces. I forgave the choir for failing to sing, and so did the council chairman.'

Ah, those close calls that bring out the sweat and naughty words, and once again a microphone was at the centre of the trouble. Many years ago, an organist was giving an organ concert at Southwark Cathedral in London, where the organ loft was far removed from his audience. A microphone was placed nearby so he could introduce each piece. The microphone was usually switched off before playing. Except for one memorable time during his playing of the delicate Pietro Yon *Toccatina* for flutes. Although an excellent player, he suffered from nerves and was addicted to industrial language. Each slip was accompanied by expletives of a colourful kind, clearly heard by the audience.

Robin Coxon was in splendid isolation in the Southwell Minster organ loft deputising for a weekday Evensong with the choir. Robin's view was restricted to the music and the conductor on the CCTV. Suddenly, halfway through the Magnificat, the screen went blank.

'During the 2nd Lesson, I tried everything I could; switched the monitor off, then on again, checked the leads were secure. Still no picture. The Nunc Dimittis was one where at the conductor's signal I held the opening chord and then he brought the choir in; he didn't know that I couldn't see him. I waited until I thought they'd be ready, played the chord and off we went. Then as the choir sang *To be a light to lighten the Gentiles* the picture came back.' Timing is everything.

Computers know exactly when to be awkward. It was Philip Bailey's rehearsal time for Rossini's *Petite Messe Solennelle,* which unusually features a harmonium and piano accompaniment. With limited funds, the choir had accepted the offer of a choir member to provide the harmonium sounds via computer rather than hire a real harmonium.

All went well initially, until the week when his laptop decided to update itself just as the rehearsal was starting. Eighty minutes later, and after the beginning of the second half of the rehearsal, the harmonium rebooted itself and started making noises.

Philip decided that he might as well treat the MIDI keyboard as a dumb keyboard for the practice, and started playing along.

'It must have looked convincing because the conductor at one stage asked me to give a note for the choir. I then had to confess that the harmonium was only 40% updated —.

'At one point I hummed the bass note of a long-held chord just to say I was still there and supposed to be doing something.'

Stuck with an all singing, all-dancing new digital super-duper electronic machine while the usual pipe organ was being restored, a young organ student had been left to explore the rest of the buttons. After trying out the myriad of percussion effects, he thought he would leave a surprise for his teacher to discover on Sunday morning. Finding the loudest possible bass drum hit and cymbal crash, he turned the percussion volume up to full and set the tempo to the slowest available. This combination resulted in the organ letting out a huge drum hit and cymbal crash every couple of minutes or so.

When the student turned up for his next lesson, his teacher looked at him accusingly.

'Every few minutes in the service, there was an almighty crash from the organ. It wasn't until some of the women came up and pushed and poked everything they could find on the console that they were able to stop it and the service could continue.'

The student grinned . . .

WISHFUL THINKING

A visitor to the Möller organ factory shop in Hagerstown saw a large 4-manual console being renovated for a college chapel. The organ had a solo stop called Trompette, and above its draw knob was a small plaque beautifully engraved in Old English type: '*Lead us not into temptation.*'

In a smaller shop which did custom console engraving, the same visitor also noticed that amid the usual labels (Swell to Great, Great to Pedal, etc.) was '*Bourbon to Organist*'. The shop owner confirmed that this was to be installed on the organ, and was not a key-chain ornament, nor merely the figment of a deranged organist's wishlist.

The restored Hill organ at St Paul's, Newcastle-under-Lyme in the UK, was rebuilt by George Sixsmith & Sons to incorporate a most sympathetic stop — the Tibia Liquida. When drawn, a miniature cocktail cabinet is revealed above the stop knobs of the Pedal and Swell divisions, complete with liquid essentials.

Similarly, in Ratzeburg Cathedral, the Rieger installation includes a stopknob labelled 'Rauschwerk'[17] (which can be translated as 'Intoxication Division'). Pull out the stop, and a drawer of libation goodies emerges smoothly to the left of the organist.

Ratzeburg Cathedral, Germany (Rieger)

Photo: Sean Tucker

When the late George Bayley was organist-choirmaster at two different churches in the USA, he had a Chivas Regal 4/5 stop knob installed which operated the Tremolo (what else would a bottle of whisky give you, other than the shakes?). George reported that at one of the churches an organist snob sniffily asked him what kind of Baroque stop that was meant to be. When George told him it was a joke, the snob was not amused, turned on his heels, and left in a huff.

Two cats, Felix and Sylvester (owned by the late organist, Stephen Ridgley-Whitehouse), are immortalised as the names on two Solo organ stops at the 1992 organ in St Peter's Eaton Square, London: the Tibia Sylvestris and the Viola Felix. What would they have done if the cats had been dubbed Tiddles or Snugglepussums?

Sean Tucker was organist at Saint Aldhelm's, Branksome, UK, when the organ needed a rebuild. Sean and his colleague fancied a stop "Choir to Pub" so included it in the specification.

'We had also planned to connect it to a small trap-door in the side of the console, which formerly housed the piston selector-board, but this has still not been connected. Apparently, the engraver queried it twice before he would produce the stop head.'

A potentially intoxicating stop is the Chivas Regal 4/5 (obviously a close relation to the Chivas Regal 4.5 whisky), in the Noehren organ in St Richard of Chichester Church, Chicago. Pulling it out turns the light on in the Swell. In First Presbyterian Church, Buffalo, New York, the Bombarde division contains a Chivas Regal 4/5 as a nod to the favourite tipple of the organist there, Squire Haskin.

Uh? Well, that's helpful.

NOTICE THE NOTICES

————❦————

Die Stadtkirche bleibt wegen wiederholter Einbrüche bis auf Weiteres geschlossen. Der Kirchenvorstand

"*Due to repeated break-ins, the city church remains closed until further notice. The Church Council.*"

(Well, that's handy. The concert is today.)

THIEVES OPERATE

IN THIS AREA
ST MARY REDCLIFFE CHURCH

DO NOT LEAVE ANY PROPERTY UNATTENDED

Today's church staff: clergy, verger, organist, thieves, flower arrangers, welcoming teams. . .

Please note,

Organist Rehearsing

Do let the organist know if you would like to Pray quietly.

Thank you

Hmmm. And this was found in the noisiest church in the UK. Correction: World.

"Back to Church" Sunday in Melbourne, when people were invited back to church, from the pew sheet:

"*All families who have attended for baptism, and those who were married or buried in the last 5 years have been invited back for a special family eucharist*".

Musicians & Choristers Only

Think about it.

Order of Service typo for the First Sunday of Easter:
O Sons and Daughters,
Let us Sin.

A member of the congregation said he had been coming to church for years hoping to get such permission.

INSTRUCTIONS FOR STARTING ORGAN

1. Switch on and listen to the pump motor accelerating. After 2 or 3 seconds the motor will stop accelerating and stay at a contant speed. When this happens ...

2. ... immediately switch the motor off then on again quickly. The motor should then start accelerating again until it stops accelerating (after 2 or 3 seconds – as before) then ...

3. ... as before switch motor of and on again quickly. Motor should start accelerating again.

4. This procedure should be repeated until the motor reaches full speed.

5. If you think the motor should be accelerating but isn't then switch off for a while then start starting procedure again. If motor is allowed to continue at a constant speed without accelerating (yet hasn't reached full speed) the heat protection thermostat will throw out the overload relay. If this happens ...

6. ... reset the relay by pulling out the red STOP button and pushing in the green START button. The relay is in the box enclosing the motor in the organ loft – the little access door to the relay is at the end of the loft furthest away from the door. The key to the loft hangs behind the console mirror at the top. Having reset the relay, repeat the starting procedure. If the organ still fails to start check the single phase fuse in the starting motor circuit. This is located on the switch board in the choir robing room.

****

Note: The key to the organ console is on a bunch of keys in the cleaners' cupboard.

Photo: Christopher Templeton

The simple process of how to start an organ in Christchurch, New Zealand

A shove coupler on a Dutch organ displayed this notice: *"Everyone who dares to couple whilst playing will be punched, shot, hung and quartered"*

Console notice, Royal Festival Hall, London

DEFINITELY
NO SMOKING
AT THE CONSOLE

Photo: Bryan Moseley

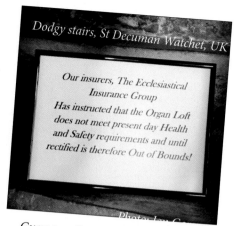

Dodgy stairs, St Decuman Watchet, UK

Our insurers, The Ecclesiastical Insurance Group Has instructed that the Organ Loft does not meet present day Health and Safety requirements and until rectified is therefore Out of Bounds!

Guess practice is out of the question today

"Members of the congregation found interfering with this organ will be severely reprimanded & forbidden to practice with the choristers."
Reverend T. Hardie Fallus
Rector of Brenton

ABOVE: A curious urban myth plaque, which despite its clear fallacy, has been reproduced as a plaque from Canada to Scotland since the beginning of the 20th century. It has even been sold in auction rooms as a genuine item.

KEEP CALM
AND
PLEASE
DO NOT
INTERRUPT
THE ORGANIST

Photo: Larry Reynolds

Sign next to the organ console at Hallgrimskirkja in Reykjavik, Iceland

In St David's Cathedral, Wales, in the 70s there was a "*Do not disturb the driver whilst the vehicle is in motion*" sign.

INTRODUCTIONS
To respond call 1902 242 527

MEN SEEKING WOMEN

CONCERTS

EUROPEAN male seeks relationship w/Filian Indian lady. Bollywood Fan. View perm relationship VMP 536079

University of Sydney presents
FREE ORGAN RECITAL
Sun 2 Sept, 3.30pm Great Hall
Martin Setchell (NZ)

WOMEN SEEKING MEN

ASIAN lady 50 y.o. widow, good looking, good cook, happy, lucky person, lived in Australia 7 years seeks permanent relationship VMP 101076

CHINESE Lady 24yrs, student, living in Australia for 2yrs would like to meet a young man between 24yrs-30yrs who is educated, honest and a good worker for initial friendship and long-term relationship. VMP 140085

INTRODUCTION AGENCIES
Phone: 13 25 35

Syd Asian Ladies
80% ladies are permanent residents. View photos and

Where else do you place an organ concert but in the "Personals" columns? *Sigh*

DEPENDABLE DEPS

Filling in for absent organists ('depping') is a way of life for many church musicians. A Deputy is also the life jacket of forgetful others. Maggie Pemberton, one of thousands of such Deps around the world, helps churches in Vienna. Each time brings new challenges, and this is a typical example.

THE SEARCH FOR AN INCREDIBLE *CREDIBLE QUEEN?*

One New Year's Eve, Maggie was sitting in her hostel in Vienna with a mug of hot tea and a cheese sandwich when her mobile rang; it was 17:23. "Can you get to the XYZ church for 18:00?" Change of plan —

'I jettisoned the tea, rushed up to my dormitory to grab everything, and tore down the street to the underground station. The church was fairly central, but of course the city was chock-a-block. Somehow I got there at 17:46, which was good, as I knew the church, but not the organ. The first challenge was to get into the building. I raced into a dark courtyard and frantically tried doors, eventually bursting into the sacristy.

'A Kind Lady materialised and gave me a hymn list, and the sacristan took me to the gallery door. With minutes to spare, I ran up the spiral staircase and searched for switches. As I was finding which stops were on which manual, another Kind Lady appeared and told me I would not need to play during the communion. I flipped open to the first hymn just as the Mass bell sounded, not realising that the fun part was yet to come.

'Just after the *Gloria* the complete music desk, including the massive two-kilo hymn book, calmly detached itself and crashed down on my knees. Well, it had been glued on, so it was only a question of time. Although I carry small screwdrivers, sticky tape, elastic bands, etc. with me, I had not brought an electric drill, so I put the desk on the floor and wondered how to continue. In a dark corner, I discovered an antique metal music stand, which I dragged to the console, but it proved to be too tall.

'Time was against me and I had to play the *Hallelujah* next, so I balanced the unwieldy book beside me on the organ bench. There was a bit of loose wood hanging in front of the music lamp on the organ, and I was able to clip the photocopies of the final voluntary and a hymn prelude onto that. It's always good to have clothes pegs with you. It was hard to read the music with the bulb shining through the paper, but it was a change from the twisted neck and swivelled eyes.

'We got as far as the sermon, where I finally had time to read the second half of the hymn list. This was a bad shock — the final hymn had no number, only a name. The name translated as *Credible Queen*, which I had never heard of and thought must be a local favourite that I might find in the music cupboard next to the organ. This, however, contained hymns in Hungarian. I had no choice but to sneak down and consult one of the Kind Ladies under the wary eye of the preaching priest. It emerged that the hymn name was a typo. After much page-flipping we agreed on *Queen worthy of glory*, and found the number in the Diocesan appendix.

'When we got to the communion, I sat down at the front of the gallery to take a breather, and a Kind Lady announced that there would be a CD of music by Mozart.

Well, I could have played some Mozart, but maybe they had good reason to prefer CDs? Before I could ponder further, I saw the priest waving at me. "Play us something!" he commanded — the CD player had broken down.

'So I vaulted back onto the bench, pushing in the louder stops I had prepared for the final hymn, and launched into a piece of Handel that happened to be lying at the top of my music pile. After that, one of the Kind Ladies announced the final hymn number, as the bemused congregation had been issued with the same hymn list as me.

'Before the blessing the priest thanked me for turning up at the last minute and even playing the correct hymns. After the voluntary, I brought down the music desk to hand over to the sacristan, as in my experience simply reporting "something broken in the gallery" may make no impression or soon be forgotten.

'I appeared at the back of the nave, where all the Kind Ladies were lined up to congratulate me. Their mouths fell open when they spotted the gigantic piece of solid wood I was clutching under my arm. I told them they were lucky there had been any music at all after the *Gloria*'.

Winnie P. went to Poke-it-with-a-Stick to play the organ after the organist died.

'The first thing I noticed was that, in the absence of both organist and parish priest, the choir assumed rather a lot. One man sat in the curate's stall and announced the hymns. His presence there blocked the view of the altar through the carefully positioned (and expensively mounted) mirror. When announcing the hymn he had a 50/50 chance of getting it right.

'The first time he got it wrong, it occasioned considerable panic at the console with frantic glances at the hymn boards. The congregation didn't seem to care, so I played the one I thought it should be. The 'announcer' had a curious whistle as he breathed in and out, and a pronounced limp. He was not alone; all the choir seemed to walk oddly. I would guess their combined age would be close to 900.

'Over the next year I came to know them better. When the church offered me the position I declined, telling the vicar privately that the choir was the reason, as it was a pastoral problem to which I had no solution. After one candidate for the post withdrew and there were no others on the horizon, I gave them a chance

of getting an organist. I offered to take a few practices, just to hold them together.

'As for the rest? The married couple: He declined to stand for more than one verse of a hymn (but only in practices) and she was singularly badly named Joy. A refugee from another choir turned up only once, and his reluctance was incomprehensible. If ever there were a bass who had no clue what to sing, and who needed help, here he was.

'There was a good tenor, and I have no idea how he stood it. The other 'tenor' didn't read music, he told me proudly. His speciality was the tune down about a octave and a third. Whistler never turned up at all.

'Singing in unison was not a strength of the women, and rhythm was probably too Roman Catholic for them. Coming in, as one, a full beat late was a regular occurrence I had to tackle. I should have tried something simple, like pushing a pea up a mountain using my nose. Corrected one week, the next it would be back to "usual practice". Playing over a hymn didn't convey to them the speed or exactly when to come in. I explained how to calculate the gap between verses. Alas, nothing worked.

'Thrice is enough. I shall miss the depping fees.'

As a deputy, Marilyn Oakes has played organs where notes did not sound, where they sounded randomly, and a couple of memorable organs where the notes trilled with themselves.

'One organ had a nice 16' pedal stop that was unusable because if you played C, it sounded C sharp. One hideously decrepit organ would fall out of tune with itself while you were playing. It had to be turned off and restarted to get it to play in tune. That's just danged awkward and disruptive when you're in the middle of an organ work or a hymn.

'There was another complicated task for that organ where you punched all the transposition keys and got it to retune that way, but my eyes glazed over while reading the instructions and I decided not to attempt that one. Plenty of organs had lights that needed replacing. Without the lights, you couldn't tell if a stop was on or off. One organ had pistons locked in theatre organ settings.'

The orchestral effects sported by the organ in St Michael's, Folkestone, were a marvel to all who heard it; bass drum, bells, cymbals, kettle drum and all manner of 'kitchen department' clatterings were available to the organist — as long as they knew what all these accessories did. And how. Which is unfortunately what one innocent deputy was unaware of when he nonchalantly leaned back to listen to the sermon.

'Immediately the kettle drums started into action to the astonishment of the congregation. The noise became louder and louder as the involuntary [and totally oblivious] creator of so much uncelestial harmony pressed back and gazed upwards in fruitless endeavour to discover the cause. The noise went on for a considerable time and there is really no knowing how long it would have continued, had not the mystery been explained, which was, that the organist by leaning back was pressing the vital button which put the drums into full play. . .'

A deputy in the south of England arrived at a church an hour before the service was due to start, since he always likes to make sure he avoids any possibility of error. Forty-five minutes later, another organist turned up — the real one whom the church had booked.

'I occasionally wonder where I was supposed to be that Sunday. . .'

A friend asked Bruce Steele to deputise for him at a wedding in a university chapel. A rehearsal with a soloist was arranged for half an hour before the ceremony. Bruce arrived early in the loft, which was in a high gallery, and began finding his way round the organ.

'My soloist (male, teenage, blond and blow-waved, wearing a grey sequined suit) arrived breathless at the top of the long, winding stone staircase, clutching a roll of music. He took one look at the gallery and said "Hey, where's the mike?" He looked over the edge at the void below and turned a pale shade of green.

'The music was *We've only just begun*. Exactly. In all fairness, he made a reasonable fist of the song. The wedding party, however, escaped without paying me. Next day I rang the college to find a contact phone number so I could extract the fee, only to be told "not known at this address".

Flashing red and blue warning lights should spell trouble ahead to anyone who is asked to take their own organ to anything. A shame that Erik Cannell did not sense danger when he was told to take his own keyboard for a funeral at a cemetery chapel in the East End of London. When he arrived, he found the chapel crammed with no significant spaces and seating for fewer than 70 people.

'They needed the front of the chapel for the coffin, so I was forced to the back row where the only room for the keyboard was by lying it diagonally between the seat of one pew and the back of the next, with the music also propped up against the back of the next pew. I had to play sitting at a 45 % angle to both, playing in one direction on a slant, and looking in another direction straight.'

'Afterwards, I had to go after the hearse to get the fee.'

Victoria Barlow showed up to play at one of her local crematoria to discover it was missing a pedalboard. It does possess a full pedalboard, but the staff '— aren't allowed to attach it, in case someone trips over it.'

Are you serious? Why?

"Health and safety, luv, sorry".

As an example of blind ignorance, some dimwit tried to hand Marilyn Oakes a CD while she was in the middle of substituting for the resident organist at a service.

'First, and most important, I am playing and I don't have a free hand, let alone free attention. Second, I don't know how your sound system works. Third, even if I did, you could have done this before I started playing. This has happened several times while subbing, at several different churches.'

Don't touch!

A crib sheet (which has nothing to do with the lining of a nativity bed for the baby Jesus) is the first thing a deputy looks for when reaching the organ bench. With luck the incumbent organist has listed top tips, traps, and notes to keep the Dep out of trouble.

Crib sheets come in varying degrees of helpfulness or hindrance. I was welcomed once by a note which urged the player "whatever you do, don't touch the **** (word completely obscured as blur-smudge-odd-indecipherable-marks) as it won't go off again." I was too terrified to touch anything other than basic stops and the notes. When nothing happened I figured that the resident organist's warped sense of humour was behind the warning. Revenge will be sweet.

Another crib sheet provided for another dep had this seemingly constructive instruction:

'Play before the service. When the altar party enters through the door to your right, play over the first hymn.'

The organist played, and played, and played, keeping his eyes to the right, wondering what was the delay. Unfortunately, since the organist had written the crib sheet, the console had been turned around 180 degrees. The door the deputy should have watched was to his left.

Other organists leave nothing to chance when handing over to a deputy. Many years ago Robert Coates deputised in a now demolished church in Southwark. The crib-sheet was extensively detailed. Among other things: *'Sermon: 10 minutes. If you want to smoke, use boiler room. But don't touch my brandy!'*

Giant posters everywhere bellowed instructions to an organist deputising at a church in Vienna: *Before playing this organ, call this number* (in the middle of the night?); *the use of couplers isn't allowed; don't stand on the pedals;* and on the case behind the console somebody had fixed a cigarette stub with a tape and the words:

SMOKING IS FORBIDDEN HERE.

Near the console, graffiti with the 'dos and don'ts' of the ages was everywhere on the historic wall: a drawn hand with a pointing finger, and the information: here is the blower switch, there is the light, written over and over again.

The drawstops were dotted with mysterious stickers — a red "X" or the number "13"— with no relation to the stops. It might have been a warning, or just to irritate substitute organists. The two manuals were not allowed to be coupled. The organist, shocked, kept exploring.

On the first manual, someone had written on the soprano A note in felt pen the words "DON'T PLAY!!!" A short test on the pedals showed the middle D and F did not work. Terrific...

The organist tried bending and twisting to play the pedal line an octave lower, but the D# down there was also broken. Playing the bass line of the hymns would be possible only with strange leaps of the feet, and his head was already spinning. That was a challenge for the Schubert *Sanctus* in Eb Major, and for *Silent Night* in B Major.

So what could he play for the Postlude? Apparently nothing in D or F Major. He decided on a decadent piece of French Romantic, without needing to change the pedal part, where the A appears only once in a fast movement. The poor organist hoped he could avoid it somehow.

The organ accompaniment 'books' were single tatty sheets, smeared with religious comments ("Oh!! His eternal Love!! Oh!! His eternal forgiveness!!") and unrealistic dynamic (pianissimo) information. It was like stepping into another world.

Philip Norman tells of a church which complained about a former Oxbridge organ scholar. They claimed he could not follow a complex liturgy and warned that he should be used for only simple services. A few weeks later, Philip played at the church himself. He found:

a) The organ was in a west gallery, with the organist facing westwards, away from the chancel. There were no console mirrors, so to see the liturgical action you had to turn your head so far round you could not keep contact with the manuals at the same time.

b) The person promised to "cue me" didn't show up.

c) The instruction was: "Play the first hymn as the altar party enters, which is indicated by three loud rings of the sanctuary bell. This will happen at about 5 past 10." At 3 minutes to 10 there was a faint ching (was that it?). By the time I established it was my cue, the party was in.

d) In the written instructions: Play xxxx before (crossed out), after (crossed out) etc. No other help was given —

Potential confusion lurks around every corner for the beleaguered substitute organist. It's a marvel that anyone, anywhere, is prepared to deputise at all.

Making it all up ~ improvisation

Improvisation — the skill of extemporising unscripted and spontaneous music — is the heart and soul of jazz. In the organ world a strong tradition of improvisation permeates French and Dutch music especially, but in other traditions it is not so actively taught. JOHN RILEY recommends developing this skill for the following eventualities:

- The bride is very, very, late, possibly having mistakenly been taken in the Rolls to the other St Mary's (of a different denomination), or down the wrong motorway going in the opposite direction. You have used all your music, including *Why are we waiting?*, *She'll be coming round the mountain when she comes,* and *Time to go home* and she has still not appeared.
- You have left your music on the bus.
- You are on your way to give a recital but have left your music bag unattended momentarily at the airport, and the security services have blown it up.
- A thief has stolen your music bag without knowing what was in it.
- A jealous professional rival has stolen your music bag knowing exactly what was in it.
- You have been asked to play a boringly plain accompaniment for a singer of the opposite gender, whom you are keen to impress.

- You are hosting a concert of world premieres of some recently rediscovered works, by an equally recently rediscovered member of the Bach family. Half an hour before the concert is due to begin, the world-famous recitalist (after some less than perfect counterpoint in a recent romantic liaison) arrives at your church in a profoundly intoxicated and less-than -perfect emotional state. Worse still, they have just thrown the scores in the nearby river. Many of the world's leading Baroque musicologists are in the audience. To avoid disappointment and embarrassment all round, you must delve into your resources of improvisational ingenuity (and Baroque pastiche).
- During a voluntary of some modern French music, somebody opens a side door and your illegal photocopies get blown off the stand. You must quickly invent a section for manuals only in order to kick the music

to one side; followed by one for pedals only, so you can pick it up.

- You are playing the final (and distinctly challenging), piece in a recital of obscure Baroque music. You have not had time to get to know the work thoroughly and are therefore relying on your fluent sight-reading skills to carry you through. Since you are due to go straight from the recital to the airport, you save luggage weight by working from loose photocopies. As you approach the grand climax, your page-turner inadvertently turns two of the photocopies at once. Your squeals of anguish and panic result in emotional osmosis, and a reciprocal reaction in the page-turner who, albeit with the best of intentions, replaces all the pages in the wrong order, upside down, or off the stand altogether. You now have to rapidly collect yourself and draw upon all the stock Baroque devices of repetition and extended climax within your armoury to bring the piece to a dignified and idiomatic end.
- Some notes on your organ have suddenly developed multiple potential ciphers à la Russian roulette, and only an especially composed piece is likely to avoid them.
- You firmly believe that music should underpin elements within the service. A sermon touching upon the ethics of genetic cloning might, therefore, inspire a Toccata on *I wanna be like you*, or an announcement that the proposed repairs to the organ have been cancelled with a Fugue on *There might be trouble ahead.*
- While playing an obscure contemporary work, (the composer of which is mercifully out of the country or deceased), you lose your place in the 'music'. Since no one knows or is capable of comprehending the work, and it is extremely unlikely to be performed again, you can complete (and probably improve), it à la mode with impunity.

Musical interlude

David Sadler (with apologies to Fauré)

Who lives inside your organ?

Given that organ pipes are open receptacles, it is not surprising that bizarre objects find their way into them. Apart from the understandable bats and birds, other strange discoveries need imagination (and a good sense of humour) to figure how they got there. Or why.

Ever since I watched amazed as a technician reeled giddily out from the case in Notre Dame in Paris after Olivier Latry had thundered through a lengthy and thunderous improvisation, I realised all manner of creatures might choose to regard the chambers as a home away from home. The oddest object that organ builder Ken Aplin ever found inside an organ case in Wellington, New Zealand, was a bed. A complete bed. Among the pipes, trunking and general paraphernalia. Perhaps the sermons were long, or services too frequent, but whatever the reason, the organist made sure he was comfortable. Until the vicar found out.

Having foreign bodies inhabiting organs is nothing new; the *Te Aroha News* of July 9, 1887, reported the curious story of an impulsive clergyman imprisoned in an organ pipe.

'The Archdeacon of Winchester, who is a very little man, whilst showing some ladies over the cathedral a few days ago, must needs prove the monstrous size of the pipes of the organ in the course of repairs by creeping into one which lay on the floor. He then stuck fast in the pipe. He had the key of the cathedral in his pocket, and had locked the door, so the

situation was critical until the workmen who were repairing the organ came back after dinner and pulled the venerable adventurer out.'

Perennially curious cats forever cause trouble in organs. A tiny kitten was responsible for bringing a major London show to a halt, as reported by the *New Zealand Herald* in 1934.

'A kitten taken into the Prince's Theatre, London, to bring good luck to "On with the Show", stopped the theatre's giant organ at the first matinee. Given a free run of the theatre, the kitten got into the organ chamber and climbed into one of the larger pipes.

'When the organist began to play, five notes failed to function, and he was compelled to bring his performance to an early close. Meanwhile, the kitten having climbed 2ft up the pipe, found itself trapped. Eventually, it was hauled out safely with a walking-stick.'

Although not strictly inside a pipe, a homeless man was found sheltering inside the organ of Scotland's biggest cathedral in 2015, according to staff.

The man is thought to have entered St Mary's Episcopal Cathedral, Edinburgh, by climbing 18m of scaffolding and entering by a hatch. He then laid a plank between the interior stone wall and the back of the 14m-high organ pipes of the 1879 Father Willis organ, which was installed when the building opened. After crossing the plank, at least 15m above the stone floor of the nave, the back of the organ offered many access and repair platforms that provided a cosy sleeping space — until the organist switched the instrument on.

During World War II, seven people lived among the organ pipes in the Breeplein church in Rotterdam.[18]

The church warden of the local Breepleinkerk and his wife, Jacobus and Annigje de Mars, built a special room behind the organ (not in the organ itself), disguised so that no one could see the secret hatch. A Jewish couple, 17-year-old Rebecca and 25-year-old Maurice Kool, began hiding there in 1942. Maurice's parents, Meijer and Ida Kool, joined them.

Gerrit Brillenburg Wurth, pastor of the city's Dutch Reformed Church, and his wife, Gerda were quite unaware of the families hiding in their own church when they approached the warden to help hide another couple, pharmacist Chaim and Fifi De Zoete.

So a second secret room was built, mirror-image on the other side of the pipes. Life carried on as normally as possible; Rebecca Kool gave birth to a son, Emile, on January 6, 1944. This happened in the home of the church warden, with the help of an ophthalmologist (whose knowledge on giving birth was based only on a book) and a nurse. The baby was raised by the warden and his wife.

Despite some close calls, all seven survived the war.

George Henry Jr, the organist at St Mark's Cathedral in Salt Lake City, Utah, went to practise and noticed a tiny head sticking out the tallest pedal pipe on the old Holtkamp organ. Curious, George pulled out that stop and played the corresponding pedal note. Hey presto! It was shredded tweet time as feathers (and not feathers) came flying out of the pipe. A pigeon had lodged itself inside. There it was — stuck but still alive.

George immediately called the technician in charge of the instrument to deal with the problem, who then, with the sexton, climbed ladders and surveyed the situation. Pulling out the large pipe to free the bird was more than two people could handle safely. But then they had an idea. They built a small perch, lowered it into the pipe, then brought it up under the poor animal who did what comes naturally to birds: it hopped onto the perch. The pair then pulled the perch up and freed the pigeon, happy to escape. Not a bird-brained idea at all.

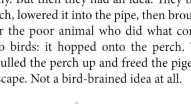

Look what I just found!

Smaller, yet no less intriguing objects somehow find their way inside organs. Members of the Facebook group "Organ Memes" gleefully listed some of the trophies they had discovered inside organ chambers and pipes.

- Organist shoes (almost new, but not used in a decade), an empty bottle of wine, an owl, countless rats, mice, and bats, unidentified poo, dead flies enough to fill two vacuum cleaner bags. Once even a 50 pfennig German coin from 1890
- A large plug of original packing paper, inside a trombone pipe, of an organ installed 30 years previously
- Human ashes
- Car and train magazines
- The plastic tray out of a biscuit packet
- A deflated beach ball, a water bottle (empty), paper balls, old homework, a rodent, a pencil. All at the same school
- A used condom. (*'There is a story to go with the finding. It's the romantic organ, which the owners were trying to "save" by moving it to my church. It was sitting in a church that had been converted to a youth church where they don't use organs, altars and pulpits. Except for this creative use,'* notes the finder)
- All the handheld percussive instruments for the praise band, on the bellows
- 100 Italian lire and an image of Saddam Hussein
- A flock of birds that flew out as the first strains of the bridal march began
- A sparrow which was set free, and a bat
- Tulips
- Human excrement on top of the ancillary bellows
- Cardboard rolls used for paper towels/toilet paper
- The leg of a dead bird sticking out through the mouth of a front display pipe
- A cat that had crawled into the console
- Half a rank of pipes
- A takeaway cup of coffee, with flies
- An orange
- Maple syrup in the bird whistle
- Waxing strips
- Champagne cork
- First generation iPhone
- A pigeon's egg
- Beer bottle cap
- Cough drops
- An old sock
- A thong
- A French baguette on the manuals

Sordid tales from the keyboards

The much-loved, treasure extraordinaire, 'Pavarotti of the Organ' Carlo Curley was a larger-than-life, much-loved giant in the organ world until his early death in 2012. He was acutely aware of the detritus that spoiled the organist's environment.

Carlo's performances, extrovert character, and musical exploits are well known, but many of his peers would be unaware of his almost fanatical bid to get organists to clean up their act.

He waged war on those who let their manuals become discoloured, grimy and sticky from inattention. He was an adept hand with duster and cleaning cloths before even thinking about playing. In Carlo's words:

'As I sat casting my gaze over my workstation for the next two days, it was all but impossible not to notice the encrusted dirt and grime that was in evidence on the thick-cut, bone keyboards, on the coupler-rail's tilting-tablets, and almost every one of the numerous thumb pistons as well. Even the builder's nameplate was corroded with dirt of one sort or another — how did this happen? Perhaps the organist longingly caressed and fingered the nameplate during the sermon by way of special homage — who can say?

'In spite of the impending revolt I sensed lurking within, I proceeded with my normal audition of the various voices, seeing how this and that blended with this, that and the other. I was never able to forget that the ever-important tactile side of playing the organ had been violated once again simply because the incumbent musician couldn't be bothered to take a few minutes each week to purify the keys, stops, couplers and playing aids. It felt as though my digits were wallowing in the slurry of a pigsty. Additionally, the remains of many enthusiastic rubber-eraser sessions (termed affectionately by an English colleague as 'eraser droppings') were clearly in evidence, both on the music rack and on the manuals. Is it necessary for organists to attend a course in basic console hygiene to learn how to maintain a clean console? Perhaps this is a basic curriculum which should be offered everywhere organ performance is taught.

'I sympathise with highly-strung organists whose nerves set them on tenterhooks when performance time arrives. But I recall the early 1970s as though it were yesterday when visiting a large church in western Pennsylvania, not far removed from Lake Erie, home to a spanking new digital instrument whose console sported four rows of gleaming, highly polished hollow plastic keyboards.

'The organist, while being one of the kindest and most ebullient chaps one could ever hope to meet, was absolutely terrified as the Sunday 11am service rolled around. He revealed that he experienced not only shortness of breath and slight dizziness but his hands copiously perspired, rendering the keys wet with his exudation.

'Sadly, his was not the bog-standard variety of perspiration but included some heinous, pestilent essence that could only be considered acutely toxic. After about six months of regular use, ridges, bumps, bubbles and the like showed on the playing surfaces, and the most exercised areas had worn splits, cracks, and holes right through into the keys. Such damage was the first time I'd ever seen first-hand such a disturbing phenomenon, and it was no surprise that it became necessary to replace all four keyboards over time.

'A couple of seasons ago before a concert in Texas, I asked the organ service man to bring a vacuum cleaner and remove the pedalboard, as it was obvious there was much to expunge from beneath this important clavier. We collected 16 pencils and ballpoint pens, several small pencil sharpeners, some pads of 'PostIt' notes, a slightly rusted letter-opener, two dollars and 84 cents in small change, a great many McDonald's sandwich wrappers, and quantities of mouse droppings.'

Carlo collecting his dusters ready for another console cleaning job.

Carlo also relates a story from an organ builder who found a glass eye under the pedals. The organist claimed it as his, having lost it when he got carried away during a postlude.

Then, reports Carlo, there was the small matter of the organist in the 1950s who used his pedalboard as a spittoon. This was reliably recounted in a letter from the Estey Organ Company who had the unenviable job of tending to the inevitable repairs necessary on the pedals when it was used for this purpose.

It gets even grubbier

Ernest Nichols relates his experience with an organ of a different variety, but with the same problems for the organist.

Ernest had to provide four shows daily for three months on a Wurlitzer in a 2800 seater auditorium of the Malco (now returned to its original name of the Orpheum), and rejuvenated to inspire and entertain a wealth of modern-day performers and listeners. Here is his story:

'Pre-opening rehearsals with the Wurlitzer went smoothly, after what appeared to be bushel-baskets of ancient buttered popcorn were removed from the pedal area. The manual keys were a feculent black; a disgusting, dark sepia caused by the 'filth of the ages' being glued to the ebonies, ivories, and other console mechanicals by copious layers of sticky ooze. This ooze was the residue of soft drink, flung wildly into the pit by audience members, who inconsiderately considered the gaping abyss to be a massive garbage receptacle for their personal use.

'The gentleman who restored the organ was interested only in everything functioning and that all the notes played — a commendable desire, of course. But console cleanliness did not appear on his dance card. Everything functioned, but he never got all the notes playing, which is another story in itself.

'It took three rolls of damp paper towels, an equivalent number of rolls of the dry variety, and careful manoeuvring to clean all that nastiness. Nothing could be so sodden that water would run down onto the old contacts and cause some major technical mishap.

'The instrument had not been tuned and would not get a full-temperament tuning for the entire time I was there. Touch-ups were the order of the day, and only for something howling miles out of tune.

Opening night for Ernest was on Thanksgiving 1959.

'The console rose, the ancient lift vibrating like a car with four flat tires, well past the sell-by date, as I enthusiastically bashed out the Sillman *Never Seen Us Before* theme to cheers from the amazed audience, most of whom had no idea that the theatre even had a pipe-organ. Then, suddenly the top of the pedalboard went dead. I looked down to see what was amiss. As the brilliant, carbon-arc follow spot was illuminating everything, I spotted something colorful between the gaps of the pedals.

'Like a trouper, I continued, my gaze fixed upon that object beneath my right foot. Finally, the opening number ground to its conclusion as I discerned a slight bit of faded red jutting out from the right of the pedals.

'There was an entire, empty orchestra pit to my right. Danger! My intention was to grab the protrusion at once and fling it into the scary, seemingly bottomless void, which I tried to do.

'The audience stopped applauding as if on some unseen cue. I wrenched the fabric, almost falling off the lift, and flung back a piece of tacky velour. It revealed a small mountain of popcorn, candy wrappers, and other items which it had covered for at least 30 years, all of this easily visible from every seat in the theatre, and under a bright spotlight.

'The ensuing cloud of mucky debris was colossal and resembled a test on an explosives range, most of the rubbish flying back onto me. The audience gasped, then applauded, and laughed hysterically, finally breaking into cheering. I, of course, being the consummate professional, took a bow. That set them off more.

'As I tried to return to my place on the Howard Seat (Oh, dear God!), I noticed that my left foot, the most important limb one can use when playing a Wurlitzer, had a strange object firmly attached at the toe and likewise on the sole. I ignored the obstruction, much to my misfortune.

'When the next number began, featuring the charming Chrysoglott and a handful of ultra-keen Wurlitzer Violes, I had difficulty negotiating from one note to the next because I discovered the encumbrance was two enormous wads of gluey bubble gum that had become affixed to my shoe. Not a pretty scene, rest assured. No wonder that chewing and bubble gum are banned by law in Singapore.

Not the result of misuse, but an organ in Christchurch New Zealand abandoned after earthquakes. The end result is the same.

THE JOURNEY OF
ORGANICUS GRINDUS

A rake's progress, of sorts, as confessed by JOHN RILEY; whose own deeply personal love of the instrument qualified him to become a regular recipient of the local 'neighbour from hell' award.
(The names of churches have been changed to protect identities)

From a tender age, I took every opportunity to hijack the organ at the family church and make lots of impressive noise. Moreover, the temptation to play an organ better than my own was never far away. From time to time, the lure of a fine-looking instrument in an unlocked state would prove too much. With nobody about, I would start the motor and have lots of loud fun. Eventually, though, one of the clergy or the lady doing the flowers or, worst of all, the organist, would appear without warning. With the echo still bouncing around the building, denying knowledge of the dastardly deed proved to be futile.

Being caught red handed and chased out of churches became wearisome. However, having gained a place in a higher education music institution, more genuine organ-playing opportunities gradually emerged.

It all started reluctantly in a small way, but playing for mid-week funerals at a local church soon became a regular necessary source of income, not least to finance a growing passion for organ LPs, mainly the expensive continental imports.

This was during a period of increasing tension and turbulence in the local area. The Ladies' knitting circles and Inter-denominational turf wars were hitting new and ever more grisly heights. Meanwhile, many members of the local criminal classes were meeting increasingly mysterious and eccentric fates, usually in remote or unorthodox locations. One after another was perambulated up the aisle, and the vicar would perform great pyrotechnic feats of theology and biblical

interpretation in bringing the character and deeds of the deceased into the Christian fold.

The primarily unchurched nature of the congregation would be betrayed by a marked lack of synchronisation in kneeling and standing, genuflecting helplessly in response to every part of the service, or dutifully clapping after the bible reading. The hymn, on the other hand, became a regular duo spot for solo organ and obligato clergy.

The search for a regular organist post led deeper and deeper into more strange worlds. In a moment of rash acquiescence, I agreed to help out with the organ playing for a local evangelical vicar. The regular organist had suddenly 'left', but it was only the ensuing months that would yield some clues as to his fate.

Holy Sepulchre church was the size of a small cathedral, but by the time that they had got to the organ the money had run out, and even the five-second acoustic could not hide its limitations. The church heating system had packed up beyond repair shortly before my arrival. During the winter, the congregation had the luxury of a few gas stoves. Sixty feet up, however, even three jerseys, a coat and fingerless gloves could not remove the sensation of physical and spiritual numbness.

The organ was little more than a bunch of second-hand pipes strung together in the church attic. Access was by a ladder, which, for someone who is phobic about heights and enclosed spaces,

created a weekly bout of fear. Pipes had been removed because of incurable ciphers, and it was one of these, a giant 16ft open wood, that I knocked over one memorable Sunday. I narrowly avoided crushing my foot but succeeded in creating an enormous dull crash followed by clouds of dust, and a level of excitement and alarm among the congregation probably not experienced since the World War II air raids.

The congregation was among the nicest that you could hope to meet. Nevertheless, the many virtues found in the church were becoming more than outweighed by the damp cold, the wretched organ, and the ever-present physical hazards. The more that I signalled the wish to leave, the greater the affection and warmth showered upon me by all concerned. The vicar's wife, in particular, was stunningly expert at dissipating all moral grounds for leaving and inducing guilt that one should have ever considered such a thing.

It was only a matter of time before some bodily injury would be incurred. Sure enough, one evening I came down with a rapidity and spectacle of which Frank Spencer would have been proud. While being a thoroughly unpleasant and unpremeditated event, this proved to be most useful in promoting a case for leaving. Aided by some fiction about a growing emotional connection with the minister's daughter from a church on the other side of the town, I was finally able to make the break.

Just a short distance up the hill was an entirely different world and an affluent suburb crowned with the Victorian glory of St Philip's and St George's; here I finished my student days as one of the organists. This large and popular church had an organ to die for, an excellent choir, and a rich social scene of students and young professionals.

Alas, sightings of UFOs (Unattached Female Organists) were rare, and even my ingenious five–part fugal expositions on the last hymn and other feats of musical prowess seemed to leave the objects of my attentions curiously unmoved. So my halcyon student days — and many high hopes — met their inevitable end, and with it the equally inevitable and unpleasant prospect of having to make my way in the real world.

I decided to offer my services as a freelance musician, aided by a CV that miraculously combined truth with a misleading, inflated representation of my abilities and experience. An advertisement in a church newspaper offering my services as organist in return for lodgings eventually secured an 'arrangement' at a church in an important university town in Southern England.

The vicar at St Peter's was an educated man in many ways but almost frighteningly absent-minded, confused, inarticulate, and inept at any moment of crisis. His wedding sermons would be a white-knuckle ride that effortlessly eclipsed the best man's speech for revelations of family secrets, postnuptial practical advice and other content guaranteed to keep any listener in a state of nervous apprehension. One highlight was the free interchange of the names of the bride, bride's sister and mother, their family pets and recently deceased relatives, all to interesting and, on one occasion at least, rather tragic effect.

The church had a large congregation that was a truly democratic institution, to the point that nobody knew how far the delegation went. There were two unofficial music coordinators, neither of whom coordinated much with the other, so both the music group and organist would start to play a hymn or musical item at the same time, or wait, expecting the other to be doing it.

The biggest irritation was a young electric guitarist whose ego, talent, popularity, volume and wish to project his creative personality almost equalled my own. Even after he had finished his spot, his endless tuning, practising and doodling jammed every silent part of the service in which I wanted to play.

Worst of all, just before launching into a perfected voluntary that I knew the congregation would love, he would often receive a visitation of the Holy Spirit, manifested in charismatic and unbounded musical form.

This became too much to bear. One Sunday before anybody arrived I undertook a delicate reordering of the wires in the back of his amplifier (the equivalent in guitar terms of sabotaging the organ blower). However, the effects went some considerable way beyond what was intended and indeed proved to be most spectacular. Shortly afterwards the guitarist left and — with, I am assured, his bandages now completely removed

— was last heard leading a Christian rock band tour round Russia.

Guitarist apart, playing music before the service became pointless. Half the congregation would jam the door just after the official starting time. The music groups would arrive late and still be tuning and testing the microphones when the service was supposed to start.

The service would eventually grind into action a little after 10.30 and consist of readings, music, announcements, a dramatic presentation, interviews with members of the congregation, visiting missionaries or other celebrities. This would be crowned by the sermon, which seemed to expand in direct proportion to the visible signs of boredom from the congregation, or in the case of a visiting preacher, the distance that they had travelled to be there. Everything was thrown into the pot without any real coordination or understanding of how each item complemented the other or added to the total length.

If we had not reached the final hymn by noon the vicar would panic and chop the hymn or, worse still, the extroit, which the choir had rehearsed for several weeks beforehand. The final voluntary was often interrupted by somebody grabbing the microphone to make an announcement, or to inform the driver of a car that they were blocking the driveway, had left their lights on, or that their children were trying to drive it away.

Sundays were blessed with opportunities to invent preludes with subtly embedded melodies related to some aspect of the sermon, or other pertinent aspects of the service. However, one Sunday, a prelude that embodied a secular melody pertinent to a distinctive aspect of the vicar's wife's new outfit was delivered with less than customary discretion and ambiguity. Noting the rapid embodiment of hell's fury on her face — and mindful of the saying that it is better to jump with a parachute than be kicked off the plane without one — I duly signalled my imminent departure.

Next, I was installed at my current post as organist at St Edward's; a church blessed by its position in an affluent part of town, and able to provide a handsome salary.

The organ upon my arrival at the church was a less happy affair. It had only recently been rebuilt and enlarged by a small builder from the Midlands who then promptly retired to Spain and declared himself bankrupt. The instrument promised far more than it delivered, and was deteriorating fast. One evening, while inside the organ trying to fix yet another cipher, I was overcome by a spectacularly cathartic orgy of violence and malice that resulted in kicking over and jumping on the offending organ pipe. With this new clarity of mind came the realisation that since things were unlikely to get any better with this sad instrument, a rolling phased programme of subtle sabotage might be used to force its replacement.

By coincidence, about the same time a solicitor who was a man of exceptional charm and persuasion joined the congregation. His unerring logic in all matters biblical persuaded many wealthy individuals about the divinely ordained enhancements in this life and beyond, which would ensue in return for donations towards certain good causes. The funds soon materialised and, after an interregnum that was served by free trials of electronic instruments, our magnificent new pipe instrument was installed.

This organ is the pride of our parish and a draw to many less fortunate local organists, who are only too happy to deputise for merely musical reward when higher callings elsewhere detain me on a Sunday. Through regular concerts on our spectacular instrument, I am privileged to be able to raise much-needed funds for a variety of good causes of which I am in sole charge.

Like a plughole in an emptying bath, the organ is the centre around which the rest of life happily revolves; for true organists know in their heart that even on the bleakest of days, the sound of the organ will communicate a voice of beauty and truth amid a cruel, insensitive, and incurably ciphering world.

Don't ever tell an organist that the donkey is getting restless.

Organists v. Congregation & Audience

What makes an appreciative audience or congregation? Sometimes an organist is merely grateful that anyone at all is left in the pews as they play their outgoing voluntary, and not just because they are swapping tales of inflammatory bowel diseases and grandchildren.

Adrian Marple reckons that if the number of people at a concert is more than the number of performers it is a good start, but guarantees nothing. He writes:

'An eminent English Cathedral organist of extraordinary playing talent and an entertaining raconteur tells the story of his recital in a country church where he made his grand entrance to an audience of three. After introducing himself and his programme, one person left, as she had come on the wrong night for her flower arranging. Of the remaining two, one had come only to open and lock the church.'

Adrian has played to a venue that was designed to hold 2000, but on the night that he was engaged to accompany a group of singers, it housed four in a small embarrassed huddle. Another event was a jazz band of five playing to a full house of three, where two-thirds of the audience were girlfriends of the band.

On a recent concert tour of Germany, organised mainly by email, Adrian's St Mary's choir of 25 was accompanied by parents and loved ones to all their venues, thus guaranteeing an appreciative audience.

'But one place managed to leave all the stops well and truly in when not even the person with the keys turned up. The church was in a beautifully sleepy village and was thankfully open for prayers. This was just as well, as I was offering up plenty when it became apparent that the bloke with the keys for the organ had not appeared, and we had 30 seconds to go before our choristers burst into song.

'Have you ever faced an audience with a choir on whom the organ was an important prop, armed with a programme of music written mainly for choir and organ, but without the aforementioned box of pipes? No? I don't recommend it. And the audience that came to hear us, apart from the parents? Yes, you guessed it — three.'

Particularly during free concerts in churches, there is no guarantee that people will behave themselves. I have watched, gape-mouthed, as tourists have strolled up the aisles during concerts, taking selfies; and one holier-than-thou hopeful who noisily made a mission of inspecting all the confessionals up one side aisle then down another, before leaving with a snort of disgust after finding no priest ready to hear his confession.

You can never be sure what members of the congregation are thinking — and perhaps it's better not to know. Kris Emmett was idly eavesdropping at the back of the church post-service while his visitor friend played the organ for him. Kris overheard an elderly member of the congregation remark to her companion that the 'resident' organist got 'better every week.'

Organists soon learn that what might be music to their ears can be regarded as aural pollution to others. When aged about 12 or 13, Peter Tandy used to practice in Holy Trinity, Stratford-upon-Avon, UK (allegedly the site of Shakespeare's Grave). The organ has a magnificent full Swell and a fine Great principal chorus so what had to be done? Yup, play on the Great and gradually open the box to let the 16', 8', and 4' reeds and Mixture through. Cue stroppy verger: 'Keep it down Sonny, the visitors can't hear themselves talk'. It's a wonder Peter got any practice done with cruel comments from the great unwashed to contend with. Peter was in the embryonic stages of trying to learn a new piece which was really beyond his capabilities. A visitor to the church asked, 'Are you tuning it?'

Weddings bring out the — yes, it has to be said — drongos. Frequently ill at ease and unused to churches, some behaviour is so extreme, that only those who have seen the most bizarre happenings believe it possible. Lighting up a

cigarette, shouting, and generally behaving as if they were in a football stand or a pub, wedding guests stretch tolerance to breaking point. Even blissful ignorance can cause problems for those trying to create the magic of a wedding ceremony. Take the example of the organist who was playing a wedding in the organ loft on a small instrument.

'After the opening hymn, I sat on a pew nearby and a flustered mother walked in with her children in tow. She went to deposit her handbag on the organ keyboard, so I stopped her. Her attitude was: "Oh I didn't think the organ was being used".

'I asked her what instrument she thought was usually used at weddings. It was this same woman who, later in the service, while holding a child on her hip, stood behind me during one hymn rocking her infant while I was getting booted in the back. The words that were going through my head were not repeatable.'

One organist was forced to extract a child from the pedalboard during the signing of the marriage register. It happened so suddenly; the little boy appeared, vaulted over the organ bench and landed feet first at the top end during what was supposed to be a sensitive rendition of Bach's *Air on the G String*. The organist was distinctly unimpressed.

'It's an unfortunate sign of the times it appears, where clergy (bless 'em) seem to encourage children to run around unsupervised'.

Free-range children are like the pestilence to anyone trying to concentrate on their job. Another player describes her nightmare experience of playing at a wedding where the children were allowed to play and run unchallenged. Owing to the proximity of the organ to the families, one child decided to take a run at the organist.

'He was trying to kick my leg when I glared at his father and loudly told him that he would have to remove the child. The dad looked at me strangely, so I stopped playing until he complied.'

Wily (and professional) organists know to check which verses of each hymn will be sung for the hymns before a service. Which is what Tim Howard did; and he also noted with interest that *Hark the Herald* had an unusual fourth verse, *Come Desire of Nations, Come*.

'During verse 1, my *Carols for Choirs* volume disappeared off the music stand and fell between the pedals somewhere. I played on from memory. By the beginning of verse 3 it had been retrieved for me by an elderly lady, so I played verse 3 with right hand and pedals, with the book on my lap, while frantically trying to find the Willcocks descant to do in verse 4.

'With one bar to spare, by some miracle, the music was back on the stand with the right page open. I played the first two chords of verse 4 and there was absolute silence from the church. I stopped and glanced at the screen; yes, that verse is up there, did I miscount? No, it turned out that everyone stared at it in unfamiliar disbelief and didn't sing. The leader called out "Yes!" so I started again.'

Give a congregation a tempo and they will either race ahead or dawdle as if they were going to the dentist. A church meeting group dragged behind the organ so much in the opening hymn that organist Jo Sorrill got a full line ahead of them.

'I stopped, rose to my feet, faced the group and said, "Folks — this is the last time I'm waiting for you". After much laughter, we started again. They never lagged after that.'

There are odd occasions when an organist comes in useful and is appreciated for unexpected reasons. Colin Jenkins was told after his appointment (by one of the clergy — bless 'em) that most of the strange people at the church were in the choir.

'I found this was not always the case. One character who frequently wandered into services had a necktie for which he found many uses including using it as an arm sling. He was usually quiet, even on the days that he wore his underpants over his trousers. However, one morning just before the final blessing, he suddenly came forward and started screaming fortissimo at the officiating minister who was unable to break in, let alone calm him down. I decided that the solution was to forget about a benediction and launch into an extended postlude on full organ. Yes, I was appreciated that day.'

ORGANISTS V. CHOIR

H. Compigne Andrews was teaching his probationer choristers about 'time'. After explaining the use of bars and counts in a bar, he asked a few questions.

'What do you mean by "two in a bar"?' he asked a dull boy whose father kept an inn.

A long pause, then the boy replied: 'I heard father say one day there were two in the bar and three in the smoke room.'

Choirboys have challenged the patience of every organist and choirmaster since they were invented. Eric Booth trained boys from a rough area of North London in the early part of the 20th century, and he was constantly exasperated by the bad speech of the boys in his charge.

'One evening, the boys were practising *All People that on Earth do dwell*, the last line of which runs "And for his sheep He doth us take".

'The boys' rendering of this particular line was "And for 'is sheep 'e doth a steak".

Choristers never change and were as mischievous last century as this. Manchester

341

Cathedral organ at one time had a device whereby sitting on the stool turned on the hydraulic blower. James Kendrick Pyne was quite proud of it until a visitor said it reminded him of the automatic flush in a railway station lavatory. But even better, the choristers discovered that by raising the seat and turning the lever over they could reverse the action, so that the blower turned off when the player sat down, and the wind ran out during the opening voluntary.

Adrian Marple remembers playing for an excellent but nervous tenor, during a large and important service at All Soul's, Langham Place, London.

'It was a massive gig; in addition to the four-manual organ we had a full symphony orchestra, brass band, fanfare trumpeters, a choral society, and some celebrities doing readings. I was excited about accompanying this particular fantastic tenor on the magnificent organ, with the choral society acting as the 'backing chorus'. The tenor rose from his seat, and I gently rippled the opening bars of *O Holy Night*.

'The audience was hushed, expecting something superb and memorable. They were not disappointed — the tenor's singing was beautiful, his diction measured and clear.

"O Holy Night! The stars are shitely brining . . ."

Peter Hignett was in his first appointment as organist and choirmaster of a fashionable Sussex village church in a picturesque position on the South Downs. He had inherited a loyal and committed but elderly choir with a few boys, and he was building the numbers. The repertoire was conservative, and his predecessor had been afraid to try anything new.

'I was committed to the RSCM and its principles, and my new vicar was sympathetic and wanted to take advantage of my background. Being young, I was keen to bring the repertoire up to date, particularly the psalter.

'The vicar and I prepared the choir for this new venture which, for some of them, appeared to be a massive challenge. Two rather abrasive elderly couples in the choir were a clique whom one was constantly trying not to upset. This quartet was furiously, opposed to any changes, particularly if advanced by a young whippersnapper like me; but the vicar and I agreed that progress could not be held up by a few. The other adult members were supportive.

'We ordered the necessary copies of the Parish Psalter. Not long afterwards I received an abusive and threatening letter from this small group. At the next choir practice which I had regarded with some trepidation, the four troublemakers were absent. I was sitting with my back to the door when it opened; an apparition entered, covered from head to foot in black leather riding gear with a vintage pilot's helmet, came past the piano and sat with the choir members. I thought it was someone in fancy dress — the whole vision startled me considerably. It turned out to be the vicar, an avid motorcyclist, who had decided to come to our practice.

'Thank goodness he did, as soon afterwards the door burst open, and the four troublemakers came towards me shouting abuse. They hurled their hymn books and psalters at me, hitting me and the piano. They then rapidly left, slamming the door, leaving a stunned silence in the room. This stunt was their parting shot before the four of them left the choir — to everyone's relief. I was shaken and upset, but everyone rallied round and after that the choir improved by leaps and bounds.'

Organist / choirmaster / directors cannot prevent choristers from performing in stage productions during the week, but the *Auckland Star* in 1879 maintained there were considerable dangers in mixing the two genres. At that time Gilbert and Sullivan operas were top of the pops, and *The Star* smugly reprinted this account from the Milwaukee Sentinel:

'It is all wrong to let your church choir go off singing in the opera of *HMS Pinafore* between Sundays. A dreadful thing recently happened on this account at a California funeral. The pastor, a tall, white-haired man, much resembling an admiral, arose in the pulpit and had no sooner finished, in a sing-song tone, remarked: "We miss him in his usual haunts," then the choir sprang to its feet and shouted in return, "And so do his sisters and his cousins and his aunts." For our younger readers, this is a popular refrain from *Pinafore* (But before we get too carried away, this little yarn has appeared in several journals with variations on the account, so much salt is possibly a good accompaniment to it).'

Choirs have long memories (for some things). One year when April Fools' Day was on a Sunday,

Steve Best prepared copies of the service bulletin for the choir with a deliberately incorrect processional hymn listing. After momentary confusion, the choir caught on, switched to the correct hymn, and all was well.

Seven years later, April Fools' Day came again on a Sunday, but this time Steve didn't give it a second thought. Until the processional hymn — when no-one processed.

'At that point, the pastor explained the hiatus to the congregation, the choir processed to spirited laughter, and the service continued. I thought I was home free until it was time for the anthem.

'We were singing unaccompanied that day, so I gave the choir its starting pitches and began to conduct, at which point the choir started singing a different piece. They had searched the music library for an anthem that began on the same chord as the one that was scheduled, gathered at a choir member's home to rehearse on their own, and sang with wonderful spirit. I enjoyed every moment of it.'

ORGANISTS V. CLERGY & VERGERS

The carefully chosen and rehearsed pre-service music is something which most organists take pride in; setting the atmosphere for the coming liturgy is a crucial part of the musician's role. What you hear is not just a random plucking of whatever happens to be on the top of the organ console (hopefully). Despite the hours spent setting the scene so that the atmosphere is 'just-so', thoughtless others can undo all that in a trice.

When Marilyn Oakes was in graduate school at the University of Kentucky, she was allowed to play some of the services at the church of an organist friend.

'I had practised hard and on Palm Sunday I was ready to play the Dupré *Cortège et Litanie*. About half way through the work, the pastor's wife walked up to the bench and said, "Could you please hurry up? The donkey is getting restless."

'They had a live donkey in procession. I'm not sure which genius thought of that plan. The live donkey, apparently, didn't like Dupré.'

Marilyn's message to the pastor: 'Don't ever tell an organist, whether incumbent or visiting, that the donkey is getting restless. We don't care. Really, seriously, we have spent a lot of time getting ready to play, and we don't care.'

The sabotage of music specially for an occasion can come from anywhere. A bishop playing the ukulele from the pulpit is not a common occurrence, but this is what the auxiliary Bishop for the Archdiocese of Detroit, Donald Hanchon, does, especially at youth masses. One night the Bishop pulled out his ukulele during his homily at a Confirmation Mass in Detroit's most conservative parish, Assumption Grotto, and began to sing and strum *This Little Light of Mine*. The resident organist joined in with full organ accompaniment, which finally brought the bishop's ukulele thrumming homily to an end. A vigorous debate about the rights and wrongs of both parties banged on for months.

Sometimes the congregation just don't get it. At the Catholic Cathedral of St John the Baptist in Charleston, South Carolina, for one Christ the King Sunday Timothy Tikker played Reger's *Toccata in d op. 59 no. 5* for the prelude, figuring that a major feast encouraged full organ.

'My music director was on the main floor during the prelude, during which some parishioner asked him, "why is the organ so loud?" My director answered sharply: "because it's the Feast of Christ the King and not Christ the Wimp!"'

Ahhh, the sensitive clergy, bless 'em. Erik Cannell was playing for a service which was sufficiently important to have a bishop presiding. At the end of the service, there was to be no gap between the final hymn and the start of the voluntary. At the end of the last hymn, Erik burst triumphantly into the opening fanfare of his piece carefully selected to complement the final hymn, but after half a bar, the vicar of the church made some urgent, shouty noises asking for attention.

'I stopped playing thinking there had been some accident or the place was on fire, such was the tone he took. He, then more softly, announced: "I forgot to mention during the notices, young Jenny here has a birthday, so shall we all sing"?'

The church wardens where Andrew Burling played warned him that when people made loud microphone announcements over the top of voluntaries while he was playing, he shouldn't be upset, shouldn't stop playing, and certainly shouldn't make a fuss. So Andrew resigned.

'Perhaps I should have stayed on and made up for it by occasionally playing throughout the readings and sermon.' An excellent idea.

A little knowledge is a dangerous thing. Last century a rector's wife asked organist Frederick Pugh to play *Hail Bright Abode* from Wagner's *Tannhäuser*. Knowing it pays to obey wives of clergy (bless 'em), he agreed, but later found he had no copy of the music, so he substituted the *Prelude* to Act III from *Lohengrin*. In the evening, the same woman asked for *Lohengrin*, so he promptly played it again.

After the service she said, 'I do not know which of those pieces I like best. They both thrill me so.'

If the clergy (bless 'em too) spouses have a mind to take charge, watch out. Bruce Cornely played Bach's *Toccata* in *d minor* as a pre-service prelude (a request from a church member), and was afterwards taken to task by the wife of the clergyman who said she had received complaints (although Bruce had received compliments).

'After that, all composers and the preludes had to be hymn-based and approved by her. This from a "musician" who had never heard of R. Vaughan Williams.'

Bruce's grandmother was the organist for a Methodist church for more than 25 years and, since ministers were reassigned every three years, she had survived many.

'Once, when a new minister arrived, he commented favourably on her longevity there and asked if she had any advice for him. She replied, "Regarding your sermons — if you can't strike oil in 10 minutes, don't bore for 20." She outlived him, too.'

Clergy (bless 'em) have their fair allocation of the ignorance gene when it comes to organs. Needing to upgrade his church's organ, Timothy Tikker presented a plan to add three ranks to it. When the vestry approved his plan, the priest announced it the following Sunday, although adding: 'You'd think the organ already had enough pipes.'

Some time later at a staff meeting, the minister asked him offhandedly how many pipes were being added.

'I said 96. She suddenly became very upset. "96? I thought it was only 5 or 6!" I explained that it was three ranks of pipes, and each rank had 32 pipes, as there are 32 notes on the pedal keyboard and each note requires its own pipe.

'My explanation fell on deaf ears; she promptly reported to the Building and Grounds Committee (which had nothing to do with the organ previously) that I had misrepresented the project and was adding many more pipes to the organ than I had said we would.

'I finally got our organ technician to intervene with the committee and explain to them what was really going on; but that had to be done without the priest present to ensure that anything would be accomplished.'

Even those who should know better continue to astound, as Philip Bailey who was playing a recital on an organ that had been recently rebuilt discovered to his cost. The organ had eight general pistons and 12 channels of memory, so Philip had chosen the programme for his recital accordingly. But:

'When I arrived, I was told that the rotating switch that selected the piston channel had a problem, and channels 1—6, when set, would replicate themselves on channels 7—12, halving the number of channels available.'

The organist beamed serenely and reassured Philip: 'Don't worry, you can use all of them'.

Philip rehearsed, and used five channels, leaving them set for the concert the next day.

'I arrived an hour before the concert and checked the channels. The switch had decided to do its worst, and all 12 channels were now holding the settings for channel 1. So I took a deep breath, and decided that the eight generals left to me had to be used for the Reubke *Sonata on the 94th Psalm*. I would have to wing the rest. I was charging

through the pages, setting madly from memory (I hadn't written down each combination, but I could guess what they were) and playing occasional snatches to confirm that, yes, I could reach pistons at certain points.

'Then someone came up behind me and boomed: "Can't you do this some other time? We've got a flower festival on." It was the vicar, who had just walked past the board by the church's front door announcing Philip's recital and knew it was scheduled.

'No', he replied. 'I've got an organ recital in 40 minutes.'

The vicar turned on his heels, and never talked to Philip again. This same vicar was, incidentally, a Fellow of the Royal College of Organists, and yes, he should have known better.

Twelve-year-old Bruce Cornely was deputising in a large Methodist church where he was a member. The minister announced the first hymn, but by mistake gave the number of the hymn on the opposite page from the one in the printed sheet.

'I thought the congregation would catch the error so I began playing the hymn indicated in the leaflet. The minister turned around, leant over to me and said, "Bruce, you're playing the wrong hymn." Being just the kid that I was, I replied, "No dummy, YOU announced the wrong hymn," right into the microphone hanging round his neck.' Out of the mouths —

I know only too well the heart-stopping experience of waiting for a vicar with dyslexia to announce a hymn number, and the split-second

346

decision whether to go with his mangled call or stick stubbornly to the prescribed hymn on the board. I have weathered the fallout from befuddled officiants announcing numbers from a completely different hymnal (with sanctimonious confidence that's hard to ignore). The more important or solemn the occasion, the worse it is. This is nothing new. A Mrs Thorp, writing to the *Musical Opinion* about 100 years ago suffered the same agonies at a funeral.

'To my horror and embarrassment, the vicar gave out the wrong number for the first hymn and read out the first line: *Let us sing with praise and joy.*' Ouch.

Timothy Tikker played a funeral for which the soloist told the minister beforehand that she would sing an *Agnus Dei.* Speaking to the officiating minister before the service, Timothy noticed the minister had dutifully written the title in his notebook as *An Unused Day.*

HYMNS
350?
530?
035?
305!
(bingo!)

Organists v. Organ

Investitures held by the Venerable Order of St John are impressive ceremonies, beginning with a procession by the members of the order in ceremonial robes; among the dignitaries on this occasion was the Governor-General, Sir Keith Holyoake, as the Prior of the Order in New Zealand. Think Pomp and Circumstance writ humongous.

Peter Averi played the preliminary organ music for the ceremony, and waited for the signal to begin the processional hymn for the vice-regal party to enter the Wellington Town Hall.

'I saw the hand wave to launch into the hymn and began the introduction. But the fuse failed on the high-pressure blower and instead of a majestic full-throated sound, the organ emitted a strangulated wheeze; the diapasons were starved of air, and only a minimal amount of wind fed the few flute stops on low pressure. It needed a split-second decision.

'I leapt off the bench and scrambled down the steps to find someone off stage to stop the Governor-General entering the hall until we could drag a piano on stage.'

Luckily for Peter and the Governor-General, the message got through, and the procession was delayed until Peter was seated at a battered upright piano, offering a feeble introduction to that normally magnificent and stirring hymn *All people that on earth do dwell.*

Playing for a prestigious graduation ceremony at Bruce Steele's university on an organ praised for its suspended tracker action, Bruce chose the Bach *G major Prelude & Fugue* for the exit music. The long and colourful procession began as he launched into the manual-only opening bars.

Then, horrors. At the first pedal entry, the D on the pedalboard sounded; and sounded, and sounded — was it a cipher? Time for any organist to have a fit of the vapours. Bruce lived up to his name as a man of steel as he kept calm when he realised, uh-oh, the tracker had come adrift somewhere inside the organ.

'The Bach G major is not Percy Grainger's *Immovable Do* — you can't really play it against a dominant drone. While improvising around the stuck note with one hand as I gradually removed all the pedal stops, the procession wound on its way to something suitably stately, but most definitely not Bach.'

An organist was filling in for the late Sam Swartz with the Redlands Symphony and choruses on Mendelssohn's *Elijah*. He had forgotten in the heat of the performance that the University Chapel Casavant organ in those days had a few quirks. For example, the Pedal 8' Trumpet would already be ON when the organ was fired up.

'I turned the organ off at the interval, but did not pull the trumpet out and retire it after turning the organ blowers on again. Needless to say, the final chord of *Cast thy burdens* will always stand out in my mind not so much for the firm, gentle 32' pedal note as for the loud, brief squawk of a trumpet note not quite as in tune as it might have been.'

Don't always blame the organ. How about this for a bit of misguided self-help, reported in the Leeds Mercury July 22, 1873:

'The organ in a village church midway between Bradford and Halifax being out of repair, a professional organ builder from Leeds was called in to see what the instrument required. The Leeds gentleman was surprised to find that damp was ruining the organ, the woodwork was decaying, and the bellows leather was rotten from moisture. Close to the instrument was the heating apparatus of the church, and it was incomprehensible how the organ could have suffered so severely from damp.

'The sexton, who has charge of the church, was called to account, and he excused himself with the statement that the man who manages and plays upon the organ had erected a barricade between the heating apparatus and the instrument, with the view of keeping the organ cool. Not only had he done this, but he had poured water onto the bellows, and otherwise troubled himself to keep the instrument cool and moist, the result being deterioration and decay. This remarkable instance of ingenuity in keeping an organ cool has caused no small amount of fun in the village and the neighbourhood, at the expense of the sapient individual who tried this experiment.'

Organists know that organ stops — whatever age or whatever organ — have minds of their own. The organ at St Andrew's Church, Lismore, NSW, Australia, is a 2-manual beast from the past. One of its problems is that the stop knobs fall out when pulled. Not the complete stop, just the annoying knob.

During a service early one Sunday, the stop flew off, and the exasperated organist threw it over his shoulder. After the service, a 10-minute search looking for the wilful knob was fruitless. No sign of it anywhere. Some time later, one of the choristers came back into church carrying the stop which had managed to land, unobserved, in her open choir bag. Try doing that again.

Music desks, music stands, racks: they are called many names including unprintable ones when they are designed without thought for the player.

Richard Elliott, the principal organist of the Mormon Tabernacle Choir, was in St Joseph, Missouri to play a recital on an old pipe organ with a retrofitted music rack light fixture that obscured the stop tabs for the Swell and Choir divisions. He had to bend down to see the stop names, and since the organ had only 15 general pistons and no multiple memories, he had to register several pieces by hand and also had to reset pistons a few times during the programme.

'I set up a soft trio registration for a transcription of the Siciliano from Bach's *Flute Sonata No. 2*, and things went beautifully the first time through the A section. When it came time for the repeat of the same section, I moved my right hand to the Choir manual to play the flute melody on the charming clarinet stop.

'To my horror, what came forth was not the sound of a clarinet, but that of the Festival Trumpet stop, which was immediately next to the clarinet. Usually when this kind of thing happens, one can kick on the crescendo pedal (see page 152) and pretend that it was intended that way, but with such a delicate and exposed texture, I just kept playing on the Festival Trumpet until the third phrase, when I reached over, changed to the clarinet, and hoped that the red glow of my ears and neck were not visible to the audience members seated nearby.'

An organ in Stuttgart is burdened by a desk with a wide ledge and a back that tilts so much that it obscures the bottom part of the music. Martin Setchell's solution was to pile several volumes of the ubiquitous *Gotteslob* hymnal behind the music on the desk to move it forward and make it readable. So far so good, and the system worked well during the daytime rehearsals. But he had not reckoned on fading daylight — this was an evening concert. Come the second half of the programme, when the natural light disappeared with sunset, the only remaining source of illumination came from a lamp stationed behind the music. The score became increasingly less visible, until by the end of the concert the organist was squinting myopically into the spotlight of the lamp like a bewildered owl.

Organists v. Practice

The Chairman of the Board of a church filed a formal complaint about an organist, as follows: 'What's with all this practising? Every time I come down here he's in there practising. I thought we hired him because he knew what he was doing. If he needs to practise he ought to be doing that on his own time —'

That sort of thinking might well have suited some of Steve Best's college students who invented original excuses for not practising. One young woman told Steve in all seriousness that she had not practised because her guinea pig had produced babies. A male student skipped practising because his girlfriend's husband came to town.

But the worst (or best) excuse ever came from a student who arrived at her lesson with injured fingers — scraped and bruised. On reflection, Steve thought he should just have sent her home. But he asked what had happened.

'With nary a pause, she said: "I was wrestling with my boyfriend and my hand got caught in his zipper." I was speechless. Just speechless. One can only imagine the possible responses I could have given. But I was too stunned to speak.'

Practice became such a rare commodity for Marilyn Oakes she threatened to send her pastor a bill for concierge services. At one time, she had to practise on a console on the floor right inside the front door, and the place was like Grand Central Station. The interruptions were endless and went like this:

- *No, I cannot sign for your package. No, I cannot sign for pest control services.*
- *No, I don't know where the pastor is. He doesn't check out with me. No, I don't know when he'll be back.*
- *No, I don't know where the bookstore manager is, or when he'll be back.*
- *No, we don't have a concert series here, must be another church with a similar name. Yes, I'm sure.*
- *No, there isn't another Mass today. No, I don't know the Mass schedule but it's in the bulletin. The bulletins are in the narthex. Oh, no bulletins?*
- *No, I don't know where there are extras. No,*

I don't know where the Mass Intention envelopes are.

- *How nice that your (mother, aunt, cousin, next door neighbour, third cousin's second ex-wife's niece) played the organ.*
- *Oh, you play guitar in a band? Lovely.*
- *Oh, you brought small children with you while you pray? Joy. Get them off the pedalboard!*
- *NO, I don't know where the pastors are right now and I'm really sorry you need confession so badly but I cannot hear your confession!*

'It usually didn't slow them down. I charge in my other job to hear people confess, and I do not have the power of Holy Mother Church to forgive sin. Never mind. I was handy, so out came the story.

'Besides uncompensated concierge duties, it

Mary Comer's difficulty was an unadjustable bench coupled with her small frame. She tackled the visibility problem by cranking up the music with crackers.

was just danged difficult to get uninterrupted time at the organ. Our pastors prayed in the church. A lot. They also meditated. They were not good about sharing space. I had a wireless headset that completely silenced the organ but they could hear my feet tapping the pedals, so that was out. One swore he could still hear the organ even when I used the headset. That's impossible and it was his imagination at work. It's lovely to have praying pastors and they prayed on a set schedule, except they varied the schedule without warning. By trial and error, I figured out blocks of time, but then, things shifted and I didn't get to practise.

'They said I could practise in the choir room. The organ was in bad shape but I could do detail work. Except when they sent a runner and said it was too loud. Sometimes, one stop was too loud. Sometimes I went to the piano in the library, sometimes I gave up and left. One memorable day, one of them came into the church to hear a confession. I grabbed the wireless headset so as not to disturb them, and he unceremoniously ordered me out.

'I said, "But not even with the headset?" "NO. You're not going to practise while I'm hearing confessions." Hmmm —.'

A pastor asked why one organist found it necessary to practice so much. He told her:

'After all, playing the organ is just like typing; you get a few lessons and then just do it.'

I wish.

The only time I nearly succumbed to an urge to boil someone in oil was in Leicester Cathedral. Our rehearsal during the day — the only time possible — was constantly interrupted by visitors who looked as if they had wandered in from a comedy film set, chattering at full volume and clattering around as if it was a hockey match.

Things were looking desperate with the concert looming. The quieter stops on the organ were almost inaudible, and we hardly dared play more than a few chords to test the balance with the huge tuba. Despite being respectful of the space and people walking round the cathedral, Martin still had to set his registrations which he did as quickly as he could. Even this was too much for a woman who suddenly materialised in the loft beside him.

'You will stop playing NOW,' she boomed. 'We have come all the way from Ely, and I can't hear the guide.' Having delivered her salvo, she galumphed triumphantly downstairs to where I was trying my best to listen and not laugh.

I assumed what I hoped was my best subservient colonial face, and (yes, I'll burn for this) apologised.

'So sorry, we've come from New Zealand. Perhaps you'd like us to go home and come back here in the morning?'

In a former East German cathedral, Martin and I had been setting registrations to the noisy accompaniment of restorers and archaeologists also working in the church after closing time. By the time they left we still had much to prepare for the concert the next day.

Suddenly a door from somewhere in the darkness slammed open and an angry bee-like figure buzzed up to me sitting in the nave. This agitated creature fizzed and hissed at me in angry

German that I chose not to understand. He was clearly upset. A play was being performed in the cloisters, he bellowed at me, and they did not want to risk any noises off-stage, so the organ had to stop. I looked (I hoped) like an innocent English idiot who had nothing to do with the organ and had no idea why he was tongue-lashing me.

Mr Bee was joined by another man who

outlined their problem in English, and in return I explained our dilemma. We needed some of the louder stops to chose registration, as well as doing a basic play-through of the programme. The verger joined our little hive of discussion, before they swarmed out, humming together irritably.

It was dark when the first buzzy-bee returned, marched to the stairs, looking like he meant business. I radioed up to Martin to lock the upstairs door to the loft and sit tight. I scuttled unseen behind a pillar, and turned off all my lights while the resident bats dive-bombed me. The theatre man gave up when he could not get into the loft or find me, and he stomped out, frustrated and fuming. We kept registering as quietly and rapidly as we could, but doubted any noise would have disturbed the play in progress outside.

After the concert, a member of the audience complained that he thought the pieces were all too soft. I nearly hit him.

Brian Fahey was an organ student where the chapel was conveniently across the street from his college dorm, so he practised early morning and late evening on the 3-manual Moller pipe organ. The console was in front of the pipe work, in a pit. The chapel was carpeted, and the doors closed silently.

'My friends and I liked to play tricks on each other. Their trick on me was to scare the bejeebers out of me while practising.' They would

sneak into the chapel, gather round the wall of the console, jump up when Brian was engrossed in the music, which set him back every time. He needed a way to stop them.

One day the professor, a strict and prim Southern woman, said she needed exclusive use of this organ for an upcoming recital.

'So one evening I excused myself from study with my friends and said I was going to practise. I went to the chapel, but once inside I headed into the loft at the rear and sat behind a pillar.

The professor was practising the organ, and it was dark in the chapel except for her lights over the console. Sure enough, the bait worked. My friends soundlessly filed into the chapel, surrounded the console wall, then jumped up to scare 'me'.

'The professor was scared witless, and she retaliated by throwing books at the students. They, in turn, were taken aback by the switch and fled the chapel. I silently took the stairs to the basement and let myself outside. They stopped trying to frighten me while practising.'

ORGANISTS V. NOISE

Sometimes the audience can see the organist's face in the organ's rear vision mirror. That's not necessarily a good thing, of course, because if you can see her, she can see you. Everything: all your fidgeting, rummaging in your shopping bags, nodding off, chatting to your neighbour about the weather, and using your mobile phone. That means either talking on it, checking email, or recording the concert to upload to social media. Or worse.

Martin Setchell was engrossed in a piece when a man answered his phone and held a loud and prolonged conversation during the concert. The audience was aghast. It would have been less horrific if the piece at the time had not been Debussy's whispering soft *Clair de Lune*.

Unless you are taking part in an experimental digital concert using phones and special apps such as that held in Cologne Cathedral some years ago, put them away, and savour the moment. If you hear someone having a loud chat, let us know and we'll arrange to tap them over the head with a large façade pipe or two.

Dr Jeannine Jordan and her husband David were to perform their concert celebrating the history of the organ arriving in America at the First Baptist Church in America. The church building, restored to its original beauty, was the largest existing frame building from the 1700s in America. The perfect place for their historic American concert.

They arrived in Providence, Rhode Island during a heat wave at a church surrounded by four busy streets and sidewalks. They discovered that the church, restored as a national historic landmark building, had no air conditioning. It was boiling in the historic building, especially for the organist high in the back balcony.

The evening of the concert was a scorching Friday and all the windows were wide open to let any breeze through the baking, humid building; on the streets surrounding the church, traffic was snarled with honking horns and yelling people. The audience arrived sweltering after dealing with impossible traffic and nearly nonexistent parking.

'Early American organ music is not "big" music,' said Jeannine. 'The organs were small and the compositions petite, and what I call, simply elegant — not bombastic in the least. In the narration before a voluntary by Francis Linley, I told the gathering: "The quiet sublime sounds of this piece played on a small one rank organ in a land without the tumult, noise, and commotion of our existence, were fascinating to

Organists v. the Unusual

a people who had never heard such a thing as an organ." I then began to play on a lovely 4' flute stop — a sound that brings a hushed silence to an audience.

'As those delicate sounds wended their way from the organ high in the balcony to the audience far below, an awful bellow burst forth. Again and again and again. I thought a fire truck followed by a rescue vehicle had entered the church and were driving down the aisle.

'Yes, the tumult, noise and commotion of our existence in the form of fire trucks, rescue vehicles, and police cars (from the emergency station across from the church) brought the sublime moment to an abrupt end. Was this a sermon without words?'

Given that organists sometimes have to break into or out of the buildings in which their instruments are kept, it is a wonder that relatively few fall foul of the law. Famous Parisian organist Jean Guillou thought he was headed for a spell in clink when he was accused of stealing a piece of luggage containing valuable papers belonging to a politician.

Guillou became aware of this only when a policeman arrived at the organ console in Sylt where he was to play, and asked Guillou to accompany him to the station to answer a few questions about some stolen luggage. The innocent explanation was that Guillou's travelling companion, conductor and organist Karl Richter, had tried to help with the bags at the airport, and mistakenly picked up a case belonging to the politician, thinking it belonged to Guillou. Case (literally) solved.

A genuine criminal came unstuck in a church in Northeast England, which had a large and somewhat dilapidated organ occupying the space between the choir vestry and chancel. At some time, the trigger swell pedal had been replaced by a balanced one. The balancing weight — a substantial piece of lead — was suspended from a pulley let in to the ceiling above the vestry. David Bridgeman-Sutton describes one eventful harvest festival.

'The church was unusually full, the singing lusty. Part of the way through *We plough the fields*, the organist noted a stiffness in the swell pedal, which became increasingly unwilling to close. Exasperated, he gave it a good kick with his heel. A loud crash signalled that the frayed cord of the balance weight had parted and the weight fallen to the tiled floor of the vestry. In the silence that ensued when the singing faltered, a cry of terror and the slamming of the vestry door was clearly heard. A passing police patrol was interested to see a figure, carrying a surplice and two organ pipes fleeing the church.

'When he was apprehended, the thief complained that the organist had been throwing dangerous objects at him and ought to be arrested. The possibility of claims for compensation was raised — and promptly dropped.'

Rame Church on the Rame Peninsula in Cornwall is tiny, with no electricity and a one manual hand-pumped organ; it is not the kind of church accustomed to dealing with conflagrations at the console.

During a reading as part of a candle-lit carol service, Annie Dawe, the organist, was arranging her music for the next carol when it caught fire. Not unexpectedly she tried to put it out, but in the process, she banged the music down on the keyboard.

The pumper who had been daydreaming (and who was quite oblivious to the smell and sight of smoke), heard her and thought she was trying to play so immediately started to pump the organ. As well as fanning the flames, the noisy attempts to extinguish the music successfully drowned out the reader. To say nothing of the damage inflicted on the music — and the nerves of the organist.

Organists need strong hearts. Jane was churning her way through *Amazing Grace* for the quillionth time at yet another funeral when she began to get palpitations and feared she was having a heart attack. Organists are renowned for their stubbornness and devotion to duty so she ploughed on, with thoughts of imminent demise in her mind, and palpitations throbbing in her chest.

Before she could get too alarmed, they stopped. It was only then she realised that it was her mobile phone, set to vibrate and plunged with unthinking haste into her ample bosom as a handy receptacle.

The earthquakes of 2010-2011, which devastated much of the city of Christchurch in New Zealand, left most of the pipe organ-rich churches without an instrument; organists had to use whatever was available, where ever it was.

The Christchurch Westpac Stadium sports arena became the biggest venue that could be used for large gatherings, and an aged digital organ on loan was the only source of music there for some time. Russell Kent was playing for a school graduation ceremony in the stadium when flashes went off in a spectacular fashion. The heat and resultant flame triggered the fire alarm and sprinkler system. Doused in a cascade of water from above, Russell and the orchestra together made a mad dash for the doors in keeping with the athletic nature of the original purpose of the building. Russell just had a chance to see a wave of water swirl around the organ as he sprinted to safety.

At least as far as disasters went, it made a change from aftershocks.

Sometimes the church council or concert organisers tell the visiting organist the most inconsequential details ('Our Bring and Buy stall every month is the most popular event we have here.' Um. Thanks for that) and forget to tell us what we really need to know: where are the on/off switches, where are the lavatories, or even how to get out of the building. The advent of video cameras in the loft, a great boon for introducing an audience to the manipulations at the console, has sent many concert organisers into a spin as they are often unsure about the organist's reaction to this new-fangled contraption, and forget to pass on more useful tips.

One such concert organiser at an English church rushed to greet us and his first (and only) bit of advice was to the point:

'Don't do anything disgusting,' he said. He was solely concerned that the video would show any misdemeanours at the console; obviously previous organists and their helpers must have had a lot of fun.

A Dean under whom June Nixon served in Melbourne had an exceptional talent for raising money.

'One of his more imaginative ideas was to sell the pigeon droppings which had been accumulating in the Melbourne Cathedral tower for some 60 years. This product was sold at $5 a bag as a garden fertiliser. Two strapping young men would climb the tower armed with shovels and bags, sometimes so engrossed in their task they would forget that evensong was about to begin. I should perhaps mention here that the choir stalls in St Paul's Cathedral lie directly underneath the tower.

'I well remember that evensong, when during the Magnificat, a large open bag lurched from the tower, swung perilously then landed between the choir stalls with a loud plop, scattering its contents liberally over the choir on its way down.

'Of course, this may well have just been one of the more imaginative critical comments on the singing that day —'

ORGANISTS V. THE MESSIAH

Handel's great oratorio of 1741, *Messiah*, is one of the best-known and frequently performed choral works in the Western repertoire, but that doesn't mean it is easy. Far from it. In fact, *Messiah* comes in for more than its fair share of 'unfortunate mishaps'. A major stuff-up by one 'assistant' turner landed the unfortunate Bass soloist and organist well and truly in the poo.

During an amateur, but well-prepared, intense performance of Handel's *Messiah,* the over-zealous assistant thoughtfully set up the music for the organist so the page was open at the bass aria *Thou art gone up on high* immediately after the interval.

So far so good; the bass waited for his entry with music in hand, and the organist began the play-in. The pair continued together as expected for the first 12 bars or so. Then the bass faltered and stopped, but the organist persevered for a few more bars. After a short hiatus, they restarted. And again the bass stopped at the same place, unable to continue. By mutual and rapid agreement they abandoned the air, and moved on to the next section, the organist keeping his cool, and the bass slinking back into his seat, embarrassed and perplexed. The same piece had gone without hitch during rehearsals, so what had gone so wrong for the soloist and organist?

Simply, dear Mr Handel had written two versions of the air *Thou Art Gone up On High* — one for bass and the other for alto solo. The alto version was the next in the edition used by the organist, so that is precisely what the page turner turned to. The bass aria was in fact much later in the edition as an alternative movement. The organist, who had at some time or another played and annotated all versions, never noticed this error since his part was identical until midway through the piece. As a result the organist and bass (but not the real culprit, the page turner) were left with so much egg on their faces they were omelette-looking.

Some mistakes are impossible to find a suitable punishment for. But in this case, 50 lashes is probably about right.

A different organist, still traumatised years later, writes of the time a new, disorganised Director of Music caused complete chaos where none had existed in all previous performances for which he had played the organ.

'Our town is blessed with a large church of small cathedral proportions which has maintained an excellent music tradition. Every year we perform Handel's *Messiah* and invite young singers studying at one of the capital's music colleges to be soloists. After many years

of service, our Director of Music retired and a young, new director was appointed.

The church has a large mechanical action organ in a rear gallery from where I play continuo throughout. Only the back of the soloists' heads and the conductor can be seen in my rear view mirror. Choir risers are erected below the organ gallery and the orchestra sits in front of them with the congregation seated facing the west end. Often there is standing room only for this annual concert. The church choir is augmented by members of the local choral society.

In past years, in addition to the regular choir and orchestra practices, one night was set aside to rehearse with all the soloists and another night was set aside to rehearse all the choral movements. We all came together on the night of the performance.

The new director (who, we discovered later, had never conducted a *Messiah*) had different ideas. This year there would be one rehearsal the night before the performance.

'We arrived by 7.30pm, expecting to start

promptly. The first notes of music were not played until 9pm. At 11pm, people in the choir started leaving, although we had rehearsed only some of the choruses, and none of the arias and recitatives.

'Previously we always had cuts, particularly in the third part, to keep the performance down to about two hours plus an interval. Many of our scores, including mine, had pages clipped together to jump over the cut sections. Using the Watkins Shaw edition, many recitatives and arias exist in more than one version and key, so the version not performed was crossed out or its pages clipped together to skip. There were many new players in the orchestra and we had not rehearsed any of the soloists' movements, so they had no idea which versions we were used to doing — and neither did the conductor.

'No-one had seen a programme before we entered the church to begin the performance as they were still being photocopied and were handed out to the audience after the performance had started. Being up in the organ loft, I could not speak to the conductor — or anyone else — to ask which version we were about to play. None of us realised that the conductor had decided to perform a 'complete Messiah'. This meant there were several choruses the choir had never sung before, as well as arias that some of the soloists had never sung or prepared.

'Well, you can just imagine. Several times I gave a chord such as G minor for a recitative, only to have some of the orchestra play a D minor chord while others played my G minor chord. What note would the soloist begin on? We always used the 12/8 version of *Rejoice greatly* which is in the back of the book. I turned to the back and started playing in 12/8 time while others played in 4/4; I launched into an aria while the orchestra launched into a chorus that had always been cut. The choir had to sight-read and hope for the best, after they had unclipped their pages to find the normally cut chorus half a page after it had started. At one point, our vicar walked up to the conductor and suggested we needed to have an interval. . .

'I have never been so happy to see the *Amen* chorus but as soon as it was over, the conductor called out for us to do the *Hallelujah Chorus* as an encore. The audience leapt to its feet and several reviews spoke of the standing ovation given for that year's performance. . .'

Last bars of Handel's 1741 manuscript of the Hallelujah chorus

"HELP! Am being held prisoner by a man-eating organ."

Ready. . .   *aim. . .*   *fire!!*

In Mainz Cathedral, a chamade trumpet rank, known as the "Kardinals-trompeten" was installed in a Renaissance chamber as a generous surprise gift for a cardinal. Used for high days only, (such as the visit of the bishop) the chamades are activated from the organ by a switch which opens the two windows, and the battery of pipes moves forward, ready and primed for action. When President George Bush visited Mainz, the entire city went into security lockdown. His wife Barbara was taken to see the cathedral, and as befitting a politically important visit, the organist decided the Cardinal's Trumpets would be an appropriate welcome. He didn't reckon on the zealousness of the bodyguards; when he opened the chamade chamber doors, the 'cannons' moved forward, and the tribe of secret service boys simultaneously sprang forward to thwart the 'gunmen'. A swift change to the Star-Spangled Banner apparently saved the day (and presumably the organist).

ONE GOOD TURN

Organ assistants need to
turn over a new leaf

Page-turning is easy-peasy? Stop-pulling is a doddle? Moving bits of paper around and thrusting little knobs of wood in and out of other bits of wood is child's play? Uh-uh. It's not for the faint-hearted. Implacable souls gibber in terror at the thought of page-turning or stop-pulling. It is a huge responsibility.

Apprentice page-turners tend to flap ineffectually around the score like a jellyfish on a piece of elastic unless they are Olympians—musically and physically. It can be so cramped in the jaws of a massive pipe organ that assistants should hone their gymnastic skills before taking on the job.

The duties of an assistant at the console? Page turners cope with pages that are glued together, or even more amusingly, rip from the binding altogether and fall under the pedals. Registrants (stop-puller, sequencer-pusher) will be confronted with stop names in a multitude of languages that vanish, or refuse to budge, or seem to do nothing that was rehearsed earlier. Some stops have no name at all. Doing either job means standing for hours on end.

Combine these two jobs and the responsibility turns into thinly disguised horror. With two, or even three registrants, the potential for disaster during a recital is right up there with dodgy rollercoasters.

A typical scene: I stretch my puny 5'2" frame to the max to reach the music while balancing with one foot between pedal pistons and the other on the bench. I then rush to the other side of the console in 0.3 seconds while keeping an eye on the score and mentally cursing the 7'10" orangutan organ builder. I must look like a deranged spider about to strangle the organist, who is thinking the same. (Some advice: Avoid tight skirts and dangling sleeves that catch on stop knobs or stick between notes. Trust me on this.)

A love of risqué adventure is good. On a steamy hot night in France, I had to clamber

over Martin on the stool to get from one side to the other of the organ console at an organ with a Rückpositiv. I also poured water down his neck to keep him cool. We would have come close to being charged with public indecency if anyone had seen us.

Besides being a good reader of any kind of music score — manuscript, tatty, illegible, illegal photocopy, or 19th century hand-me-down facsimile — the turner must be a mind reader to judge how many beats ahead of the organist they must turn. Does 'gruuunt' means 'no', and 'arghghg' mean yes? Or vice versa?

There is one good point to all this. It means organists must be really very, very, very, very nice to assistants before concerts.

CO-PILOTS MESS UP TOO

Thanks to the advent of modern sequencers and stepper systems, an organist can survive at a console alone and unaided during a concert. Mechanical action organs with unmodernised consoles may have stops that are not only heavy but difficult to reach. Such examples are common in Northern Germany, France, the Netherlands, and elsewhere in Europe. These goliaths pose an entirely different scale of challenges. Enter the mighty army of registrants (or stop pullers) who become essential to the organist. Their contribution can make or break a performance.

The organist-assistant relationship is like a marriage minus the sex; lots of compromise, give-and-take, and forgiveness, and making up after a contretemps. Good humour goes a long way, too. Philip Bailey was turning pages for a friend during a recital.

'I must have had something on my mind as after one piece, he looked at me and said "I thought you could read music"?'

Indeed, reading the dots may not be entirely necessary; some assistants wonder why organists bother with printed scores when playing extreme avant-garde music. One luckless turner was unexpectedly propelled into action with an ultra-modern organ score, minus any barlines, and little reference to conventional notation. With no clue amid the cacophony as to when to turn, he still wonders why the music was necessary in the first place.

Of course if you are fortunate enough to have a prodigious memory, confidence, and bravery in bucketloads, doing away with scores altogether is another possibility. It has all the attraction of walking a tightrope over Niagara Falls with ants in your pants.

Frank Resseler knows the potential terrors of a registrant all too well, and his misfortunes would be typical of many of us 'helpers'.

The first rule for the player-assistant relationship is: don't get rattled. Frank and his father were assistants for a well-known Dutch organist giving a recital in the Allemanskerk in Oudkarspel in the Netherlands. They positioned themselves either side of the organ bench. After a late page turn, the organist snarled at Frank's father, which made him understandably nervous.

'During a piece of Franck on the softest Swell stops, my father prepared for the next change in registration by holding the four loud reed stops, ready to pull them out. However the organist misinterpreted this move, and he immediately ordered my father to pull them — in the middle of the softest part.

'You will understand the reaction of both organist and stop assistants (not to mention the audience) when the four Swell reeds came thundering on.'

That same organist (on different organs) used Frank's skills on many other occasions, despite the odd glitch which included adding a wrong stop (the organist hissed: "You are killing my piece"). Each time the organist seemed to forgive and forget, and he was always happy to have Frank's help. Frank progressed his stop-pulling vocation with greater and more diverse mishaps, crowning his achievements with a spectacular misfire in the Grote Kerk in Maassluis. The same organist was playing his final piece, in which the middle section ends on a soft unison note. Frank was hauling out almost all the stops of the Bovenwerk (third manual) for the following Fugue. While the organist held the single note on the Hoofdwerk, Frank mistakenly pulled the Bovenwerk to Hoofdwerk coupler, bringing the full weight of that manual unexpectedly into play.

'So that got the same effect that my dad achieved in Oudkarspel. The organist was rather disturbed, so the fugue was a bit inaccurate.'

Frank adds that he has also made 'soft' bloopers. With the same organist ('I assisted on many occasions well, so he still asked me; you may think I messed it up too much'), this time in Naarden. Again it was a piece with a crescendo to full organ, but after that a sudden pianissimo of two bars on the Viola 8', the softest stop available. So Frank had to push many stops in as quickly as possible to bring the sound right down.

'Unfortunately, I pushed in all stops including the Viola. So, no amen, until the organist pulled it himself. No one seemed to notice.'

Picture the setting: a major organ recital, during the final piece of extraordinary difficulty, and the thunderous climax fast approaches. With a flourish, page turner John Riley turns two loose photocopied pages at once, then tries to make amends. Amid panic and distinctive noises of anguish from the recitalist, he puts back the remaining pages in completely random order, and, for good measure, one upside down. Full marks for a spectacular re-arrangement.

Luckily for any maladroit page turner having a bad day, organists have learned to rescue blunders without much ado. Adrian Wintle still cringes at his memory of turning pages in 1959 for Mervyn Byers at St Andrew's Cathedral in Sydney for a lunchtime recital.

'Well into the D Major fugue of Bach, the music ticking over like a well-oiled sewing machine, I whipped the page over and was shocked to note a new key signature of three flats. Frozen in fear, all I could think was "*Bach doesn't do that.*" In a nanosecond, Mervyn flicked the page back to the rightful two sharps and proceeded on his way without missing a beat.'

Page turners can be too helpful; in this case the word 'assistant' becomes an misnomer. Turning back for repeats in the music which the performer is not observing, or turning too early, are common slip-ups that can happen unless turns are rehearsed beforehand. But much worse is possible.

Take this award-winning performance by a page turner who had to care for not one, but two organists. Here is the account from Mark Quarmby who was part of this disaster duet.

It was an important academic occasion in the Great Hall of the country's leading university, with many top scholars present. The musical item was to be an organ duet, the Australian premiere of a work by Jean Langlais; *Double Fantaisie pour Deux Organistes.*

'My teacher was the university organist, had studied in France, and knew many of the great French church musicians. He asked me to play the secondo part, and he would take the primo.

'My teacher was a perfectionist and even though he regularly performed the most challenging works in the repertoire, he was always extremely uptight during a performance. One wrong note played in a lesson, and you thought he was going to have a seizure.

'We rehearsed on the organ, fastidiously registering everything, making sure everything was secure. My teacher had asked a young university organ student to turn pages. She attended our final rehearsal to practise and to become familiar with the work.

'We were well prepared and confident of an exciting premiere. Everything was going well until the page turner forgot that the left page was my part (secondo) and the right page was the primo part of my teacher. I wondered why my teacher was becoming flustered and getting increasingly agitated as I continued playing from my left-hand page onto the right-hand page when the page didn't go over, albeit reading the treble clef notes as if they were still in bass clef.

'After some improvisation on both our parts, my teacher thrust the page over, and we continued from the first bar of that page. Unfortunately, my teacher then started playing the left-hand page but in the treble clef while I was playing it in the bass clef.

'I tried to work out what was wrong as my teacher came closer and closer to having a stroke. The tears started rolling down my cheeks from suppressed laughter. I wanted to burst out laughing — it was all the funnier for knowing that I couldn't.

'Meanwhile, tears were running down the page turner's cheeks for entirely different reasons. She was totally lost by now and blamed herself for ruining the performance. The audience packing the hall sat silently absorbing this premiere performance.

'There were repeats. With all that had gone on, one of us forgot to go back for a repeat while the other carried on. The piece was falling apart everywhere, but we kept going and never broke down. The music was getting more and more removed from the written score as we both became improvisers in the grand French style.

'In desperation, my teacher lifted one hand from the keyboard. He thrust it at the music, pointing at a rehearsal marking, and shouted: "From HERE!" We were playing loudly when most of this happened so the grunts and yells would not have been audible downstairs. Obediently I jumped to this section but again on the primo page where his finger was pointing and continued playing in bass clef.

'How we ever finished the piece I cannot recall. I could barely read any of the notes by this time for the tears had flooded my eyes, streaming down my face. I tried my best not to laugh, while my teacher looked like he needed a defibrillator. Somehow we did make it to the end and over afternoon tea with the guests in the anteroom, we marvelled at how many of those learned men relished the performance and wished they could hear it all over again.'

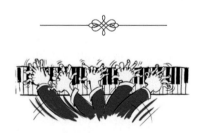

BUILDERS AND OTHER
ORGAN CAREGIVERS

Organs, organists and organ concerts would not exist if it weren't for the builders. They deserve a book to themselves, but meanwhile here is a taster of their connection with the people who depend upon their dedicated workmanship. And let's not forget the now extinct organ blowers, who for centuries gave their muscles for music.

An elderly organist told Christoph Saure that many years ago, when a tuner from the German organ building firm of Weigle worked on organ maintenance, he always smoked cigars while working. With the cigar in his mouth, he couldn't say 'next' or 'one back' as tuners normally do, so he grunted 'mmh' for 'next', and 'mh-mh' for 'one back', balancing the cigar between his lips. One time the tuner became angry and burst into a stream of swearing. The organist holding notes for him at the console stayed calm, but was understandably startled and concerned. The tuner reassured him: 'No, don't worry. All is okay. But my cigar got so short, that I burned my mouth'.

Later, while working for Paschen organ builders in Kiel, Christoph was asked to tune a Weigle organ. Entering the case, he realised immediately who the tuner was. The clue? Cigar stubs in the case.

Ciphers! The bane of the organist's life. Organ tuners and builders too, find them problematic, and are on such high alert about ciphers that they can mistake the real cause of a dreaded long-sounding note. A voicer in Helsinki tells of the time he helped a Russian organist playing the large pneumatic Walcker organ in the Johanneskirche, Helsinki. Suddenly the assistant heard a cipher, which made him extremely nervous. Did he pull a wrong stop? Was it a technical defect? But the organist kept playing, oblivious to the sound. The assistant then discovered the cause: the cipher was the organist, humming along to her playing — out of tune.

Strong lads were frequently called upon for the tedious and thankless task of pumping hand-operated organ bellows. In the 1920s in Christchurch, New Zealand, a suburban church used boys from the Bible Class to pump for the curmudgeonly organist who regularly complained about the lack of constant air pressure. The blower room was a windowless affair behind the organ console, so to pass the time during the sermon while no pumping was necessary the boys would puff away on a forbidden cigarette or two.

One Sunday the sermon ended before the cigarettes did, so the two boys on duty sprang immediately into action at the pump. Unbeknown to them, the bellows inhaled the smoke from inside the small room and puffed it out through the pipes into the body of the church where the minister, choir, congregation and organist got the full benefit. The service came to a standstill while the source of this was investigated, and the culprits were caught fag-handed, so to speak. They were made to pump vigorously for the rest of the service and then had to crawl home to face the wrath and punishment of their parents who were unimpressed.

That was the end of the Bible Class Boy Blowers, and six months after that, the hand-pumped bellows were replaced by an electrically operated (and well-behaved) pump.[19]

Care to flex your muscles and operate the bellows, anyone? You have a choice.

Right: by hand, in St James, Kinnersley, UK, or above, by foot, treadmill style, in St Augustine, Paris.

TAKING NOTE

Organ-tuning notebooks are left on a console so disgruntled organists can leave succinct messages for the organ tuner about problems with the organ. Sometimes it is more of a problem with the organist than the instrument. Naturally, it pays to be as specific as possible, but as can be seen from these examples below, that doesn't always happen:

- *Tuba fails to go in on General Cancel (very dangerous!).*
- *If you bang Great very hard, Choir notes squeak. Tuner: Don't bang it, then.*
- *One of the front pipes has fallen out. Tuner: I might not have noticed that.*
- *It makes a funny noise on the top keys. Tuner: Can you be slightly more specific?*
- *SW to Grt stop dosent (sic) make any sound the bottom notes go wah-wah-wah all the time now.*
- *Evidence of pedal felt falling off. Organ tuner: Evidence removed*
- *Can you put some trumpets in next time pls*
- *That odd noise is STILL there. I told you about it last time. Please can you remove.*
- *My ring rolled under the pedals. Can you look for me please. Cant (sic) see it but you might. I lost stamps & pencils so if there's stuff like that can you get it too.*
- *Hate the Voix Celeste. Would it be possible to change it when you tune at Christmas? Not change whole thing Hahahah but Id (sic) like something with guts pls. Can you make it kind of fuller? tks.*
- *Please leave Swell Box open when organ not in use. If you don't, it causes un-tuning of the sound!!!*
- *Swell Cor de Nuit and Unda Maris having an argument (throb) when together.*
- *Bottom E Violone sounds like a skill saw going through a nail.*
- *Loud droning (no pitch) coming from on high. Definitely not angelic.*
- *Also, can you lessen the tremulant so that it sounds less like Mrs Miller.*
- *At Westminster Abbey: Please could you move the Bombarde reeds to the high altar? P.S. The nearer the clergy, the better. (Organ builder:) Sorry, didn't have time today — will look at this on the next visit.*
- *Organ tuned to the best of my ability but would suggest that it's put on a life support machine as soon as possible.*

Town Hall, Birmingham, England

Music
is the
eye
of the
ear

~ *Thomas Draxe*
Bibliotheca, 1616

BUT OH,
THE JOYS!

ON THE PLUS SIDE

I think that the powerful and unchangeable love which an organist comes to have for his instrument is based upon its endless possibilities, the constant unfolding of mysteries, the giving forth, piece by piece as it were, of the unfathomable secret of soul appeal.' [20]

— G. Waring Stebbins

INNOCENT PARTY: *Are you going away for Easter?*

ORGANIST: *Are you mad?*

Ceiling bosses,
Chester Cathedral,
England

Glorious spin-offs

If so much about being an organist is such hard work, why do we do it?
The music, the music, and the music. And let's be honest: the power. The
thrill of controlling a thundering great beast and filling a huge space with
sound. Or the heart-rending sound of a solo flute soaring through an
aeons-old cathedral, or the spirit-lifting dance of bright mixtures in the latest
architecturally designed concert hall in the galaxy. That's a great part of it.
But there is so much more.

The music is the reason organists submit to regular daft schedules, often for little reward or even voluntarily. Nothing, but nothing, in the world compares to the sound of a large organ thundering out at full gargantuan throttle. Or the same organ tiptoeing meekly, almost inaudible.

The organ is an instrument for making the hairs on your neck stand up, dropping your jaw, or making you cry. It manipulates the listener, stirs every molecule and demands a reaction. It is the complete musical instrument. Even non-meglomaniacs understand this thrill.

Consider the sights we see. Imagine standing within arm's reach of some of the world's most historic architectural treasures; able to view close-up the intricacies of the art of the woodcarver or artist. You can take your time and watch as the light fades, colours mutating from the sunset through the stained glass.

In Chester Cathedral the loft affords a closer view of spectacular ceiling bosses (left). Cherubs with their cohorts provide a private art gallery testifying to the skills of artisans now dead for centuries. The journey up the impossibly narrow steps to the organ for this alone is worth it.

To be silently cosseted by a building that during the day throbs with life, is a particular pleasure. It is saying: 'Now I'm all yours; look at me as I really am.' And I do.

In centuries-old buildings I take time to walk around, read the plaques on the wall, the headstones in the floor, the dedications on the furnishings. The effigies come to life, and I meet the husbands and wives with their dogs leaping up from their feet now that no-one can see them dance. I read their stories and regret yet again I do not remember my Latin.

But these sculptors were so clever they hardly need words. Here is a young woman, dead in childbirth, leaving a deeply grieving husband and motherless children; or there are the four sons of the squire who all went to war — but nothing more is said. What happened to them? Then there was the glowing plaque from a man — about himself. Really? For the curious and inquiring, life on the concert trail is paved with gems.

Accommodation during tours can be almost anything, short of pitching a tent in the nave (no doubt that will come). We have dossed down in monasteries, a chateau, bed and breakfast, posh hotels, backpackers, private homes, slightly sleazy dives and once, only once, a Retirement Home.

Sight-seeing is relegated to 'if we have time' after the concerts when we can relax, but we have become adept at spotting the fleeting charms of beauty in the small things: signs, tombstones, marks made by humans who have trod this way centuries before us, the wonders of massive cities that are nothing like our own, the fun of making our way in foreign languages. The novelty of everything. The joy of it all.

The following pages include just some of the delights of this absurd life of the organist.

THE POIGNANCY OF PIPES

*Organists have the privilege of being present at the rites of passage
for the full range of humanity. It is a privilege that brings with it the
responsibility of choosing the perfect matching music for the occasion.
Jeannine Jordan expresses the anguish of the organist when faced with
the decision of what to play at these important times.*

'Our church, known for being a place where non-members could get married, also was a church where non-members could hold funerals for loved ones. Those were the funerals I played for people I had never met; those were the funerals I will never forget. Those were the funerals for people who had died abruptly and tragically.

'Those were the funerals where the "ritual" was broken down by people who did not know the pastor's strict adherence to routine. Those were the people who did not want the *Lord's Prayer* sung but wanted *The Marshmallow Man* played. Those were the people who could not celebrate life at that moment.

'Vivid images of a mother

draped over the closed casket of her 16-year-old daughter killed on her way home from a skiing trip on Mt Hood will always be with me. What did I play for nearly 30 minutes while a weeping mother in an empty church convulsively said goodbye to a daughter she would never hold again?

'What did I play for the grief-wracked, guilt-ridden family of a prominent businessman who had locked himself in the cabin of his sailboat as it sank in the river? What did I play for the parents of a precious, perfect two-day-old baby whose life had been snuffed out as quickly as it began? What did I play for a friend of 35 years after his death from an inoperable brain tumour? Does it matter?

Introducing children to organs

Fiona Broughton Pipkin thoroughly approves of children coming to church, but she is not in favour of free-range children treating the church as an adventure playground, noisily ignoring what is going on, while their parents either smile benignly or try to pretend that the little horrors belong to someone else.

'After one such service, which included rabbits, I remarked to a churchwarden that I was thinking of getting a T-shirt with "Herod was right" on the back, the only part of me visible at the organ. He looked gloomily at me for a minute, before asking: "Would you make that two shirts"?'

MOMENTS OF SERENDIPITY

A representative of the Casavant Frères Organ builders in Ottawa suddenly appeared in the church sanctuary with a companion while the church's music director, Jo Sorrill, was practising.

'They were doing an organ crawl, looking at the various instruments in that area. When the two of them reached the console, I was flabbergasted when I was introduced to Sir William McKie, retired Organist and Master of the Choristers at Westminster Abbey.

'As he sat down to try the organ, he said to me: "You're a very fine organist". When he finished playing I said (boldly) to him: "You're not bad yourself", whereupon we both erupted into gales of laughter. It was one of those moments you remember all your life.'

When 18-year-old Anthony Newman was studying organ, piano and harpsichord at the Ecole Normale in Paris, he noticed an old man walking around the Ecole who would pick up trash, put it in a rubbish bin, and survey the premises. Anthony figured it must be the janitor.

'When it became time for my piano exam I walked out into the hall and noticed the same old man sitting on the gilded chair with the other judges. I asked my piano teacher who it was. She said 'Why, that's Alfred Cortot of course!'

Philip Chant relates the story from many years ago that on a winter's day, the organist of Down Ampney church walked through the mist towards the beautiful church, intent on some practice. Approaching the porch through the church yard he was surprised to hear the organ being played. On entering he saw a large man with a craggy face and muddy boots improvising on the famous hymn tune *Sine Nomine*.

'The organist was very annoyed that this upstart was playing around with such a beautiful melody. The intruder profusely apologised and explained that he had written the tune and had walked all the way from the railway station at Cricklade to his birthplace.

'It wouldn't be often that you would find the likes of Ralph Vaughan Williams playing the organ in your village church.'

Late one starry night, after a concert and carousing in Valletta, Malta, Kevin Bowyer and his wife were picked up by a huge, silent, unsmiling taxi driver, who was to take them back to their hotel in Sliema.

'We sat in the back, behind the unspeaking driver. At some point on the way the taxi turned off the road and began a journey through the still night, on minor roads with unlit old buildings on either side and no sign of life. We looked at each other, fearing the worst.

'After some time we drew up on a black and deserted quayside. The driver stopped the car, switched off the engine, opened his door and got out. He opened the passenger door on my side and beckoned with his finger that we should get out. I thought, "this it: he's going to rob us, kill us and dump our bodies in the water."

'Trembling with the anticipation of execution, we got out of the car and stood on the quayside in the placid Mediterranean night, the stars overhead and the lights of Valletta across the water. He spoke for the first time, throwing his arms out passionately towards Valletta: "This is my home. I just wanted you to see my beautiful home. This is Valletta — my home"!

Laughter in the loft of Saint-Nicolas du Chardonnet in Paris during a Requiem service is unusual. Requiems are meant to be solemn affairs. But one Saturday morning in the mid-1990s, during the *Dies Irae*, the titulaire of Saint-Nicolas, Marie-Agnès Grall-Menet, and singer Ghislaine Victorius (who was in the loft with her) could not contain their fits of giggles.

The cleaning lady (what was she doing up there during a requiem?) arrived to polish the wooden case, and in particular one of the handsome Atlas figures supporting the weight of the case above.

The housekeeper sprayed her polish cheerfully over the great body, then under his armpits, blissfully unaware that her housework looked for all the world to the performers alongside as if she was treating him to some overdue under-arm deodorant. Admittedly, supporting a tribune is sweaty work. . .

While working in Nottingham, England, Fiona Broughton Pipkin sometimes practised during lunch in an inner-city church. The organ loft was up on the north wall of the nave, approached through the vestry, and there was little view of what was going on below.

'I was trying to learn a Bach fugue, and was determined to get one particular section straight that day, so I kept repeating left hand, right hand, pedals and all combinations thereof, but very softly. I was vaguely aware of occasional rustles from the nave, but nothing more. Just before 2pm I thought "OK. Play through and go" and did, still on soft stops.

'I locked up, went downstairs, through the

vestry — and stopped, aghast. Perhaps 20, mostly elderly people were sitting in the nave, the women in respectable, rusty black, the men wearing the suits in which they were probably married a long time ago, black armbands prominent. The coffin stools were by the chancel steps, waiting. As quietly as I could, I started to tiptoe down the side aisle but heard the patter of feet behind me. Feeling thoroughly guilty, I turned to apologise. A tiny, elderly woman looked up at me, bright-eyed, and laid a confiding little paw on my arm. "Oh, me duck, thank you. Thank you ever so much. Oh, George would have loved that. We told vicar we couldn't afford no music. Thank you".

'I couldn't say anything for the lump in my throat, so I just patted her arm in turn, and slipped away.'

Appointed professor of music at Dublin University in 1862, Sir Robert Stewart was held in considerable awe because of his skill at the organ. None was more impressed than S.J. Rowton, a student who watched Stewart playing in the loft at Dublin's Christ Church Cathedral, and was agog at what he witnessed.

'While accompanying the conclusion of the service, playing from only a figured bass and transposing as before [down a tone], Stewart with his left hand took a half-sheet of paper and wrote a pencil note of instructions for his assistant who was to play in the afternoon—and

all these things simultaneously without for a moment ceasing to whisper to me about other matters. It was a remarkable instance of a man being able, with perfect composure, to divide himself into a number of distinct parts, all independent of each other.'

Peter Averi was assistant director of music at Wellington Cathedral when there was a funeral for a much respected doctor.

'Just before the eulogy, there was a sharp earthquake. We all froze, hoping there was nothing worse to follow. The sub-dean began the eulogy with a reference to the deceased's early career, during which she was one of the first doctors to be in Napier on the day of the 1931 earthquake which killed 256 people. It was an eerie coincidence that at this woman's funeral an earthquake occurred, almost as if it were a bizarre reminder of that terrible event so many years ago.'

I NEVER UNDERSTOOD HOW MAN COULD DARE
TO WATCH A CITY SHAKEN TO THE GROUND,
TO FEEL THE TREMORS, HEAR THE TRAGIC SOUND
OF HOUSES TWISTING, CRASHING EVERYWHERE,
AND NOT BE CONQUERED BY A SICK DESPAIR.
ALTHOUGH HIS BUILDINGS CRUMBLE TO A MOUND
OF WORTHLESS RUINS, MAN HAS ALWAYS FOUND
THE URGE TO BUILD A STRONGER CITY THERE.
WITHIN MY SOUL I MADE MY TOWERS HIGH.
THEY LIE IN RUINS, YET I HAVE BEGUN
TO BUILD AGAIN, NOW PLANNING TO RESTORE
WHAT LIFE HAS SHAKEN TO THE EARTH; AND I,
IN FAITH SHALL BUILD MY TOWERS TOWARD THE SUN
A STRONGER CITY THAN WAS THERE BEFORE.

Plaque from Napier, NZ

St Paul's Cathedral, London, England

The joy of having access after dark, alone, to some of the world's great tourist spots — minus throngs

Temple Church, London, England

Lincoln Cathedral, England

There is no-one else.

Exeter Cathedral, England

Ottobeuren Abbey, Germany

St Nicholas, Blakeney, England

Bath Abbey,
England

Sunsets on vaulted ceilings and pipes are a bonus

*Saint-Germain
des Prés, Paris,
France*

Other times, it is the peace of the solitude of rehearsal in a cavernous concert hall in China . . .

. . . or the thrill of a crush of wall-to-wall audience in a small mountain church in Italy.

Limburg Cathedral, Germany

Organists find themselves in beautiful
places at magical times

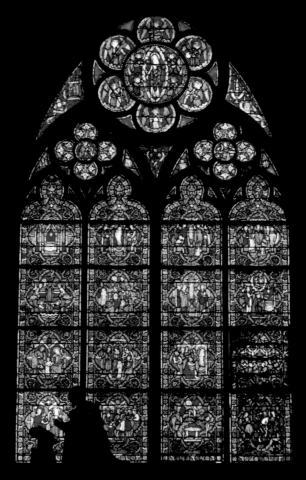

Notre Dame, Paris, France

Which ordinary visitors never experience

ORGANISTS HAVE
TIME MACHINES
AS THEIR
WORKPLACE

Gasping for breath,
we often muse on the
dubious inspiration
of trudging the steps
up to the same lofty
heights to which
Handel . . .

Marktkirche, Halle, Germany

St Blasius, Mühlhausen, Germany

*. . . and Bach
climbed in their
time*

*Simply, organists get to play
the King of Instruments*

It doesn't get much better than that.

St Sulpice, Paris, France

APPENDIX

LINKS TO TERMS USED

Keys to montages

Up close and personal

Fat and Thin,
Textured and Plain
Page 82

1. Exeter Cathedral, England
2. St Franziskus, Pforzheim, Germany
3. St Stephen's, Seattle, USA
4. Bridlington Priory, England

Prettily Painted
Page 83

5. St Peter's, Akaroa, NZ
6. St Mary's, Hay-on-Wye, Wales
7. Soldiers Memorial Hall, Tanunda, Australia
8. St Andrew's Cathedral, Sydney, Australia
9. St Michael's, Tenbury Wells, England
10. Ely Cathedral, England

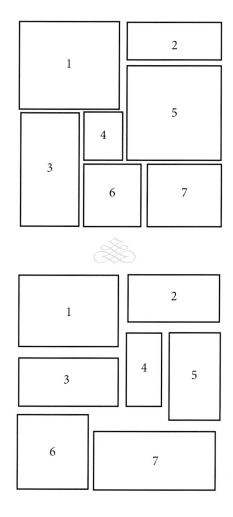

THE CARVER'S ART, RUN RIOT
PAGE 102

1. Andechs Monastery, Germany
2. Fulda Cathedral, Germany
3. Kaysersberg, France
4. Bath Abbey, England
5. Ely Cathedral, England
6. Weingarten Abbey, Germany
7. St Leodegar, Lucerne, Switzerland

CHERUBS AND ANGELS
PAGE 103

1. Chester Cathedral, England
2. Albi Cathedral, France
3. Breda Grote Kerk, Netherlands
4. St Anna, Limburg, Germany
5. Oliwa Cathedral, Poland
6. Lebuïnuskerk, Deventer, Netherlands
7. Saalkirche, Ingelheim, Germany

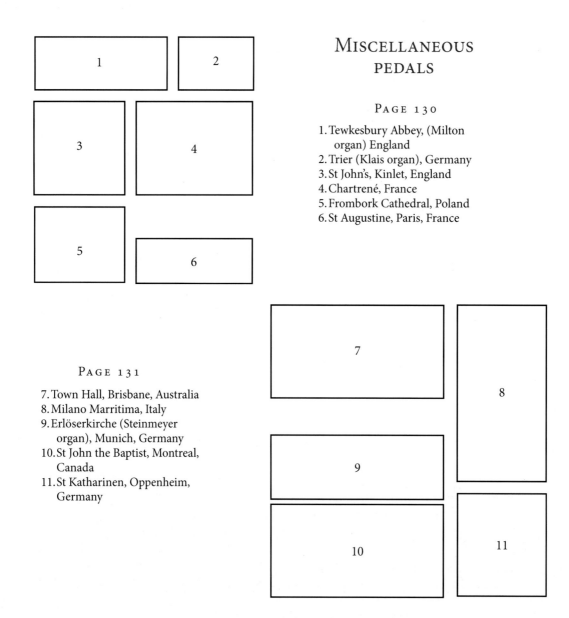

PAGE 130

1. Tewkesbury Abbey, (Milton organ) England
2. Trier (Klais organ), Germany
3. St John's, Kinlet, England
4. Chartrené, France
5. Frombork Cathedral, Poland
6. St Augustine, Paris, France

PAGE 131

7. Town Hall, Brisbane, Australia
8. Milano Marritima, Italy
9. Erlöserkirche (Steinmeyer organ), Munich, Germany
10. St John the Baptist, Montreal, Canada
11. St Katharinen, Oppenheim, Germany

Thirsting for more?

~ Recommended Reading

- Introduction to the Organ — Austin Niland, (Faber)
- The Auckland Town Hall Pipe Organ Book, text & Illustrations by Ksenia Bönig. Produced Orgelbau Klais Bonn; Souvenir programme Auckland Town Hall Organ Book, 2010
- The Organ, (The New Grove Musical Instruments Series) Peter Williams and Barbara Owen, Macmillan ISBN 0-393-30516-3
- King of Instruments, A History of the Organ, Bernard Sonnaillon 0-8478-0582-4
- Making Music on the Organ, Peter Hurford, Oxford University Press ISBN 0-19-322264-7
- The Cambridge Companion to the Organ, ed. Nicholas Thistlethwaite & Geoffrey Webber, ISBN 978-0-5215-7584-3
- The History of the English Organ, Stephen Bicknell, Cambridge University Press ISBN 0-521-65409-2 (1998)
- Understanding the Pipe Organ, John R. Shannon, McFarland ISBN 978-0-7864-3998-0 (2009)
- Elizabeth Stirling and the musical life of female organists in nineteenth-century England, Judith Barger, Ashgate ISBN 978-0-7546-5129-1 (2007)
- Bach's Feet, David Yearsley, Cambridge University Press ISBN 978-0521-1990-18 (2012)
- All the Stops, Craig R. Whitney, Public Affairs™ ISBN 1-58648-262-9 (2003)
- Organ Loft Whisperings — the Paris correspondence of Fannie Edgar Thomas, compiled and edited by Agnes Armstrong, Sticut Tuum productions ISBN 0-9747338-0-6 (2003)

WEBSITES

- Organ website links: pipelinepress.com/links.html
- Encyclopaedia of Organ Stops: organstops.org/
- Worldwide Organ Database: die-orgelseite.de/index_e.html
- National Pipe Organ Register (British): npor.org.uk/
- Friends of the organ (German): gdo.de
- Organ Historical Trust of Australia: ohta.org.au
- Organ Historical Society (USA): organsociety.org/
- Halle Handel House: haendelhaus.de
- Christchurch Town Hall Organ: nzorgan.com
- Auckland Town Hall organ tour: aucklandorgan.org.nz/the-organ-tour/
- Pleasures of the Pipes: pleasuresofthepipes.info/PoP.index.html
- American Public Radio Pipe Dreams with Michael Barone: pipedreams.publicradio.org/
- Organlive — Organ music around the clock: organlive.com
- Types of organ pipes: savetheorgan.org/pipes/pipes.htm
- Jigsaw puzzles of pipe organs: nzorgan.com/organ-jigsaws.html
- Dr J. Butz Music Publisher: butz-verlag.de/engl/index.htm

1. (p.85) flagpipes.com: The Glass Memorial organ built by Xaver Wilhelmy as part of a memorial proposal for ground zero. In the proposal, one pipe would have been created for each victim of the events of that day (3000 pipes, one pipe for each person to remember their life interactions in sound and music). The memorial proposal was not approved or these 14 pipes would be part of a much larger existing display of light and sound in memory of the fallen. The largest pipe is six inches in diameter and is 10 feet and two inches tall. For proper display and performance, the instrument needs a minimum space of 14 feet in height. It is presently working but in storage.

2. (p.87) 'French fries' is a nickname for the 2004 Rosales organ opus 24, in the Walt Disney Concert Hall, Los Angeles, California (rosales.com/instruments/op24/).

3. (p.93) Positiv organ, attributed to Adam Ernst Reichard, Nuremberg, 1710.

4. (p.96) The organ in San Francisco's Legion of Honor was given to the people of San Francisco by John D. Spreckels in 1924 and the apse in the Rodin Gallery is thin cloth, trompe l'oeil, painted to look like marble in order to allow the organ to "speak" through the dome. (legionofhonor.famsf.org/about/skinner-organ).

5. (p.100) John Ruskin, *The Seven Lamps of Architecture, (1849) — The Lamp of life.*

6. (pp. 105+114) Reichel positiv organ of 1664 in the Halle Marktkirche Unserer Lieben Frau on which Handel had early organ lessons.

7. (p.120) wanamakerorgan.com/: the organ has 464 ranks, 28,750 pipes, six ivory keyboards, 29 colour-coded stop tablets, 168 piston buttons (under the keyboards) and 42 foot controls. The largest pipe, made of three-inch-thick Oregon sugar pine, is more than 32 feet long and the smallest is a quarter-inch long. The organ's String Division (with 88 ranks of pipes and 6,340 pipes) forms the largest single organ chamber in the world.

8. (p.121) boardwalkhall.com/arena-information/pipe-organs: Seven manuals: Choir, Great, Swell, Solo, Fanfare, Echo, Bombard. There are 1,235 stop-keys, consisting of 852 speaking registers, 35 melodic percussions, 46 non-melodic percussions, 18 tremolos, 164 couplers, and 120 swell pedal selectives — for switching the shades of the swell boxes onto the six swell pedals (a seventh pedal is the crescendo).

9. (p.123) huygens-fokker.org/instruments/fokkerorgan.html. The 31-tone system of tuning espoused by the Foundation in Amsterdam, The Netherlands.

10. (p.123) The organ at Memorial Church, Stanford University, Fisk Opus 85, combines elements from the Renaissance and the Baroque. This dualism shaped the tonal design and extends to the tuning of this unique organ. By means of five additional pipes in every octave, a large lever

can switch the Werk, Rückpositiv, Seitenwerk, and Pedal divisions from a Renaissance fifth-comma meantone to a well-tempered tuning like those J. S. Bach knew. The Brustpositiv and the Brustpedalia are fixed in meantone. They offer two sub-semitones, or split sharps, per octave: D sharp/E flat and G sharp/A flat. Meantone tuning expert Harald Vogel worked closely with Charles Fisk during the development of this system and shared much valuable knowledge.

11. (p.125) Sir George Smart, after viewing a German organ with pedals at the Crystal Palace in London, William Leslie Sumner, *The Organ* fourth edition, p.185 (London: MacDonald and Jane's, 1973)

12. (p.172) "This was a sort of double-bicycle-saddle arrangement, supported on minimalist steel tubing. The idea was to give patrons an uninterrupted view of the organist's pedal technique." (nzorgan.com/harry-remembers-3.html)

13. (p.216) The Weingarten Basilica of St Martin organ was ground-breaking in many respects. It was Germany's first detached console when Joseph Gabler built it between 1737 to 1750, as Gabler was instructed to avoid blocking light from the six rear windows; his unique solution was to build the organ around the windows. The 4-manual, 169 rank, 63 register, 6,890 pipe instrument includes special stops: a Carillon (shaped like grapes, hanging above console and played by the pedals); a Rossignol (three pipes dipped head-first in water to imitate song of a nightingale); a Glockenspiel, Timpani, a Cuckoo, a Cimbalum, and a stop which sounds like a storm, called, unsurprisingly, La Force.

14. (p.217) Sydney Town Hall pipe organ was built by Hill and Sons between 1886-1889, and has one of only two 64-foot stops in the world. The full-length 64ft Contra Trombone (the largest pipe of which is 20 metres long) is among the 9000 pipes of this organ which was the largest in the world at the time of its construction.

15. (p.297) *The Succession of Organists*, Watkins Shaw, 1991, Clarendon Press, ISBN 0-19-816175-1 (p. 74)

16. (p.300) advertisement from 1865, reproduced in *Elizabeth Stirling and the musical life of female organists in nineteenth-century England*, Judith Barger, Ashgate, (2007) (p.39)

17. (p.311) The double-meaning of Rauschwerk: From Organstops.org: "Rauschwerk is frequently used to replace [Rauschpfeife or Rauschquinte]; but for early sources [...] 'Rauschwerk' was a term denoting either a semi-Flute solo compound stop imitating a reed instrument, or a reed stop itself..." *The New Grove Organ*, Peter Williams and Barbara Owen, 1988, W. W. Norton & Company.

18. (p.326) The story behind the organ loft hiding place in Rotterdam's Breepleinkerk: breepleinkerk.nl/orgelzolder

19. (p.370) *As I Remember*, stories from Sounds Historical, edited by Jim Sullivan, reprinted 2000 Tandem Press, ISBN 1-877178-53-5.

20. (p.375) *Organ Loft Whisperings, the Paris correspondence of Fannie Edgar Thomas*, compiled and edited by Agnes Armstrong, Sticut Tuum productions, 2003. G. Waring Stebbins (1869-1930) was the Organist and Choirmaster of Emmanuel Baptist Church, Brooklyn. (p.26)

AUTHOR

CARTOONIST

Jenny Setchell's life-long interest in photography, coupled with a hands-on passion for music, has meshed perfectly with her 20-year career as a journalist with *The Press* newspaper in Christchurch to produce a third book covering organs and the people who play them. Her first offering of *Organisms — Anecdotes from the World of the King of Instruments* was well received by the public and profession alike, and translated into German. A recent international photographic essay of organs around the world and their environs — *Looking Up* — was published by Butz in Bonn. Jenny lives in Christchurch with her organist husband Martin, and two demanding burmese cats.

pipelinepress.com

Al Nisbet was raised in a cave where he learned the art of drawing on walls using the blood of politicians. He spent his early years in captivity chained to a desk in *The Press* newspaper for about 25 years, until escaping to a sanctuary for abused mammals in a secret location. His lampoons of the Great and Glorious have won him some accolades and many death threats. His favourite hobbies are leaving bizarre messages on answerphones, fishing and dribbling. His latest book of cartoons called *Faultlines* (a collection of his cartoons covering the Christchurch earthquakes from 2010 to 2016), is likely to land him in chains again. He does caricatures of suckers daft enough to send him photos of themselves.

cartoonyoo.com

Adrian Marple

has been playing the organ since the age of 13, so it's about time he started doing it better. His introduction to church music was as a result of his big sister 'eyeing up' one of the choirboys in St Peter's church choir in Wolverhampton. Some studying of music and organs continued at Durham University and the Royal Academy of Music, London, before attempting to earn some money teaching music. He is currently Director of Music and Organist of St Mary's Church in Bury St Edmunds, Suffolk, and is Director of Music at Stoke College. He is married to Ruth and they have two children, Benjamin and Abigail.

Website: adrianmarple.co.uk/

Thanks to those who also shared their stories:

Adrian Wintle; Andrew Burling; Anthony Newman (anthonynewmanmusician.org); Aram Basmadjian (organ-concerts.com); Barry Holdstock; Brian Fahey; Bruce Cornely; Bruce Fletcher; Bruce Steele; the late Carlo Curley; Carol Dziuba; Christoph Saure; Christopher Templeton; Colin Jenkins; David Scott; David Yearsley; Erik Cannell; Ernest Nichols; Fiona Broughton Pipkin; Frank Resseler (cathedralorgan.nl/); Gordon Atkinson; Harry Cross; Ian MacDonald; James Henderson-Holloway; James Lally; Jeannine Jordan (promotionmusic.org); Jo Sorrill; John Keys, John Riley; Jonathan Dimmock (jonathandimmock.com); June Nixon (junenixon.com); Ken Aplin; Kevin Bowyer (kevinbowyer.net/); Kris Emmett; Lynette Bromage; Lynley Clarke; Maggie Pemberton (MagdalenMaryPemberton.de); Marie-Agnès Grall-Menet (marieagnesgrall-menet.fr/); Mariea Black; Marilyn Oakes (marilynoakes1.com/); Mark Quarmby (mq.sydneyorgan.com/); Martin Setchell (organist.co.nz); Mary Comer, Morwenna Brett (theladyorganist.com); Pauline Turpitt; Penny Kempler; Peter Averi; Peter Hignett; Peter Tandy; Philip Bailey (wandering-organist.blogspot.co.uk); Philip Chant; Richard Elliott; Robert Coates; Robin Coxon; Russell Kent; Sean Tucker; Steve Best; Stuart Palmer; Tim Howard; Timothy Tikker (ttikker.com/); Victoria Barlow. Special thanks to Christopher Herrick (christopherherrick.org) for his Foreword.

"I cannot find the words to thank you as I would wish, but if there were an organ here, I could tell you"
~ *Anton Bruckner*

St Gallen Cathedral, Switzerland

Permissions and Illustrations

Acknowledgement to the following for photographs and illustrations: Igor Pushin **p. xv**; Scott Shaw (scottshaw.org), **p. 61**; William Henry Stone (*Elementary Lessons on Sound*, MacMillan & Co., London, p.165) **p. 80**; Schott Publishers (schott-music.com) **p. 81**; Organ Supply Industries, (organsupply.com) **p. 84**; Xaver Wilhelmy, (flagpipes.com) **p. 85**; Archiv Stiftung Händel-Haus, (haendelhaus.de) **p. 93**; Joe Routon (flickr.com/photos/joerouton/) **p. 120-121**; Ole Jacobsen (organdemo.info), Huygens-Fokker Foundation (huygens-fokker.org) **p. 123**; John Mander, Andrew Bryden, **p. 146**; Christian Boiseaux (parcourirlemonde.eklablog.fr), Claudius Winterhalter (orgelbau-winterhalter.de) **p. 147**; Sheila Hignett **p. 172**; Towser Burko **p. 177**; Martin Doering (die-orgelseite.de), **p. 178-9**; Sean Tucker (organanoraks.com) **p. 312**; Bryan Moseley, Ian Carson, Larry Reynolds, **p. 315**; Mary Comer **p. 351**.

For permission to reproduce photographs and text: Various extracts from *Tales of Organists* (Bardon Entrises reprint) — Reprinted by permission of 'Musical Opinion Ltd, publishers of *The Organ* since 1921', and Warwick Henshaw of Bardon Enterprises (bardon-music.com); Church Times published on May 10, 2013, article by Madeleine Davies, **p. 303**; The Church of Christ of the Latter Day Saints. Also thanks to Robert Matthew-Walker, Wolfgang Valerius, Christiane Barth, Philip J Wells, Sander Germanus and Agnes Armstrong for their help tracing photos, giving permission to use material. Christopher Templeton (pipeorgans.co.nz) supplied press archive materials.

In particular, thanks to the tireless Martin Doering who continues to share his vast database of specifications, stunning photography and drawings from his website die-orgelseite.de

Sub-editors at work

 PHOTOGRAPHIC NOTE

Most of the photos I shot over about 30 years, often inside churches that are dungeons of darkness for photographers. In many cases, in order to get usable images, I had to employ any resource to hand, which included hymnbooks, pew cushions, or Martin's shoulder as the only available tripod. My cameras have included a Lumix Panasonic and assorted Minoltas and Canons. These days I use a Canon 7D, with an EFS 10-22mm f/3.5-4.5 and 28-135mm f/3.5-5.6 IS USM; but in emergencies, a Nexus 5 mobile phone.

St Giles Cathedral, Edinburgh, Scotland

Sydney Town Hall, Australia